Antonio Machado's Writings and the Spanish Civil War

Hispanic Studies TRAC
(Textual Research and Criticism)
(PUBLICATIONS INSTITUTED BY THE *BULLETIN OF HISPANIC STUDIES*)

General Editors
ANN LOGAN MACKENZIE   DOROTHY SHERMAN SEVERIN
University of Glasgow   *University of Liverpool*

Assistant Editor
CERI BYRNE

Advisory Board

Don W. Cruickshank *University College Dublin*
Alan Deyermond *Queen Mary and Westfield College, London*
José María Díez Borque *Universidad Complutense de Madrid*
Victor Dixon *Trinity College, Dublin*
Gwynne Edwards *University College Aberystwyth*
Margit Frenk *Universidad Nacional Autónoma de México*
O. N. V. Glendinning *Queen Mary and Westfield College, London*
I. L. McClelland *University of Glasgow*
C. A. Longhurst *University of Exeter*
Helder Macedo *King's College, London*
Ian Macpherson *Queen Mary and Westfield College, London*
Ian Michael *University of Oxford*
Frank Pierce *University of Sheffield*
Geoffrey Ribbans *Brown University*
Francisco Rico *Universidad Autónoma, Barcelona*
Edward C. Riley *University of Edinburgh*
Nicholas G. Round *University of Sheffield*
José María Ruano de la Haza *University of Ottawa*
D. L. Shaw *University of Virginia*
Albert Sloman *University of Essex*
Colin Smith *University of Cambridge*
Joseph Snow *Michigan State University*
Arthur Terry *University of Essex*
John E. Varey *Queen Mary and Westfield College, London*

Textual Research and Criticism (TRAC) publishes Spanish, Portuguese and Latin-American texts of literary, linguistic or historical interest not otherwise available in modern editions. The texts are accompanied by a substantial introductory monograph and full apparatus of critical footnotes. The series also publishes literary and critical studies. TRAC is firmly aimed at a scholarly readership.

Scholars are invited to apply to the Editors for further information and to submit a brief summary of their projected book. Contributions will be assessed by eminent Hispanists in the appropriate areas, and should not exceed 400 pages of typescript.

Hispanic Studies TRAC
(Textual Research and Criticism)
VOLUME 10

Antonio Machado's Writings and the Spanish Civil War

JAMES WHISTON

LIVERPOOL UNIVERSITY PRESS

First published 1996 by
Liverpool University Press
Senate House, Liverpool, L69 3BX

Copyright © 1996 by James Whiston

All rights reserved.

No part of this book may be reproduced, stored in a retrieval system, or transmitted in any form or by any means, electronic, mechanical, photocopying, recording or otherwise, without the prior written permission of the publishers.

British Library Cataloguing-in-Publication Data
A British Library CIP Record is available

ISBN 0 85323 540 6 Cased
        0 85323 550 3 Paper

The Editors of TRAC are indebted to Trinity College Dublin for a subvention which has generously assisted publication of this book.

Printed and bound in the UK by Redwood Books, Trowbridge.

For Stephanie, Barbara, Anna and Emily,
and in memory of Christian

CONTENTS

INTRODUCTION 9

CHAPTER 1
'Las ideas no deben ser de nadie': *Juan de Mairena* (1936) 13

CHAPTER 2
'Un miliciano más con un destino cultural': *La Guerra* (1937) 49

CHAPTER 3
'Deberes fraternos': Machado's Writings in the Early Issues of *Hora de España* (January-August 1937) 85

CHAPTER 4
'Sobre la guerra y la paz': Machado's Writings in *Hora de España* (1937-1938) 107

CHAPTER 5
'Más fuerte que la guerra': Machado's Civil-War Sonnets (1938) 149

CHAPTER 6
'Iniquidades envainadas': Machado's Writings in *La Vanguardia* (1938-1939)... 193

CONCLUSION 241

BIBLIOGRAPHY 249

INDEX 257

Antonio Machado in 1939, shortly before his death.

Reproduced from Arturo Serrano Plaja, *Antonio Machado* (Buenos Aires: Editorial Schapire, 1944)

INTRODUCTION

Compared to the massive critical bibliography that Machado's poetry has attracted, the attention given to the prose and poetry of the last four or five years of his life is of miniature proportions. The main reason for this can be assigned to the outcome of the Spanish Civil War, in the immediate aftermath of which, in the words of one cultural historian, Spain became 'un auténtico páramo intelectual',[1] with the death or emigration of its finest artists and intellectuals; and also whereby two generations of Spaniards, and to not much less an extent Hispanists outside Spain, were denied the kind of generalized access to Machado's Civil-War writings that would have stimulated written commentary in the shape of *tesinas*, theses, articles and books. There has also been a marked reluctance on the part of critics to concede that Machado's writings from 1934 to 1939 are able to stand comparison with his two famous books of poems from the earlier period of 1899 to 1917. The later works appear to have suffered disproportionately from the reputation of *Soledades. Galerías. Otros poemas* and *Campos de Castilla*. While the publication of Aurora de Albornoz's valuable four-volume anthology of Machado's prose in 1970[2] attempted to break the silence of official Spain with regard to Machado's Civil-War writings, it was not until 1983 that a properly comprehensive collection was published by Julio Rodríguez Puértolas and Gerardo Pérez Herrero.[3] This was soon followed in 1985 by the oddly named collection of his Civil-War writings, *Antonio Machado, poeta en el exilio*, edited by Monique Alonso, in collaboration with Antonio Tello,[4] which

---

[1] J. L. Abellán, *La cultura en España (Ensayo para un diagnóstico)* (Madrid: Editorial Cuadernos para el Diálogo, EDICUSA, 1971), 9.

[2] Antonio Machado, *Antología de su prosa*, 4 vols (Madrid: Editorial Cuadernos para el Diálogo, EDICUSA, 1970).

[3] Antonio Machado, *La guerra. Escritos: 1936-1939* (Madrid: Emiliano Escolar, 1983).

[4] Published in Barcelona by Anthropos.

completes the already almost complete collection of his 1983 editors. Finally Oreste Macrì, in collaboration with Gaetano Chiappini, brought out in 1989, to commemorate the *cincuentenario* of Machado's death, what was undoubtedly meant to be the most comprehensive collection to date of all of his writings.[5] This four-volume edition is a splendid undertaking, a wonderful tool for the scholar, who at last has the vast bulk of Machado's works (excluding the plays written with Manuel, and the only recently discovered notebooks) in a form that is readily accessible for consultation. There are gaps: for example, three of Machado's Civil-War contributions to *La Vanguardia* are missing; but these can be supplied by reference to the two earlier editions mentioned. Macrì's huge Bibliography in Volume I, over one hundred and seventy pages long, has probably rendered large-scale bibliographical exercises on Machado redundant for a number of years to come. It is a pity that what appears to have been excessive haste in the preparation of the edition as a whole should have led to mistakes and misleading misprints. There is also an excellent two-volume Cátedra edition of Machado's *Mairena* prose by Antonio Fernández Ferrer, published in 1986. We can therefore confidently expect a concomitant expansion of interest in Machado's late writings over the coming years and indeed for many years into the future. For the moment, and to the best of my knowledge, this work at present in the reader's hands is the first exclusively critical book to be published on the subject of Machado's late writings.

The immediate pre-Civil War period, which in the history of Machado's writings culminated in the publication of *Juan de Mairena* as a book in the summer of 1936, is also included in this study, in order to show the process of continuity and change that the years from 1934 to 1939 represented for Machado. If the aphorisms of *Juan de Mairena* (1936) seem worlds away from Machado's political commentaries in *La Vanguardia* during the last year of the Civil War, this is due to the kind of response that was demanded of him in that final desperate period. Yet although the surface may seem different, the substance — that of seeing through postures and manoeuvres to the essential elements of conviction and truth — meant that the

---

5   See chapter 1, note 18.

bedrock of Machado's vision remained intact. One of his late aphorisms (from July 1938) is 'nunca para la verdad es tarde': I hope to show that Machado's last writings amply justify this aphorism.

I have been able to try out versions of some of these chapters in the Universities of Córdoba and Seville, University College London, the Universidad Autónoma de Madrid, the Spanish Cultural Institute in Dublin, and at the 1989 Conference in Seville to commemorate the *cincuentenario* of Antonio Machado's death. Part of the first chapter was published in a book of essays in honour of Professor E. C. Riley,[6] another part in the *Actas* of the 1989 conference,[7] while *The Modern Language Review* also published an earlier version of my chapter on the sonnets.[8]

I wish to express my sincere thanks to the Arts and Social Sciences Benefactions Fund of Trinity College, Dublin for a generous grant to undertake part of the research for this book. My grateful thanks are also extended to the Dirección General de Relaciones Culturales y Científicas of the Ministerio de Asuntos Exteriores of Spain for their generous support of this research, and to the staff of the Spanish Embassy in Dublin for their courtesy and help. Valuable financial assistance was also forthcoming from the Trinity College Dublin Association and Trust, and from the College's Academic Development Fund established by the present Provost, Dr Thomas N. Mitchell.

My thanks are due as well to Professor César Real Ramos of Salamanca University, and to Professor Francisco Caudet of the Universidad Autónoma de Madrid for their assistance. Final thanks go to those who helped with the processing of the

---

6 'The "Cubing" of Language in Antonio Machado's *Juan de Mairena* (1936)', in *Essays on Hispanic Themes in Honour of E. C. Riley*, ed. Jennifer Lowe and Philip Swanson (Edinburgh: Department of Hispanic Studies, Univ. of Edinburgh, 1989), 148-69.

7 'Las "misiones paradójicas" de Antonio Machado', in *Antonio Machado hoy. Actas del Congreso Internacional Conmemorativo del Cincuentenario de la Muerte de Antonio Machado*, 4 vols (Seville: Alfar, 1990), I, 345-56.

8 ' "Más fuerte que la guerra": The Civil-War Sonnets of Antonio Machado', *Modern Language Review*, LXXXVIII (1993), 644-65.

typescript: Gabrielle Coffey, Inmaculada Kinsella, and Patricia Keohane; and especially to María Luisa Basurka who keyed in most of the early drafts with sympathy and patience, and with a fine Spanish aplomb when dealing with my frequent *ocurrencias* and revisions. My wife Stephanie, as usual, provided just the right assistance when it was most needed.

J. W.

Trinity College, Dublin.

CHAPTER 1

'Las ideas no deben ser de nadie'
Juan de Mairena (1936)

The year 1931, as well as being a notable year in the history of Spain (the Second Republic was declared on 14 April), was also important in the life of Antonio Machado, marking his return to live in Madrid after an absence of twenty-four years.[1] Machado was able to take up a teaching post at a new Institute in Madrid, the Calderón de la Barca, in October of that year. Luis A. Santullano was instrumental in arranging Machado's transfer from Segovia, according to a *Memoir* of his, added on to José Machado's biography of Antonio.[2] Machado's interests in education were to be expanded in the same year, because a few weeks after the declaration of the Republic, the Government announced an initiative in cultural pedagogy, the *Misiones Pedagógicas*, the principal aim of which was to promote the extension of culture — literature, drama, painting, music and the cinema — to the remote and forgotten villages and towns of Spain.[3] Manuel Bartolomé Cossío was named as *Presidente* of the Commission (*Patronato*) announced by the Government to direct the work of the *Misiones*, with Machado as a member.

---

[1] José Luis Cano, *Antonio Machado* (Barcelona: Salvat, 1985), writes of Machado's 'traslado, en octubre de 1931, a Madrid, para ocupar la cátedra de francés' (171); but Macrì (I, 42-43: see note 18) gives 1932 as the year of Machado's transfer from Segovia. In reality, Machado spent long weekends and other periods in Madrid, whenever he could absent himself from his teaching in Segovia.

[2] José Machado, *Últimas soledades del poeta Antonio Machado* (Soria: Imprenta Provincial, 1971), 169.

[3] Although the work of the *Misiones Pedagógicas* was carried out under the auspices of the Republic, the announcement of a 'Comisión para la organización y dirección de una misión pedagógica' was made in a *Real orden* of 6 March 1931 (see the Report published by the *Patronato de Misiones Pedagógicas* [Madrid, 1934], 153).

(Santullano, who was Secretary of the *Patronato*,[4] states that he was also responsible for Machado's nomination.[5]) With Cossío's contribution, and that of artists and intellectuals such as Alejandro Casona, Pedro Salinas, Arturo Serrano Plaja, María Zambrano, Rafael Dieste, Ramón Gaya and Machado himself, one can see that the *Misiones* represented a powerful force for the extension of culture in the pre-war years.[6]

The main promoter of the scheme was Cossío, who had waited many years for this dream to be fulfilled. Cossío's hopes appear to have been centred on a permanent transfer of educational resources to the rural areas.[7] What he was given, in the shape of the *Misiones Pedagógicas*, was more in the nature of the traditional Catholic mission, consisting of a short visit by a small number of *misioneros* to the remote areas to preach the gospel of culture. The Decree establishing the *Misiones* set out three aims: 'el fomento de la cultura general', 'la orientación pedagógica' and thirdly 'la educación ciudadana',[8] the latter designed to encourage an awareness of 'los principios democráticos y liberales que se hallan en la base de la civilización moderna'.[9] The third aim was obviously a bold step to help consolidate the position of the nascent Republic, as the first Report of the *Patronato* makes clear. The Report, indeed, talks of 'el fin primordial de difundir ideas acerca de la cultura política actual, el espíritu de la República y el conocimiento de la Constitución', although it adds that this was to be done 'al

---

4   Eugenio Otero Urtaza, *Las Misiones Pedagógicas: una experiencia de educación popular* (La Coruña: Ediciós do Castro, 1982), 35.

5   José Machado, *op. cit.*, 172.

6   See Eleanor Krane Paucker, 'Cinco años de misiones', *Revista de Occidente*, (April, 1981), 233-68, — an excellently documented article — for the composition of the *Patronato* (261). For a personal reminiscence of the *Misiones* see the article in the same number of *Revista de Occidente*, 'Las Misiones Pedagógicas' by Enrique Azcoaga, 222-32.

7   Cossío had written of his hopes in this direction, as early as 1906: 'enviaremos, como misioneros de la educación, los mejores maestros, donde son más necesarios, a las escuelas rurales, donde hay menos recursos de cultura', in his book *El maestro, la escuela y el material de enseñanza* (Madrid: R. Rojas, 1906), 31.

8   *Patronato*, *op. cit.*, 154-55.

9   Joaquín Xirau, *Manuel B. Cossío y la educación en España* (Mexico: El Colegio de México, 1945), 309.

margen de toda intención partidista'.[10] Francisco Caudet has written of the *Misiones Pedagógicas*: 'era labor de divulgación cultural y de concienciación cívica que no tiene en nuestra Historia parangón',[11] and Eugenio Otero makes a broadly related point when he observes that 'las *Misiones Pedagógicas* no fueron copiadas de un modelo extranjero, y la originalidad de su método, no tiene prácticamente antecedentes'.[12] Certainly the *misiones* must have been conducted with great vigour and energy: the 1934 Report of the *Patronato* speaks of 'casi 4.000 pueblos favorecidos por la obra de las Misiones', in all or nearly all of which a small library was deposited: the number given as donated in the Report is 'tres mil quinientas seis Bibliotecas a otros tantos pueblos'.[13] It is possible that the title 'Misiones Pedagógicas' may have been chosen having regard to the fact that the Ministerio de Instrucción Pública was the paymaster for the programme, and that to justify the annual budget (the total sum granted between 1931 and 1935 was 2.5 million pesetas) it was necessary to include in the title some reference to a pedagogical function. Yet the pedagogical element, in the strict sense of the word, did not figure at all as a part of the programme. The first sentence of the Report begins: 'Las Misiones pedagógicas ... sin equívoco, hubiera sido, tal vez, más acertado llamar Misiones a los pueblos o aldeanos'. The very words with which the *misioneros* introduced themselves to the villages also emphasized this fact: the inhabitants were not being asked to return to school (or attend for the first time). The *Misiones* represented (to quote from the speech of presentation suggested for use by Cossío) 'una escuela donde no hay libros de matrícula, donde no hay que aprender con lágrimas, donde no se pondrá a nadie de rodillas, donde no se necesita hacer novillos'.[14] The local school building was used only for art exhibitions or as a depository for the books which were donated to the people.

Machado became a very active committee member of the

---

10 *Patronato, op. cit.*, 10.
11 'Las Misiones Pedagógicas: 1931-1935', *Cuadernos Hispanoamericanos*, DCLIII (1988), 93.
12 *Op. cit.*, 10.
13 *Patronato, op. cit.*, XXI. This figure was greatly expanded during the Civil War.
14 *Patronato, op. cit.*, 13.

Patronato, although apart from his nomination he is not mentioned in the 1934 Report, except that his poetry appears to have been a popular choice for reading aloud by the *misioneros*. Luis Santullano states in his *Memoir*: 'Antonio Machado fue hasta la última hora, uno de los vocales más asiduos del Patronato y hablando allí poco, decía siempre la palabra justa y orientadora'.[15] Santullano casts some doubt on Machado's motivation *vis-à-vis* the *Misiones* themselves, suggesting that he attended and took part in the work out of loyalty to Cossío.[16] Matilde Moliner has recalled how she and Machado worked together in establishing the small libraries of the *Misiones*: 'Machado y yo quedamos encargados de seleccionar los libros que habían de formar el primer fondo de cada biblioteca ... Se enviaban, en principio, cien volúmenes'.[17] Machado's participation in this practical aspect of the work of the *Misiones* leaves no doubt that in general terms and up to a certain point his ideas coincided with the ideological thrust of the *Misiones*, whereby all the people of Spain might have some access to the work of the great thinkers and artists of the centuries. His fictitious teacher Juan de Mairena is sharply ironic about cultural exclusivism when he speaks of 'los pobres desheredados de la cultura [que] tengan la usuraria ambición de educarse y la insolencia de procurar los medios para conseguirlo'.[18]

Juan de Mairena was the work with which Machado in all probability was most concerned during the immediate pre-war years (his notes for it date from 1933)[19] and there are many points of contact between this work (published as a book in the summer of 1936) and the concept of the *Misiones Pedagógicas*. On 4 November 1934 Machado began to publish his *Mairena*

---

15 José Machado, *op. cit.*, 172.
16 José Machado, *op. cit.*, 174.
17 'Mis encuentros con Machado', in *Instituto de Bachillerato 'Cervantes'. Miscelánea en su cincuentenario, 1931-1981* (Madrid: Ministerio de Educación y Ciencia, 1982), 303.
18 Quotations from Machado's works are generally taken from *Antonio Machado. Poesía y prosa*, ed. Oreste Macrì in collaboration with Gaetano Chiappini, 4 vols (Madrid: Espasa-Calpe/Fundación Antonio Machado, 1988). The reference will be by volume and page number, as here: IV, 1975. Subsequent references will be placed in the text. Since Macrì's edition of Machado's prose is not complete, other editions of Machado's work will be used, as required.
19 See Macrì, IV, 2127-57.

pieces in the newspaper *Diario de Madrid*; and in what Manuel Tuñón de Lara calls 'las páginas sencillas, y hasta si se quiere, plebeyas de la prensa diaria'[20] there is a suggestion that Machado wished to address a much wider public than would be normally available to the writer of what is essentially an experimental literary volume, in spite of its many popular elements. The little notebook that formed the basis for the book *Juan de Mairena*, dated 'años de 1933-34' by Machado, spans what in liberal historiography is the end of the Republic's 'bienio reformista' (1931-33) and the beginning of the 'bienio negro' (1933-35). Francisco Caudet has shown that the *Misiones Pedagógicas* fell victim to the increasing tensions that overcame the country in 1934.[21] Indeed, all the cultural and pedagogical initiatives of the *bienio reformista* were subjected to severe cutbacks under the régimes of the following two years. There is perhaps room for speculation here as to why Machado decided to begin publishing his *Mairena* notes when he did. Did his decision have anything to do with the fact that by then the *Misiones* were losing the impetus of those early years?

Manuel Aznar describes the situation towards the end of 1934 as follows, following the revolutionary events of Cataluña and Asturias: 'la represión que siguió la revolución de octubre de 1934 fue el factor desencadenante de la aceleración histórica hacia el compromiso de la inmensa mayoría de artistas españoles. Misiones Pedagógicas o populismos culturales iban perdiendo su razón de existencia como consecuencia de la radicalización de planteamiento'.[22] It could well be that the *Mairena* sketches enabled Machado to continue, albeit theoretically, with some of the ideas of the *Misiones*, having seen from his seat on the *Patronato* that these were faltering through ideological divisions, both in the *Cortes* that supported them financially and in the villages that received them. There is another possibility concerning the timing of the publication of

---

20 *Antonio Machado, poeta del pueblo* (Barcelona: Nova Terra, 1967), 235.

21 'Las Misiones Pedagógicas; 1931-1935', 105-06. See also Antonio Sánchez Barbudo's comments in *Homenaje a Antonio Sánchez Barbudo*, ed. Benito Brancaforte, Edward R. Mulvihill and Roberto G. Sánchez (Madison: Univ. of Wisconsin, 1981), 22; and Paucker, 248 and 250-51.

22 M. Aznar Soler, *Pensamiento literario y compromiso antifascista de la inteligencia republicana* (Barcelona: Laia, 1971), 71.

Juan de Mairena: that the format — that of a humorous and whimsical protagonist debating innocent-seeming topics — was a means of circumventing the censorship of the post-Asturias period of the Republic, described by J. Bécarud and E. López Campillo as 'un período de silencio obligado, debido a la suspensión de garantías, que duró prácticamente hasta enero del año 1936';[23] the same authors go on to remind us that 'Entre otros, Azaña fue a la cárcel, y destacados socialistas tuvieron que pasar a la clandestinidad'. Certainly, seeing that Sunday edition of *Diario de Madrid* in which Machado's first *Mairena* article appeared, one is left with a graphic impression from the notice that appears on the first page: 'Este número ha sido visado por la censura'. This was the result of Prime Minister Lerroux's declaration on 6 October of a State of War throughout Spain, following the revolutions in Asturias and Barcelona. (*Diario de Madrid* only began life as a newspaper on 26 October 1934, and in its first leading article stated that its launch had been delayed because of the crisis.) When we remember Machado's words of late 1938 concerning the publication of *Juan de Mairena* — that these notes, from being a 'breviario íntimo ... un día saltaron desde mi despacho a las columnas de un periódico' (IV, 2279) — we sense an energetic decision on Machado's part to commit himself in this public way to an art within the reach of all. The verb 'saltar' is apt indeed for the tireless talker who is the protagonist of the work, and also for the vigour of Machado's text: the flood of words, the bombardment of the reader with observations, analysis, criticism, paradoxes, aphorisms, questions and imperatives. During the year and a half of its publication (up to the end of June 1936) and in spite of its remarkable variety, the work shows no sign of flagging, and ends with Mairena still attempting to 'agitarse entre creencias contradictorias' (IV, 2123). Luis Santullano enters our story again, in connection with Machado's switch, one year after his first *Mairena* piece, from the *Diario de Madrid* to *El Sol*. 'Me creo parcialmente responsable' for the move, he has written in the *Memoir*, adding significantly, in the light of the question of the widening of cultural consciousness that was such an issue at the time, that

---

23 *Los intelectuales durante la II República* (Madrid: Siglo Veintiuno, 1978), 124.

El Sol was 'el periódico español entonces más leído'.[24] There may have been political reasons for the move. M. Tuñón de Lara has observed that the *Diario de Madrid* 'no coincidía en sus apreciaciones políticas con don Antonio, ya que sostenía la política del bienio restaurador'.[25]

It seems that Machado himself (he was in his sixtieth year at the end of 1934) was aware of the renewal of his own literary youth, when Mairena writes of the process of ageing as follows: 'no siempre el tiempo que plenamente vivimos coincide con nuestra juventud. Lo corriente es que vayamos de jóvenes a viejos ... pero lo contrario no es demasiado insólito' (IV, 2087). There is plenty to suggest that *Juan de Mairena*, giving a new and energetic creative impulse to Machado's contribution to culture, represents a basic commitment on Machado's part to the cultural 'missionary' ideas of the pre-war Republic. Mairena himself observes to his students in chapter XXXII:[26] 'de algún modo hemos de acusar en nuestras clases los tiempos de barullo y algarabía en que vivimos' (IV, 2039). Antonio Fernández Ferrer sees in *Juan de Mairena* 'una clara intención de "educación cívica" ',[27] and Mairena certainly has his 'missionary' tendencies: he is the author of two so-called sermons (the 'sermón de Rute' and the 'sermón de Chipiona') and his students are sometimes known as his 'discípulos'. Machado, however, does not usually localize the direction of his prose very much in his *Juan de Mairena* writings, which speak to the human consciousness, irrespective of national or historical boundaries. *Conciencia*, in its perceptual sense, is indeed a key word in Machado's prose meditations in *Juan de Mairena*, and has long-standing antecedents in his work. Using the word in a

---

24 José Machado, *op. cit.*, 170.

25 'Antonio Machado y la Institución Libre de Enseñanza', in *Cuadernos para el Diálogo*, XLIX (1975), 103.

26 There are fifty chapters in *Juan de Mairena* (1936), although they are not referred to as such, being given only Roman numbering; and a total of four hundred and twenty-two sections. We have referred to these in the text with Roman and Arabic numerals respectively. The credit for being the first to count (in print) the number of sections must go to P. A. de Cobos, *El pensamiento de Antonio Machado en Juan de Mairena* (Madrid: Ínsula, 1971), 7. Cobos was an active *misionero* in the *Misiones Pedagógicas*, according to the *Patronato* Report, 21.

27 Antonio Machado, *Juan de Mairena*, 2 vols (Madrid: Cátedra, 1986), I, 20.

letter to Unamuno in 1904 — 'todos nuestros esfuerzos deben tender hacia la luz, hacia la conciencia' — the attempt even then, as Geoffrey Ribbans puts it, is to 'alumbrar y dar conciencia a los problemas vitales humanos'.[28] In one of the Civil-War *Mairena* pieces in *Hora de España* Machado puts in his apocryphal teacher's mouth a definition of culture that embraces all intelligent thought and activity, and hence is open to all: according to this definition culture is 'el humano tesoro de conciencia vigilante' (IV, 2317). In the same vein is Mairena's praise of Velázquez: the aphorism that he uses to single out Velázquez's genius in taking a scene which belongs to our everyday consciousness and transferring it to the canvas: 'Él pinta por todos y para todos' (IV, 2037).

The setting of *Juan de Mairena* (1936) is what we presume to be an *Instituto de Segunda Enseñanza* in 'una gran población andaluza' (IV, 1954) around the turn of the century. We say 'presume' because the bricks, mortar and furniture of nineteenth-century realism have no place in this twentieth-century Socratic setting: Mairena is a teacher of Physical Education (*Gimnasia*) who gives classes in Rhetoric which are not part of the official programme of the *Instituto* (IV, 1961). This classroom setting allows Machado to expound his ideas in a way that enables him to reach a wider public, which is not necessarily interested in literature. The formula that is repeated throughout the work — 'Habla Mairena a sus alumnos' — is also of interest in the context of the *Misiones Pedagógicas*. The formula may have been used in order to introduce Mairena to each possible new group of newspaper readers, or simply to remind established readers of the fictional convention being used. But it could also be a means of reminding Machado himself to keep his non-specialist readership in mind. At the beginning of chapter V Machado tells us that 'Mairena hacía advertencias demasiado elementales a sus alumnos. No olvidemos que éstos eran muy jóvenes, casi niños, apenas bachilleres; que Mairena colocaba en el primer banco de su clase a los más torpes, y que casi siempre se dirigía a ellos' (IV, 1928). Machado may also have repeated the formula 'Habla Mairena a sus alumnos' to remind himself of what appears to be an

---

28 *Niebla y soledad. Aspectos de Unamuno y Machado* (Madrid: Gredos, 1971), 301. Both Machado's words and Ribbans' comment are on this page.

important stylistic goal of the book: the constant use of the forms of the spoken word, forms that lend themselves to a very direct rhetorical impact and hence to the maximum diffusion of the ideas that are being presented.

Mairena's approach to teaching also facilitates what we might call the technique and theme of accessibility throughout the text. The classroom scene described in chapter XXVI deserves commentary in this regard. Both registered and non-registered students receive the same courteous attention from the teacher. In this scene we see Mairena's easy, benevolent attitude, even though on this occasion he has to 'atajar severamente la algazara burlona' (IV, 2011) of some students who have been laughing at an elaborate exchange of courtesies between Mairena and one of the *oyentes*. Mairena calls his class to attention, addressing them as 'amigos míos', and speaks to them, not by standing on the magisterial pedestal but sitting casually on his desk, creating an atmosphere in class whereby, he tells us, 'muchas veces charlamos como buenos amigos'. Joaquín Xirau has described the lectures given by the *misioneros* as follows: 'Las conferencias se daban en tono amistoso y familiar, huyendo siempre de la declamación y del espectáculo y procurando dar a los temas un desarrollo vivaz, ameno y agradable'.[29] As in the *Misiones Pedagógicas*, so in Mairena's classes there are no textbooks. And the use of the reiterated phrase 'Habla Mairena a sus alumnos' is worth mentioning again: Mairena does not declaim or raise his voice. We are a long way from the closed, monotonous and petrified atmosphere of the classroom scene in the fifth poem ('Recuerdo infantil') of *Soledades. Galerías. Otros poemas*:

> Con timbre sonoro y hueco
> truena el maestro, un anciano
> mal vestido, enjuto y seco,
> que lleva un libro en la mano.

And just as in the *Misiones Pedagógicas*, Mairena's classroom is 'una escuela sin lágrimas', Mairena treating his students with punctilious respect, calling them 'señores'. Machado, too, has chosen ordinary surnames for these 'señores': Pérez, Rodríguez,

---

29 *Op. cit.*, 304.

Martínez (Gozálvez is probably the least common)[30] and for the *oyente* Joaquín García, as if to underline that when he writes in chapter XLVI 'Nosotros ... hablamos al hombre' he is addressing what he was later to call 'la prole de Adán' (IV, 2313), or its Spanish equivalent. Mairena's benevolence towards his students is by analogy an invitation on Machado's part to his readers to come into the house of culture without fear of an authority that is 'enjuta y seca'. If the *Misiones Pedagógicas* represented an attempt to democratize culture, there is also throughout *Juan de Mairena* a democratic vein in which Machado establishes a familiar 'convivencia' between text and reader. And there are times when Machado turns conventional hierarchical authority upside down, making Mairena frankly confess his limitations to his students, asking them for 'ese mínimo de respeto que hace posible la convivencia entre personas durante algunas horas' (IV, 1932-33). It is worth underlining Mairena's use of the phrase 'ese *mínimo* de respeto': Mairena, who is such a scrupulous searcher after truth, only very reluctantly asks for respect for himself, not for the sake of any hierarchical authority, but in order to keep alive the dialogue between himself and his students. At the same time as Mairena acknowledges his limitations he advises his students: 'Huid de escenarios, púlpitos, plataformas y pedestales. Nunca perdáis contacto con el suelo; porque sólo así tendréis una idea de vuestra estatura.'[31] The wry smile that we can imagine on Mairena's face as he proffers this advice points towards an essential feature of *Juan de Mairena*: the sense of humour that runs through the work — or at least 'una chispita de ironía' — which Mairena counsels for every work of prose, whether scientific or literary, because, Mairena says of such an author, 'hasta intentaríamos leerle alguna vez' (IV, 1925). Raimundo Lida has applied this comic lesson to all readers of *Juan de Mairena* with his view that in it 'se hace trizas la seriedad de todo lector que no sepa reírse a tiempo de su propia seriedad'.[32]

---

30 *Gozálvez* is the name given in the first edition; Macrì prints as 'Gonzálvez' (IV, 1914).

31 Sections 4, 5, 6 and 7 of chapter VI are missing from Macrì. We have quoted from the first edition of *Juan de Mairena* (Madrid: Espasa-Calpe, 1936), 40.

32 'Elogio de Mairena', in *Antonio Machado*, ed. Ricardo Gullón and Allen W. Phillips (Madrid: Taurus, 1973), 365-69, at 365.

A fundamental aspect of the democratization of culture in *Juan de Mairena* lies in the examination or re-examination of words, phrases and concepts that may have become hallowed or worn by time and use, and now circulate freely as part of the common currency of rhetorical usage or received opinion. By asking questions about the value of these coins and coinages Machado places the possibility of valuable cultural experience at the disposition of everybody. At the end of chapter XIX Mairena conducts a re-examination in class of the rhetorical cliché, 'las canas siempre venerables ...'. Mairena asks several questions about it, with a view to undermining the stereotype suggested by the cliché, then invites his class to continue the analysis 'hasta lo infinito' (IV, 1982), after which he himself gives several more examples of a qualified and, as he sees it, more thoughtful use of the cliché: ' "Las canas, siempre venerables; las canas no siempre despreciables; las canas, en un treinta y cinco por ciento venerables" etc., etc.'. Mairena recommends this activity to his students in the last sentence of chapter XIX as 'la "cubicación" de vuestro lenguaje que es, a fin de cuentas, la gran faena del escritor'. For Mairena the original cliché referred to is too flat and stereotyped to be an adequate account of the living reality behind the expression, hence he urges his students not to be content with a single interpretation, but to observe and analyse it 'hasta lo infinito', and to invent one's own words and phrases where necessary. Mairena leads by example in this regard, using the neologisms 'cubicación' and 'planificación' (IV, 1985) to describe the depth, or lack of it, of the language of life and letters being discussed in the classroom.[33] Party politics are not

---

33 In chapter XV Machado quotes Valle-Inclán to the effect that 'el "unir dos palabras por primera vez" podía ser una verdadera hazaña poética' (IV, 1967). Analogously, there is a sufficient number of neologisms in *Juan de Mairena* (1936) to suggest that Machado is using the neologism as another element in his attempt to make his readers aware of the remarkable creative power at the disposal of everyone: the ability at least to create new combinations of words, if not the kind of neologisms with which Machado enlivens his text in *Juan de Mairena* (1936). Macrì has noted fifty-five neologisms throughout the work (see IV, 2497-508); to which we may add the following (using the rather conservative yardstick of their absence from the 1936 edition of the *Diccionario de la Real Academia Española*, the year of the publication of *Juan de Mairena*): *roezancajos, Logística, planificación, aporética, ónticas, niño-masa, videncia, alteridad, otredad, apedantarse, infantilizarse, planificar, inconmensurabilidades*. This combined list of

discussed in class, but one interpretation of the reality behind the 'canas venerables' cliché may be that it was aimed at Alejandro Lerroux, the Prime Minister at the time of the publication of chapter XIX (23 March 1935). Later, in 1937, Machado certainly did not mince his words, describing Lerroux (then in his early seventies) as 'un hombre profundamente viejo, un alma decrépita' (IV, 2191).

The analogy of the cube metaphor may also be seen in the perspective suggested by the references which Mairena makes to his role in the stages of the transmission of opinions that go to make up his classes of rhetoric. These reminders occur in chapters VI, 8; VIII, 2; XVI, 4; XLIV, 7, and XLVIII, 9 — in other words, of the five *advertencias* two are towards the beginning and two are towards the end of the book. They serve Machado as introductory and valedictory reminders to his readers that everything in the book is the result of a view that is 'expuesta a múltiples yerros' (IV, 1932). By so doing, Machado opens up his text, enabling his readers to take an active part in its re-creation. It is also an invitation to his readers to probe the opinions of others, no matter how weighty and universally self-evident such opinions may be. Mairena's first contribution to this exercise in cultural democracy is in chapter VI, 8 ('Pláceme poneros un poco en guardia contra mí mismo'): a notable piece of self-effacement by a teacher who honestly acknowledges his mistakes to his students. It also suggests a search for a subtlety in their perception that will enable them to scrutinize the medium (here, Mairena) that is purveying opinions to them. It is not too difficult, perhaps, for the reader who is imagining this scene to replace Mairena the teacher by Machado the writer, due to the predominance of references to writing in it: 'yo soy la incorrección misma, un

---

sixty-eight neologisms may still be incomplete. Incidentally, the anomaly of the appearance in the Republic of an edition of the DRAE is explained by the fact that the same edition (and print run) was re-published in 1939 by the victorious Franco régime, which removed the original frontispiece, and replaced it with what were called 'sus emblemas tradicionales y su título varias veces secular de REAL ACADEMIA ESPAÑOLA', also giving it what the interpolated page describes as 'el sello de la nueva España imperial'. The new date is given on the frontispiece as 'año de la victoria', but the Biblioteca Nacional catalogue for the edition retains the year 1936 as the date of publication.

alma siempre en borrador, llena de tachones, de vacilaciones, de arrepentimientos. Llevo conmigo un diablo ... que me tacha a veces lo que escribo, para escribir encima lo contrario de lo tachado'. In chapter VIII the subtle distortions of truth that seep into our conscious or unconscious communicative strategies are laid bare. Again, the basis is Mairena's confession to his students that he is at times 'aparentando, por exigencias de la oratoria, convicciones sólidas y profundas que no siempre tengo' (IV, 1939-40). But the net is soon widened to include 'al orador, es decir, al hombre que habla': in all conversation there is the need to make an impact on one's listener, hence the speaker 'a pesar suyo dogmatiza, enfatiza y pedantea en mayor o menor grado'. Mairena finishes by confessing to his part in the process of distortion.

The picture of the teacher — the conventional figure of authority — who undermines his position in the interests of a deeper understanding of such authority, is a perspectivist device that sets the stage for the gentle and humorous probing of intellectual reputation throughout *Juan de Mairena*. Thus, even as Mairena is offering to his students (and Machado to his Spanish readers) elements of the ideas of some of the 'greats' of Western thought, he is at the same time demonstrating the role that his students' 'conciencia vigilante' can play when they come into contact with these ideas. This reciprocity makes the exercise a creative one that is open to all, irrespective of their previous educational background. By subjecting established intellectual reputation to due critical process, in the context of these classroom scenes, Machado opens up access to intellectual culture, not just demographically to a wider catchment area of readers, but also in the critical response required to be made to these classical tenets. While a certain degree of deference is given to the Western intellectual tradition, a marked anti-hierarchical note is also present. Mairena, exposing his own position to his students as an honest but fallible broker of opinions, looks at snippets from the history of the Western intellectual tradition, and questions the basis of past perception. Carlos Beceira has seen *Juan de Mairena* (1936) as an attack on rationalist premises themselves, on account of their remoteness from everyday existence. For Beceira the book represents the 'socarronería de pueblo ante las grandes estructuras negativas del intelectualismo racionalista, divorciado del prójimo y de la vida que pasa'.[34] Beceira's excellent article, which is mostly concerned with philosophical issues, is also a useful reminder of the potential socio-political ramifications of the philosophical 'bits' in *Juan de Mairena* (1936) and of the book's aphoristic style. In the work Machado shows that he is unwilling to accept the kind of hierarchical authority that is nurtured by traditionalist belief and the routine acceptance of the superiority of social or professional status. One can easily see how from such a position Machado's attitude to the rebellion of the generals in 1936 was, on this basis alone, not in need of fundamental revision. Machado's use of language is in itself an indicator of a view of society; and Víctor García de la Concha has ably demonstrated the radical extent of Machado's re-structuring of traditional language patterns in the *Mairena* series.[35] The list of philosophers subjected to scrutiny in the 1936 book includes, among others, thinkers such as Protagoras, Epicurus, Socrates, Aristotle, Democritus, the younger Seneca, St Paul, St Anselm, Machiavelli, Galileo, Leibnitz, Spinoza, Kant, Darwin and Nietzsche. Perhaps the most witty and humorous reflection on one of the great thinkers of the past is the remark about Socrates in one of the Civil-War *Mairena* pieces. Mairena's view was that the legendary Socratic reply to one of his students ' "Sólo sé que no sé nada" contenía la jactancia de un excesivo saber, puesto que olvidó añadir: *y aun de esto mismo no estoy completamente seguro*' (IV, 2384). As a motto for his own imaginary *Escuela Popular de Sabiduría Superior* in the 1936 book Mairena would wish to adapt the Delphic command 'know thyself' to a 'forma más suasoria que imperativa: *Conviene que procures*, etc' (IV, 2056). The gentle irony here re-examines the assured classical imperative with a combination of modesty and critical aplomb that makes the famous phrase seem over-confident. However, a little later, in chapter XLIII, Mairena tells his students: 'Dios hizo a los antiguos griegos para que podamos comer los profesores del porvenir' (IV, 2091). In the same conciliatory vein, both

---

[34] 'Una frase del "Juan de Mairena" ', *Ínsula*, CLVIII (1960), 13 and 15, at 15.
[35] 'La nueva retórica de Antonio Machado', in *Antonio Machado hoy*, I, 13-32.

Socrates 'que no quiso ser más que un amable conversador callejero', and Plato 'que puso en boca de tal maestro lo mejor de su pensamiento' (IV, 1955) are praised for their essential modesty.

Another example of a scrutiny of the classical past that combines humour, sympathy and critical detachment is Mairena's brief analysis of Democritus' opposition of opinions and atoms; the former, according to Democritus, being a subjective state and hence prone to error, the latter only (and the space between them) being real. To which Mairena devastatingly adds: 'Claro está que todo esto, señores, es una opinión de Demócrito, que nadie nos obliga a aceptar' (IV, 1951). Not content with this gentle ribbing, Mairena goes on the attack, taking his stand on the view that Democritus' isolated atoms, finding cohesive expression in the human consciousness, are also dependent on our consciousness for the existence that they enjoy: 'nuestra conciencia los engloba, juntos con los colores del iris y las pintadas plumas de los pavos reales' (IV, 1952). The image of the rainbow and the smaller-scale, though equally colourful image of the peacock's plumage challenge the bleakness of Democritus' world-view by their appeal to our enhanced consciousness of colour and shape, as against Democritus' view that colours belong to the suspect realm of opinions. This appeal to the individual human consciousness, but above all to our 'conciencia vigilante', is an essential feature of the 1936 book. Such a re-examination has the effect of turning so-called classical formulations into what we might not unjustly describe, after such re-examination, as 'classical clichés'. (Nevertheless, in the paragraph following his reply to the philosopher of the atoms, Mairena is urging his students to sing the praises of Democritus.)

Protagoras' famous dictum 'man is the measure of all things' is also subject to Mairena's rectification in the opening section of chapter XLVIII.[36] The brief section is worth quoting in full:

---

36 Part of the process of rectification may be seen in *Juan de Mairena* (1936) by a stylistic quirk in the text, of which Machado himself was doubtless aware. The adverb 'sin embargo' is one of the few words used by Mairena which is specifically commented on by Machado, who describes it as follows: 'el *sin embargo* de Mairena era siempre la nota del bordón de la guitarra de sus reflexiones' (IV, 2001). Machado's comment, suggesting the

Al fin sofistas, somos fieles en cierto modo al principio de Protágoras: *el hombre es la medida de todas las cosas.* Acaso diríamos mejor: el hombre es la medida que se mide a sí misma o que pretende medir las cosas al medirse a sí misma, un medidor entre inconmensurabilidades. Porque lo específicamente humano, más que la medida, es el afán de medir. El hombre es el que todo lo mide, pobre ciego hijo del que todo lo ve, noble sombra del que todo lo sabe. (IV, 2114)

The sophist's confident statement is glossed by Mairena in such a way that it eventually gives way to images of blindness and darkness, which have the effect of making the Protagorean statement seem too static and imperious a summary of human existence. Mairena's open-ended expansion of the classical statement, conveyed by the adverbs 'en cierto modo', 'acaso' and 'más' is reinforced by the words 'pretende', 'afán' and 'inconmensurabilidades', the length of the latter word (a neologism, in its plural form) graphically suggesting the enormity and difficulty of the human task. These words, allied to the repetitions (there are five verbal variations on, and three different uses of the original word *medida* in the four sentences) give the little section an energetic quality of searching and striving that is absent from the original statement, while preserving the noble concept of the classical dictum.

Epicurus' dismissal of the human fear of death, translated by Mairena as 'mientras somos, la muerte no es, y cuando la muerte es, nosotros no somos' (IV, 2001), is also the subject of a re-examination. For this revaluation, and to make the point that 'la muerte va con nosotros, nos acompaña en vida', Mairena enlists the help of a stanza from Manrique's 'Coplas', quoting it rather inaccurately from memory:

> Buen caballero,
> dejad el mundo afanoso
> y su halago;
> muestre su esfuerzo famoso
> vuestro corazón de acero
> en este trago.

Putting the quotations in fairly close proximity for comparison has the effect of making Epicurus' quasi-syllogistic formula

---

phrase's frequent recurrence, prompted a frequency count, which revealed that 'sin embargo' is used at least fifty-nine times in *Juan de Mairena* (1936).

seem bland and vacuous when contrasted with the stoic gravity of Manrique's lines. Neither is the elegiac line of Homer on the universality of death exempt from Mairena's critical scrutiny. Translating the famous line as 'Como la generación de las hojas, así también la de los hombres', Mairena comments that in writing it as he did, Homer positioned himself on the outside of the 'gran bosque humano', whereas he (Mairena) advises his students to consider that they will one day experience death 'desde dentro, y coincidiendo con una de esas hojas' (IV, 1956).

Of the more modern thinkers, one of Machiavelli's pieces of advice, paraphrased as follows, is subject to Mairena's rectification:

> *Consejo de Maquiavelo*: No conviene irritar al enemigo.
> *Consejo que olvidó Maquiavelo*: Procura que tu enemigo nunca tenga razón. (IV, 1918)

The blunt, laconic style underlines the gulf that separates the two philosophies. The pragmatic element, foremost in Machiavelli's maxim, is opposed by the ethical imperative of Mairena, 'contra ti' being understood in his rectification, thereby lending a depth, at once moral and perceptual that is absent from Machiavelli's aphorism. Mairena has a similar criticism of a maxim as lacking in depth, when he makes an observation about Galileo's statement that the universe is written 'en lengua matemática' (IV, 2105). Mairena, continuing the astronomer's metaphor, replies: 'Como si dijéramos: el latín de Virgilio está escrito en esperanto'. This parody of Galileo's statement has the effect (as in the Democritus passage) of shifting the argument to another plane of perception, restoring a depth of perspective that is absent from Galileo's observation. In this case the absurdity, in Mairena's view, is the attempt to account for the original condition of phenomena (the universe, Virgil's work) by re-writing it in the formulaic patterns of mathematics or Esperanto. In the Democritus passage the scientific, rational and logical view is contrasted with colourful images from nature; here the contrast is with a master of classical language, making Galileo's choice of metaphor — 'lengua matemática' — seem too unidimensional a summary of human perception. However, as with Democritus (but not Machiavelli) Galileo is praised for his clarity of thought, although Mairena adds, 'Nosotros, que hablamos al hombre, también sabemos lo que decimos' (IV, 2105).

Another apparently self-evident and hallowed maxim examined by Mairena, which will help to illustrate how Machado's instinct led him to reject what Mairena calls the 'planificación' of language and thought is the Latin tag 'Primum vivere, deinde philosophari'. Omitting mention of the full phrase, Mairena advises his students: 'Contra el sabido latín, yo os aconsejo el *primum philosophari* de toda persona espiritualmente bien nacida' (IV, 1980). If culture is the accumulated wisdom of our 'conciencia vigilante', so human birth to a worthwhile life is inconceivable without 'el pensar alto, o profundo, según se mire' (IV, 1980). During the discussion in VI, 9 between Mairena and his pupil concerning the taking of sides in any conflict, the student adapts to the human condition the Darwinian view of the animal species as a struggle for life: 'La vida es lucha, antes que diálogo amoroso. Y hay que vivir' (IV, 1934). Mairena's reply to the effect that such a life is not worth living, puts his reversal of the Latin phrase in context. By omitting the word *vivere* he answers the maxim to the effect that one cannot divorce human existence from constant reflective activity in the way that the Latin phrase does, because for Mairena (and Machado) *philosophari* is, or should be, of the essence of all reflective human life: there is no need to add on the other infinitive, *vivere*, in the way that the Latin tag does. The weaving of our 'conciencia vigilante' into the texture of human life itself, effectively exposes the lack of depth in the Latin maxim, which with its compartmentalized phraseology polarizes the active and contemplative phases of human existence, putting them on single and separate planes.

In what is perhaps the longest section of the book (XIV, 3) Mairena examines St Anselm's syllogistic proof for the existence of God ('Existence is a necessary attribute of perfection, God is perfection, therefore God exists') in order to probe Kant's contention that mathematics and physics, although theoretical, really exist. (Mairena returns to this topic in chapter XLV, section 2.) Prefacing his examination of Kant with the aphorism 'todo es creer, amigo, y tan creencia es el sí como el no' (IV, 1965), Mairena turns Kant's argument into a question of personal perspective and belief; in other words, Kant 'no cree en más intuición que la sensible, ni en otra existencia que la espacio-temporal'. This perspectivist approach by Machado is a key strategy throughout the book: it is not just the revelation of an Ortegan window on reality that inevitably affects the transmission of ideas to the viewer (or listener, or reader). What Machado adds to the Ortegan *óptica* is in effect to invite (in this case) the reader to scrutinize Kant (or Ortega) himself, to see the transmission as the product of a single view, and because of that also likely to be unidimensional. So, at the end of this section on Kant, Mairena replies with conversational pungency to the grandiose philosophical maxim *Universalia sunt nomina* ('Universal ideas have no reality except as names'): 'En efecto, eso es lo que usted cree' (IV, 1965).

As with Democritus' atomized view of the universe, Machiavelli's cynical one, and Galileo and Kant's mathematical approach, what Machado exposes here is the partisan argument which for him lacks the depth and validity that only dialogue can achieve, when our 'conciencia vigilante' is at its most perceptive. Mairena puts the argument bluntly in VI, 9: 'Tomar partido es no sólo renunciar a las razones de vuestros adversarios, sino también a las vuestras; abolir el diálogo, renunciar, en suma, a la razón humana' (IV, 1933). A good example of the kind of dialogue that could exist (but in this case does not) is implied in Mairena's discussion of the unfinished poem 'El huevo pasado por agua'. Prefacing his discussion with the remark that 'en otra ocasión definíamos la poesía como diálogo del hombre con el tiempo' (IV, 1937), Mairena lists all the basic objects used in cooking the egg, and the attendant circumstances — 'nuestra atención y nuestra impaciencia' — while waiting for the egg to boil, all these being converted to images in the poet's consciousness. They remain, however, like Democritus' isolated atoms, because 'falló nuestra simpatía por el huevo ... y no supimos vivir por dentro, hacer nuestro el proceso de su cocción', and the poem is never completed.

The first philosopher who is put under scrutiny in the book is Leibnitz. The Leibnitzian statement, paraphrased by Mairena as 'El individuo es todo' (IV, 1912), is an understandably early target for one who will define human reason (in VI, 9) as 'la comunión por el intelecto en verdades ... que ... son independientes del humor individual' (IV, 1933). If the individual is everything, asks Mairena, what then is society?

To which he answers: 'no hallo manera de sumar individuos'. Thoughts on the fragmentation of society (a social version of Democritus' atoms) lead to other thoughts on the fragmentation of knowledge through the pursuit of specialisms, another form of individualism. Then Mairena returns directly to Leibnitz, using the metaphor of the soul as a melody singing to itself with, we assume, God as 'una gran oreja' listening to the resultant symphony (or, Mairena postulates, 'una gran algarabía'). The musical metaphor, the humorous debunking, are in character, as Mairena develops the theme. In the following section a sentence from Spinoza is singled out for its absurd pretensions to knowledge (and is the target of Machado's affectionate lampooning for the solipsistic picture of God that it presents). 'Nuestro amor a Dios — decía Spinoza — es una parte del amor con que Dios se ama a sí mismo. "¡Lo que Dios se habrá reído" — decía mi maestro — "con esta graciosa y gedeónica reducción al absurdo del concepto de amor!" '. To which Mairena adds: 'Los grandes filósofos son los bufones de la divinidad' (IV, 1917). Aristotelian metaphysics is also subject to scrutiny, akin to that of Spinoza: 'Y arriba está Dios pensándose a sí mismo' (IV, 2081). Such humorous pricking of the bubble reputation and of the more absurd fancies of rational thought is of a piece with Mairena's analysis of what we might term a religious cliché in the previous section. The phrase 'amar a Dios sobre todas las cosas' is examined, in a parody of the scholastic, syllogistic mode of argument, in which Machado turns the tables on the scholastic method. The five stages of Mairena's argument are themselves a witty example of the 'cubicación' of language, as Mairena continues 'complicando ... el tema' (IV, 1931) in a pseudo-logical way.

It is likely that this debunking of classical philosophical thought was prompted by Machado's own awareness of the relative poverty of any significant lasting intellectual tradition in Spain. As a consciousness-raising exercise aimed in the first instance at his fellow-Spaniards this debunking in *Juan de Mairena* goes some way towards removing any unjustified sense of inferiority in the presence of the established philosophical reputations of other countries. (In XLIII, 5, Mairena tells his students of his wish to 'apartaros del respeto supersticioso, de la servidumbre a la letra en filosofía, sobre todo cuando pueda cohibir vuestra espontaneidad metafísica'.) In a *Mairena* piece published in February 1938 Machado gives us what is probably his most forthright view on the premium and prestige that is attached to logical thought, when he comments that 'La actividad lógica puede llevarnos a un acuerdo, pero, ¡qué poca cosa es ella en la totalidad de nuestra psique!' (IV, 2371). Assessing what contribution Spain has made (or can make) to philosophy, Mairena mentions two 'Spanish' philosophers — the younger Seneca and Averroes — only to reject their abiding influence on human thought. Other nations, Mairena says, have been able to establish and continue a philosophical tradition: Britain can look to the pragmatic tradition championed by Hume, while Germany could build on that tradition with Kant. Where can Spain turn to? Mairena's answer is to urge his students to 'acudir a nuestro folklore, o saber vivo en el alma del pueblo ... el folklore metafísico de nuestra tierra, especialmente el de la región castellana y andaluza' (IV, 2047-48). Not surprisingly, Cervantes is singled out as an author who would repay study related to the 'elementos folklóricos del *Quijote*'. The contents of the programme may not surprise the *cervantistas* of to-day, but its mode of expression is very much of a piece with the consciousness-expanding thrust of *Juan de Mairena*. Here is the paragraph (with its introductory sentence):

> Lo que los cervantistas nos dirán algún día, con relación a estos elementos folklóricos del *Quijote*, es algo parecido a esto.
>
> Hasta qué punto Cervantes los hace suyos; cómo los vive; cómo piensa y siente con ellos; cómo los utiliza y maneja; cómo los crea, a su vez, y cuántas veces son ellos molde del pensar cervantino. Por qué ese complejo de experiencia y juicio, de sentencia y gracia, que es el refrán, domina en Cervantes sobre el concepto escueto o revestido de artificio retórico. Cómo distribuye los refranes en esas conciencias complementarias de Don Quijote y Sancho. Cuándo en ellos habla la tierra, cuándo la raza, cuándo el hombre, cuándo la lengua misma. Cuál es su valor sentencioso y su valor crítico y su valor dialéctico. Esto y muchas cosas más podrían decirnos. (IV, 1997)

The eight verbs of the first sentence lend dynamism as well as diversity to the piece. This complexity is followed up by the four-fold description of the proverb as a 'complejo de experiencia y juicio, de sentencia y gracia', and by another four-fold description of the potential sources of such popular sayings, followed by a suggested analysis of their value on three levels. Yet the dynamic of the paragraph is not constituted simply by the 'cubing' effect of the piling on of examples, because the rush of ideas is made to reflect on itself by the presence of thirteen interrogative elements. Leaving aside the vast programme set out in the paragraph, the disposition of the language itself is an invitation to the expansion of thought and criticism of language. Throughout this brief paragraph on Cervantes, Machado/Mairena bombards the reader with an accumulation of observations, either in the form of a number of verbs or of a series of points. If time — and thought — are constantly moving, so Mairena aims to encourage his students to 'desarrollar [el] tema con toda la minuciosidad y toda la pesadez de que seáis capaces' (IV, 2081).

The topic referred to by Mairena in this last quotation is the Eleatic paradox, in which Achilles can never pass the tortoise because of the potentially infinite division and sub-division of the last step that Achilles must take as he attempts to outstrip his slow-moving rival. Mairena, applying the paradox to time as well as to space, comments: 'Ni Aquiles, el de los pies ligeros, alcanzaría nunca a la tortuga, ni una hora bien contada se acabaría nunca de contar' (IV, 2081). The aspect of *Juan de Mairena* that is concerned with consciousness raising is evident here, in Mairena's application of the Eleatic paradox to our consciousness of time: the 'cubing' of language is one way of attempting to saturate each moment with the heightened awareness of our 'conciencia vigilante'. 'Cubicación', then, allows both for the variety of human language which is not to be reduced by the language of mathematics and logic, and for a perspectivist depth of language, because language is itself the product of a world-view that must be scrutinized for what it is: a view or perspective.

With such emphasis on 'cubicación' in *Juan de Mairena* (1936) it is not surprising that Velázquez's *Las Meninas* is referred to (in chapter XXXII). We encounter the 'usual' perspectivism of the book in the section entitled 'Kant y Velázquez', with Mairena's references to 'mi maestro' Abel Martín, in which the comments are interlaced in such a way as to make it impossible to assign them unambiguously to either of the apocryphal teachers. In this case, however, their agreement concerning Velázquez's genius makes it easy to see Machado's own admiration for the painter, in a work such as *Las Meninas*. The first element of Velázquez's painting that the two teachers single out for praise is his consummate ability to transfer ideas and concepts into his work and onto the canvas, where they become captive 'en la jaula encantada del espacio y del tiempo' (IV, 2037). The metaphor used for this process, that of eating or drinking, is a fine example of the way that Machado could compress language by bringing together two such extreme opposites as human speculation and the physical possession of the act of eating or drinking, to describe what he calls the 'realism' of Velázquez: 'su realismo ... es el de un hombre que se tragó la metafísica y que, con ella en el vientre, nos dice: la pintura existe' (IV, 2037). The wonder expressed by Machado at Velázquez's superb aplomb is a timely reminder of the poet's own deep-felt need to bridge the gap between his meditations on the enigmas of the world, and their expression in such a form as to impress themselves upon all, very much in the way that he describes the impact of Velázquez's paintings in the last three words of the quotation. Arising from the image of eating and drinking is the second element of the painter's genius that is brought to our attention: his self-assurance and almost arrogant confidence in his achievements (which we see, incidentally, each time our eyes meet his in *Las Meninas*). At the end of the section Machado sums up this aspect of his view of Velázquez — the self-confident mastery of his medium — when he has Mairena quote Martín to the effect that 'la objetividad ... el tomarla en vilo para dejarla en un lienzo o en una piedra es siempre hazaña de gigantes'. During the Civil War Machado was to be offered in the starkest terms the challenge of rising to the needs of the hour and of expressing, with depth and the maximum degree of impact, his convictions about issues such as pluralism and peace. Ingesting and digesting ideas, imperatives and even slogans (the aphorisms of war) Machado, to judge by this description of Velázquez, must have envied the painter's spiritual strength and stature, and his genius, especially in *Las Meninas*, for representing and resolving the complexities of space captured in a given moment of time.

Since his is a classroom without textbooks, Mairena

recommends for discussion 'temas muy esenciales, que logren por sí mismos captar nuestra atención, estimular nuestros esfuerzos, conmovernos, apasionarnos y hasta sorprendernos' (IV, 1947). Thus, by a process of sifting and refinement, we arrive at what Mairena calls 'creencias últimas' (IV, 2063). Machado did not fully define what he meant by these latter until his *Mairena* article in the July 1937 edition of *Hora de España*, when Mairena described them as follows: 'Cuanto subsiste, si algo subsiste, tras el análisis exhaustivo o que pretende serlo, de la razón, nos descubre esa zona de lo fatal a que el hombre de algún modo presta su asentimiento'. The discovery of these beliefs, Mairena insists, is open to everybody — 'quién más, quién menos — a lo largo de su vida' (IV, 2340). Mairena's concern to choose 'temas muy esenciales' is of itself an attempt to extend the frontiers of culture. As an example we may note his criticism of the traditional concept of infinity, basing his objection on the proposition, as simple as it is ingenious, that

> La serie par es la mitad de la serie total de los números. La serie impar es la otra mitad. Pero la serie par y la serie impar son — ambas — infinitas. La serie total de los números es también infinita. ¿Será entonces doblemente infinita que la serie impar?
>
> (IV, 1924)

We have here a very graphic — and witty — illustration of the possibility of involvement in philosophical thought, without the need for abstruse terminology: it is an art within the reach of all. The apparently simple and even trivial anecdote of the meeting between Abel Martín and the old *sereno* assumes an added significance in this context of the democratization of culture. The old man explains to Martín that he keeps himself warm on very cold nights by squatting down with his lamp between his legs. Martín comments: 'Es usted un verdadero filósofo', to which the *sereno* replies: 'La vida enseña mucho' (IV, 2110). The 'temas muy esenciales', therefore, in *Juan de Mairena* fall very much within the spirit of the accessibility of culture preached by the *Misiones Pedagógicas*. And as the anecdote of the *sereno* and Martín makes clear, the phrase 'temas muy esenciales' may be understood as an attempt to broaden the definition of culture, because what is essential is not dependent on accidents of birth, education, fashion or historical circumstance.

The very format of *Juan de Mairena* (1936), with its four hundred and twenty-two fragments, many of them short pieces containing aphoristic sayings, or *sentencias*, as the book's sub-title informs us, may have been designed to allow access by persons who have not had much formal education. Neither is Mairena concerned to develop or conclude a topic at length: there are frequent references in the work to items of unfinished business, when he breaks off from a topic with a remark such as 'dejemos esto para tratado más largamente en otra ocasión' (IV, 2070), an occasion that rarely occurs again. Mairena refers to this lack of synthesizing intention and scope in his own teachings by suggesting that the Spanish mind is incapable of synthetic thought and that that task should be left to 'cerebros germánicos, pensadores capaces de manejar el gran cucharón de la historia de los pueblos y de las religiones' (IV, 2123);[37] but the comic incongruity of the ladle metaphor implies that the minuscule portions served up in aphoristic form by Machado in *Juan de Mairena* is part of a strategy to open the house of culture to a wider occupancy. Just as Don Quixote may be read simply, as a child's adventure story, so *Juan de Mairena* allows a reading that is simple or highly complex. The famous first piece, for example, about Agamemnon and his swineherd may be understood simply as the triumph of the native scepticism of the *campesino* over the rather self-satisfied attitude of his exotically named master, or as an epistemological commentary on the problem of perception: both of them fitting into the category of a 'tema muy esencial'. And as regards *Don Quixote*, it is significant that Machado should see the protagonists of the work, not as a knight and his squire, that is, not as representatives of a hierarchical society, but as 'dos conciencias ... complementarias, que caminan y que dialogan' (IV, 2040).

Mairena's desire to establish his *Escuela Popular de Sabiduría Superior* is within the same ideological spirit as the *Misiones Pedagógicas*. An interesting point of contact between Mairena's imaginary *Escuela Popular* and the *Misiones* is in their attitude to technical education. The 1934 Report of the *Patronato* states that the *Misiones* were approached by

---

[37] Macrì prints the last word of this quotation as 'regiones', a potentially confusing misprint.

'intereses profesionales agrícolas, médicas, de la arquitectura, de las artes y otros',[38] but Cossío (the author of the Report) comments that the *Misiones* could not become involved with them. Machado's point is directed against any method of education that does not question its own *raison d'être*. As regards practical education, Mairena comments: 'Pensamos, además, que [el pueblo] ha de agradecernos esas escuelas prácticas donde puede aprender la manera más científica y económica de aserrar un tablón. Y creemos inocentemente que se reiría en nuestras barbas si le hablásemos de Platón. Grave error' (IV, 2054). Cossío was also aware of the danger for the *Misiones* through its primary emphasis on the extension of artistic culture, in a country such as Spain, forty per cent of whose population were still illiterate.[39] In a sentence in the Report that could have been taken from *Juan de Mairena* Cossío, discussing the ethos of the *Misiones*, describes the value of '[el] humano, pero privilegiado reino de lo inútil y lo contemplativo ... que la humanidad, por miserable que sea, persigue con afán al par del alimento'.[40]

Such old-fashioned contemplative humanism was largely destined to be blasted away in the heat of the activist imperatives of the Civil War, when the *Misiones Pedagógicas* became in part subsumed into the Republic's military infrastructure and known as *Milicias de la cultura*.[41] Even by the end of 1934, and especially in the wake of the bloody outcome of the October revolution in Asturias, the *Misiones Pedagógicas* came under increased fire from the political left. Josep Renau, who was active in communist politics during the Civil War, has criticized organizations such as the *Institución Libre de Enseñanza* and the *Misiones Pedagógicas* for their 'elitismo paternalista, que consideraba a la masa campesina poco menos que como un "saco vacío" que había que "llenar" con versiones "de izquierda" de la cultura y salvo una inteligente

---

38 *Patronato, op. cit.*, 6.
39 *Ibid.*, XXII.
40 *Ibid.*, XXIII.
41 See Juan Manuel Fernández Soria, *Educación y cultura en la Guerra Civil (España 1936-39)* (Valencia: Nau Llibres, 1984), 50-53; and for details of the new military organization of the Republic's Civil-War cultural initiatives see Georges Soria, *Guerra y revolución en España (1936-1939)*, 5 vols (Barcelona: Ediciones Océano, 1978), V, 222.

investigación folklórica que paralelamente se realizaba, había una muy escasa predisposición "a la recíproca", es decir, al necesario y vital *feed-back* del pueblo sobre ellos'. Renau goes on to give his opinion that 'De los valores consagrados de la época [the pre-war years of the Republic], sólo se salvaban Antonio Machado y Valle Inclán'.[42] Eugenio Otero gives us an interesting picture of the kind of tension that could arise within the *Misiones Pedagógicas* when he cites an anecdote of Rafael Dieste, a prominent *misionero*. After what Dieste describes as a very patronizing speech by one of the government inspectors of the *Misiones* the former stood up and spoke to the people of the village as follows: 'Vosotros sois los depositarios de la lengua que hablaron Cervantes y las gentes que antaño la esparcieron por el mundo ... Vosotros que tenéis tan maravillosas canciones y tan buenas mozas y tan buena gente ¡a ver si os conserváis así!'. And he goes on to comment: 'En primer lugar procurábamos devolver la conciencia de sus propios valores al pueblo'.[43] As we are about to examine from the evidence of *Juan de Mairena*, Machado would have heartily endorsed Dieste's views, but he would not have limited himself to 'maravillosas canciones' or to the ambit conventionally assigned to culture. In this respect Tuñón de Lara has cogently summed up the range and force of the *Mairena* writings: 'su originalidad, su alcance y su vigencia ... residen ... en la temática que va desde la valoración de lo popular y las relaciones entre la cultura y la sociedad, hasta un alto humanismo'.[44] During the war itself the Republic's desperate need for what Spaniards to-day would call 'concienciación' of the war issues, gave Machado the opportunity to continue to work broadly within the same range of ideas as in the pre-war *Mairena* series.

To understand in what ways Machado diverged from the programme of the *Misiones Pedagógicas*, it is worthwhile examining some uses of the word 'misión' in *Juan de Mairena* (1936). The word is used seven times, and in a text of over four hundred fragments an examination of its use may act as a thread to guide us through the formal labyrinth made up of

---

[42] See his Introduction to the facsimile edition of *Nueva Cultura*, published by Topos Verlag AG, Vaduz, Liechtenstein, n.d., XX-XXI.
[43] *Op. cit.*, 150 and 151.
[44] *Op. cit.*, 256.

these fragments. Of the word's seven appearances we have chosen the four in which Mairena uses it to speak of his own ideals for education and culture. The word first appears in chapter XIV. The complete paragraph reads:

> Hay que tener los ojos muy abiertos para ver las cosas como son; aun más abiertos para verlas otras de lo que son; más abiertos todavía para verlas mejores de lo que son. Yo os aconsejo la visión vigilante, porque vuestra misión es ver e imaginar despiertos, y que no pidáis al sueño sino reposo.

Mairena's advice to his students to be vigilant during every second of their working lives means that his profession as teacher is essentially secondary to his true 'mission': that of encouraging his listeners to 'abrir mucho los ojos, abrirlos más', to maintain 'la visión vigilante' and to 'imaginar despiertos'. What Mairena is teaching his students is not a pedagogical programme in the commonly accepted sense of these words, but rather a way of being and living. Paul Aubert has made the same point about Machado's poetry, without referring to any specific period: 'la poesía [de Machado] no depende de ningún arte particular. Es para él un estado de conciencia, una manera de ser'.[45] As Francisco J. Díaz de Castro has rightly observed of Mairena's classroom: 'la única base de la enseñanza, el único material escolar es la palabra hablada',[46] to which we could add that the only learning methods advised are 'ver e imaginar'. Mairena is happy to be without any of the apparatus of pedagogy and culture in his classroom: without a dais, without books, without plays or paintings or the rote-learning of poetry; 'ligero de equipaje', as Machado depicted himself in his *Retrato*.

If there is any pedagogical method in Mairena's conduct of lessons, it can be seen in the context of the next occasion when Mairena uses the word 'misión'. From time to time Mairena speaks in class of commonplace and set phrases, and clichés, advising his students to study the wit and wisdom of these phrases, 'porque, en efecto, nuestra misión es singularizarlos,

---

[45] 'La cultura y los intelectuales en la obra y vida de Antonio Machado', in *Boletín de la Asociación Europea de Profesores de Español*, XVI (1977), 17-34, at 22.

[46] *El último Antonio Machado ('Juan de Mairena' y el ideal pedagógico machadiano)* (Palma de Mallorca: Universitat de Palma de Mallorca, 1984), 72.

ponerles el sello de nuestra individualidad, que es la manera de darles un nuevo impulso para que sigan rodando' (IV, 1967). This cultural 'mission' is at a great remove from that of Cossío's *Misiones Pedagógicas*, because in Mairena's statement the definition of culture has been enormously amplified: the assessment of any phrase or commonplace saying is a contribution to the increase of culture. When discussing his *Escuela Popular de Sabiduría Superior* and of its 'aspecto más profundamente didáctico' (IV, 2057), Mairena also uses the word 'misión' here in a very broad sense: 'Nuestra misión es adelantarnos por la inteligencia a devolver su dignidad de hombre al animal humano'. Everything in *Juan de Mairena* revolves around basically simple ideas such as these: the use of the intelligence, the dignity of the person. These ideas have much more to do with a way of being than with any pedagogical or cultural programme. The last use of the word 'misión' to which we will refer occurs when Mairena, speaking of his work as a teacher of Rhetoric, comments on his hopes for the students who attend his classes: 'Yo no olvido nunca, señores, que soy un profesor de Retórica, cuya misión no es formar oradores, sino, por el contrario, hombres que hablen bien siempre que tengan algo bueno que decir' (IV, 2088). This is an observation that attempts to embrace a whole mode of thinking and is a piece of advice that can be followed by everyone: 'tener algo bueno que decir', which offers everybody born to the light of reason and imagination the power of contributing to the culture of the centuries.

Therefore Machado's inclusivist view of culture makes it easy to understand how his position during the Civil War did not need any essential modification. If on all the fronts in wartime every available scrap of energy has to be used to further the war effort, so too on the cultural front these broad definitions of Machado allow and encourage the intelligent participation of all, to the fullest measure of their capacity. A quotation from the wartime journal *Cultura Popular* will help to show how Machado's ideas anticipated aspects of the cultural revolution in the Republic of the Civil War. The writer in *Cultura Popular* in defining culture attempts to create an enhanced awareness of many of the strands of the social fabric, doubtless responding to the need to harness intelligent energies to the full. Culture for this writer lies

> en alcanzar un alto grado de perfección moral en el orden de la justicia y de la libertad, en poseer una afinada sensibilidad para captar matices de lo bello, tanto en la naturaleza como en la creación artística, y en estar dotados de aguda curiosidad intelectual para escudriñar los misterios de la ciencia.[47]

The phrase taken for our chapter title — Mairena's remark: 'La verdad es que las ideas no deben ser de nadie' (IV, 1979) — is another pointer towards the way in which Machado proposed the democratization of culture, which is such a fundamental aspect of *Juan de Mairena*. Closely linked to this quotation is the part played by Machado's use of apocryphal creations in the work. In spite of the perspectivist irony that arises through the openly fictitious mode of the work, the continuous presence of the apocryphal in *Juan de Mairena* is not an evasion of authorial responsibility, but is rather another tool for acknowledging Machado's view of the essentially democratic nature of culture. Using apocryphal creations Machado removes the individualist element from the creation of culture and replaces it by a collective authority. The use of the apocryphal in the case of Juan de Mairena and Abel Martín is based on Machado's idea of the collective significance of any work that is well done. Recognizing the individual genius of Cervantes or Shakespeare, Machado none the less indicates the debt of these writers to the people or country in which they lived and worked. Mairena asks: '¿es Shakespeare inglés, o es Inglaterra shakespeariana?' (IV, 2104), and of Cervantes he says: 'Sin la asimilación y el dominio de una lengua madura de ciencia y conciencia popular, ni la obra inmortal [*Don Quixote*] ni nada equivalente pudo escribirse' (IV, 1996). Machado diffuses the authorship of his work among various personages, recognizing, as Mairena says, quoting Abel Martín, that 'las obras poéticas realmente bellas ... rara vez tienen un solo autor' (IV, 2015). And he finishes by recommending to his 'discípulos' — as Machado calls Mairena's students on this occasion —: 'Guardad en la memoria estas palabras, que mi maestro confesaba haber oído a su abuelo, el cual, a su vez, creía haberlas oído en alguna

---

47 J. Manaut Viglietti, 'El arte, instrumento de la cultura popular', in *Cultura Popular*, II (December 1937), 2.

parte'. (There are, incidentally, over one hundred references by Mairena to 'mi maestro' Abel Martín in the 1936 book.) The reverse of this delicately ironic example of the apocryphal occurs when Machado deals with the role of specialists in the work of culture. There cannot be an increase in culture, Mairena tells us, through the work of such specialists: what is increased 'abrumadoramente [es] el volumen de la conciencia de la propia ignorancia' (IV, 2023) because it is almost always someone else who knows about some problem or topic. Intellectual specialism, seen in this light, is a cultural version of the extremes of private property. Remembering Machado's words of 1919, concerning his vision of cultural life as 'una tarea común [que] apasione las almas' (III, 1603), makes us aware of how deep-rooted was the democratic spirit in the poet's ideas.

It would be inconceivable, therefore, that Machado should have voiced any serious doubts about the work of the *Misiones Pedagógicas*. It is interesting to recall that in *Juan de Mairena* itself Machado dedicated some warm and respectful words of homage to the founder of the *Misiones*, on the occasion of Cossío's death in September of 1935. The very presence of the *misioneros* in the remote villages was eloquent testimony to their solidarity with them and a recognition of their innate dignity. One only has to consult the photographs included in Germán Somolinos' work on the *Misiones* in order to see the elaborate presentation, the scrupulous attention to detail of these *misioneros* to ensure that their travelling exhibition of paintings should be as dignified and agreeable as possible.[48] The fundamental difference between the *Misiones Pedagógicas* and the ideas of cultural expansion in *Juan de Mairena* is that Machado felt himself too indebted to the *pueblo* to believe that he could bring them the experience of culture, as if to a *tabula rasa*. Doubtless Machado's residence in Soria renewed his sympathy for country life, born perhaps of his excursions outside Madrid during his days in the *Institución*, but reiterated in *Juan de Mairena* (1936), where Mairena is concerned to 'despertar en el niño el amor a la naturaleza' (IV, 1961). For Mairena there was in the countryside itself sufficient material for a complete programme of studies and recreation, because, as

---

[48] Germán Somolinos D'Ardois, 'Las Misiones Pedagógicas de España (1931-1936)', *Cuadernos Americanos*, XII (1953), 206-24.

he ingeniously and perversely points out, the countryside offers physical exercise and recreation, excites one's curiosity and scientific instinct, and one can be a student in the school of nature for the whole of one's life. Mairena's praises of the countryside in chapter XXVII are also of interest, with reference to its pedagogical or rather philosophical role in our lives: 'Tampoco hemos de olvidar la lección del campo para nuestro amor propio. Es en la soledad campesina donde el hombre deja de vivir entre espejos' (IV, 2017).

In an important paragraph in chapter XII Machado deals with the contribution to culture of the *pueblo*, in its urban setting. In the section Machado tells us that 'Mairena vivía en una gran población andaluza, compuesta de una burguesía algo beocia, de una aristocracia demasiado rural y de un pueblo inteligente, fino, sensible, de artesanos que saben su oficio y para quienes el hacer bien las cosas es, como para el artista, mucho más importante que el hacerlas' (IV, 1954). Mairena's opinion, drawing on his own particular social situation and on his position as a teacher, is that 'el pueblo sabe más, y sobre todo, mejor que nosotros. El hombre que sabe hacer algo de un modo perfecto — un zapato, un sombrero, una guitarra, un ladrillo — no es nunca un trabajador inconsciente, que ajusta su labor a viejas fórmulas y recetas, sino un artista que pone toda su alma en cada momento de su trabajo' (IV, 1954). Although one could argue that Mairena's attitude here arises from a specific situation, without any possible general deductions, Machado is consistent with these views of the *pueblo* and of Mairena's recognition of the *pueblo* as an authentic creator of culture. For Machado the *pueblo* not only has the right to enter the great house of culture, but it is already in occupancy by virtue of its own contributions, because, as Mairena remarks, '[el pueblo] sabe muy bien lo poco que nosotros leemos' (IV, 2054). Machado suggests, therefore, that the truly important cultural task of the times is to investigate in what ways the conventionally educated people, the so-called guardians of culture, may learn from the culture of the *pueblo*. Seen from this perspective *Juan de Mairena* (1936) goes beyond the 'viejas fórmulas y recetas' of a conventional culture 'hecha a desgana' (IV, 1954) and, in the recognition of the culture of the ordinary people of country and city, is an attempt to create a new culture.

The coincidence in thought in this regard between Machado and Antonio Gramsci is not surprising. Gramsci went so far as to claim that the teaching of popular culture would bring about a new Reformation, when he wrote:

> El folklore no debe concebirse como un elemento extraño, raro o pintoresco, sino como algo muy serio que debe tomarse muy en serio. Sólo de esta manera la enseñanza [del folklore] será eficaz y determinará la aparición de una nueva cultura en las grandes masas populares, es decir, colmará la distancia que separa la cultura moderna de la cultura popular o folklore. Una actividad de este tipo, realizada en profundidad, corresponderá en el plano intelectual a lo que fue la Reforma en los países protestantes.[49]

What is of interest in the respective attitude of both writers is that while Machado, too, thinks of popular culture as 'algo muy serio que debe tomarse muy en serio', he also incorporates culture into a way of living or, in the example just quoted, into an artisan's daily work, in which the artisan is transformed into an artist through the concentration given to the work in hand. The implicit dignity thus ascribed by Machado to the artisan is another indication that his transition from these pre-war writings to the urgent needs of the war itself was logical and unforced.

For this new culture one does not even have to understand a concept or to express oneself logically. In *Juan de Mairena* there is a section devoted to 'aciertos de la expresión inexacta' (IV, 2065), and for the principles of his programme of studies for a 'nueva lógica' Mairena recommends the examination of 'las deducciones incorrectas, los razonamientos defectuosos, los ilogismos populares, las confusiones verbales de los borrachos y deficientes mentales, etc.' (IV, 2008) in order to draw out the complex riches they contain. Machado's culture does not cultivate the specialism of the answer, but, as Mairena says of Socrates and Christ, one that knows how to ask questions and to wait for a reply (IV, 1969). Thus Mairena advises his students: always ask questions, without worrying whether their questions fit into any accepted logic, because 'toda incomprensión es fecunda ... siempre que vaya acompañada de un deseo de comprender' (IV, 2093). For Mairena the grandeur

---

49 A. Gramsci, *Cultura y literatura*, ed. Jordi Solé-Tura (Madrid: Ediciones Península, 1967), 332-33.

of the history of philosophical thought is that it has been 'capaz de fecundar a través del tiempo la heroica y tenaz incomprensión de los hombres' (IV, 2093). And he recommends his students to reject 'la usuraria pretensión de no equivocaros' (IV, 2005). In his *Escuela Popular de Sabiduría Superior* Mairena would rank among the most important researchers 'al hombre ingenuo, capaz de plantearse espontáneamente los problemas más esenciales' (IV, 2059). Neither would it be necessary in the *Escuela Popular* to have undertaken historical studies before entry. One is aware throughout *Juan de Mairena* that Machado is not at all concerned to situate in a specific historical context any of the many artists and intellectuals studied, 'porque somos filósofos', Mairena observes, 'hombres de reflexión que buscan razones en los hechos' (IV, 2062). The studies of the *Escuela* are therefore open to anyone who is prepared to bring a 'conciencia vigilante' to bear on the problems being discussed. Mairena's course in progress includes, as we have seen, the examination of the commonplace phrases, clichés and proverbs, that is the accumulated treasure of sayings that are worth studying from many points of view, but above all the proverbs of folk wisdom: 'ese complejo de experiencia y juicio, de sentencia y gracia, que es el refrán' (IV, 1997).

Throughout the text of *Juan de Mairena* Machado demonstrates his cultural indebtedness to the collective wisdom of everyday sayings in a way that he had made his own since the *coplas* of *Soledades. Galerías. Otros poemas* and the 'Proverbios y cantares' of *Campos de Castilla* and *Nuevas canciones*. *Juan de Mairena* (1936) is like a great *refranero* or collection of aphoristic sayings, a tribute by Machado to the ordinary Spanish people who inspired them. Given Machado's educational and philosophical interests it was not surprising that he should steer his use of the form of the proverb towards questions of perception and the acquisition of understanding through dialogue; as, for example, in his aphoristic phrases 'Toda visión requiere distancia' and 'Lo inevitable es ir de lo uno a lo otro'. As to how such an attitude to folk wisdom might have affected his view of the *Misiones Pedagógicas*: the result is that *Juan de Mairena* (1936), although to some extent within the same ideological spirit as the *Misiones Pedagógicas*, only shares it to a partial degree. Machado's position also leaned towards showing people without much or even any background in classical culture the treasury that folk wisdom has accumulated in its sayings, and how this treasury deserved study, refinement, adaptation and renewal, through the exercise of one's own 'conciencia vigilante'. Machado achieves this raising of consciousness with a dual strategy; firstly by a critique of classical culture, through the examination of examples of past thought and perception, whereby some of the great thinkers of history are scrutinized and their contribution to thought is critically — and humorously — reviewed. If there is a process of levelling down at work here, it is done on the legitimate basis of 'no authority without consensus': there cannot be, as Mairena in a Civil-War piece in *Hora de España* commented, 'idólos de nuestro pensamiento que procuramos poner a salvo de la crítica' (IV, 2340). Secondly, this idea is complemented by the rather more positive evaluation of the collective authority of proverbs, aphorisms and sayings sanctioned by widespread use, but themselves also subject to assessment, revaluation and renewal. Such a balance between the common and the classical was to act as a valuable base which Machado was soon to use in the as yet only imperfectly perceived partnership of workers and intellectuals on the side of the Republic during the Civil War. Juan Manuel Fernández Soria is right to draw a distinction between the educational policies of the Republic before and during the Civil War, as follows:

> la corriente populista [of the pre-war years] caracterizada por el paternalismo y regeneracionismo ... consideraba al pueblo como un ser receptivo, al que se le proporciona la cultura como una obra de caridad ... En el segundo tiempo de la República, enmarcado por la guerra, el populismo deja paso a lo popular; de receptivo el pueblo pasa a ser considerado como protagonista consciente en la lucha contra el fascismo.[50]

While one would take issue with the phrase 'obra de caridad' (it would certainly be unfair to characterize Cossío's view of the *Misiones Pedagógicas* as such, rather than as a work of justice), in the light of the general shift in sensibility outlined in the quotation, Machado's integrity of view, evident in these pre-war years of *Juan de Mairena*, takes on greater significance for his

---

50 *Op. cit.*, 310-11.

later role during the Civil War itself. Oreste Macrì also sees Machado's absorption and adaptation of popular culture in *Juan de Mairena* (1936) as an important element (among many others) in his Civil-War writings: 'Así, pues, éste es el Machado que se prepara para los años de la guerra civil. Bajo la especie del profesor Juan de Mairena, cuyo monumento es la edición de 1936, se ha descarnado, se ha reducido a lo elemental del arte popular' (I, 239). Therefore when Mairena praises 'el secreto de la serena grandeza de Velázquez' in the phrase 'Él pinta por todos y para todos', Machado is also writing about his own debt owed ('por') and to be repaid ('para') to the collective consciousness of the 'people', a word that, as we shall see, did not have any definitive relationship with social class, in Machado's view of it. The 'formas sencillas y populares' (IV, 1938) of *Juan de Mairena* (1936) are there not only to extend literary and intellectual culture to a wider public, but these very forms act as a recognition by Machado of the common treasury of art and intellect, and as the expression of his own debt to this treasury that had inspired so much of his work.

CHAPTER 2

'Un miliciano más con un destino cultural'
La Guerra (1937)

When Machado published *Juan de Mairena* in June 1936 it was not to be republished within the two and a half years of life remaining to the poet. Machado returned to the *Juan de Mairena* format for his contributions to *Hora de España*, which began publication in January 1937. Allowing for the upheaval in Madrid in the latter half of 1936, and the impossibility for Machado of contemplating any immediate return to drama with Manuel, who was on 'the other side' in Burgos, there is still a big, unexplained gap of four or five months (between August and December 1936) when, it would appear, Machado wrote very little. The combined efforts of Machado's recent editors, Julio Rodríguez Puértolas (with Gerardo Pérez Herrero), Monique Alonso and Oreste Macrì have only managed to unearth less than twenty pages of text, approximately one third of which are interviews. Machado's references to his being 'viejo y enfermo' (IV, 2166) during the early months of the war may help us partially to understand why he did not compose very much at that time. The poet's brief words to the *Quinto Regimiento* on the occasion of the evacuation of artists and intellectuals from Madrid to Valencia towards the end of November, in which he refers to himself in the terms just quoted, are confirmed by a photograph of Machado at a dinner (in the issue of *El Mono Azul* that was published on 5 November 1936), in which he looks very tired indeed. Of the early days in Valencia José Machado has written that Antonio 'llegó a estar de una nerviosidad y extenuación realmente alarmante'.[1] Machado's poem on the death of Lorca, published in *Ayuda*, no. 22, on 17 October 1936, is unquestionably the most important of

---

1   *Op. cit.*, 137.

his writings in the last months of 1936. An earlier article, 'Los milicianos de 1936', is dated 'agosto 1936' by Machado. Both these pieces, although referring to the violence of war, maintain a more metaphysical concern for the consciousness of the individual when faced with death. They are essentially the reaction of an individual (Machado) who hears or reads news of the war, and sees in the response of Lorca, or the militiamen (or the Cid, in another epoch) a proof of their *hombría* (IV, 2164) and that they are to be counted among 'los mejores' (IV, 2165). Both these texts were included in *La Guerra*,[2] the only book of original material published by Machado after 1936, and which included pieces written between August 1936 and May 1937.

On his arrival at Valencia, however, Machado gave an interview that is a stark contrast with the quieter, more contemplative note that dominates 'Los milicianos de 1936' and the last two sections, at least, of the poem to Lorca. His words amount to a veritable artistic and intellectual manifesto in the face of the conflict that had engulfed Spain, but also with wider ramifications for the whole of humanity. The interview is titled 'Declaraciones de Antonio Machado en la Casa de la Cultura de Valencia, noviembre de 1936'. In all probability the principal motivation for Machado's direct and very blunt tone throughout the interview arose from his experience of the sustained aerial bombing of Madrid, earlier in that same month of November. 'He visto', he is reported as saying, 'las huellas de las bombas dirigidas a estos dos templos de la cultura [the Museo del Prado and the Biblioteca Nacional]' (IV, 2169). Machado's theme throughout the interview is that fascism intentionally sets out to destroy culture — the manifestation of the spirit of humanity — because it is the negation of this spirit. Machado then derives three consequences from this position. The first is the recognition of a debt of gratitude to the rank-and-file militia who have been guarding these 'templos de la cultura', without any reference to social class or political ideology: Machado cites

---

2   Antonio Machado, *La Guerra. Dibujos de José Machado. 1936-1937* (Madrid: Espasa-Calpe, 1937). The title is printed as LA GUERRA, which makes it unclear whether the second word should be capitalized, since the first is not. Because the title *La guerra* could mean *War* as well as *The War* (that is, in the latter case, the Spanish Civil War) I have opted for this more definite second meaning by capitalizing the second word.

the example of the communist militia guarding the palaces and treasures of the Duke of Alba in the centre of Madrid. (The Duke of Alba was Franco's agent in London during the Civil War.) The second consequence is that Spanish artists and intellectuals should act upon this debt of gratitude by becoming cultural militiamen in the struggle for the preservation of the intellectual and artistic life of Spain. Thirdly, because culture is the heritage of humanity, intellectuals all over the world should rally to the cause of the Republic, which is the cause of humanity.

Our chapter title is taken from this Valencia interview, in which Machado states that 'una obligación inmediata e imperativa tiene todo intelectual: la de ser un miliciano más con un destino cultural' (IV, 2171). As we have already indicated, the book *La Guerra* spans a period before and after this interview, and the pieces included in it enable us to obtain a real insight into the way that Machado expressed his response to the Civil War during its first year. There is in the book a blend of contemplative and active elements, exhortations to thought and action that, however it might at first sight appear to be a miscellany of isolated pieces of poetry and prose, gives it a unity: the solidarity of the intellectual and the soldier, especially the *miliciano*, in their common effort to win the war. Or as Jaume Pont has expressed it: 'El último libro de Machado redimensiona el compromiso del intelectual'.[3] *La Guerra* acts as a focus for the collaboration of arms and letters in defence of the Republic. This extraordinary alliance between education, culture and the military war effort in the Republic of the Civil War, and which is so faithfully mirrored and expressed in *La Guerra*, is a vast area of study, but may be summarily revealed, perhaps, in an interesting statistic quoted in *Ayuda*, no. 43, of 20 February 1937. *Ayuda* quotes the Republic's budgetary estimates for the year as, 'para las atenciones del Ministerio de Instrucción Pública y Bellas Artes se destinan 496.559.668 pesetas. Mucho más que para el Ministerio de la Guerra, que son 407 millones'.

In the November 1936 interview from which we have quoted, Machado's use of the phrase 'un miliciano más' rather

---

[3] 'Sobre *La guerra* de Antonio Machado', in *Antonio Machado hoy*, I, 477-86.

than just 'un miliciano' emphasizes the solidarity of the intellectual with the ordinary militia. In *La Guerra* Machado shows himself to be 'un miliciano más', not only because he shares the composition of the book with his artist brother José, but because of the forty-eight drawings contributed by the latter (amounting to half the space of the book), thirty-seven are sketches of what appear to be rank-and-file soldiers and militiamen (none has any badge of command). The reiterated presence of these portraits makes them to some extent become the protagonists of the book. The portrait that heads the book is that of General Miaja who had become well known for his part in the defence of Madrid. What we see of his uniform makes him seem more like a waiter in a popular restaurant than a general. That is, his dress is popular and democratic rather than hierarchical and militaristic.[4] Miaja's wire-framed glasses give him the appearance of a scholar or intellectual who has emerged from a library to take part spontaneously in the defence of the Republic. The portrait therefore brings together aspects of the alliance between the different sectors in the Republic, of manual, intellectual and military work. (The other ten drawings comprise six Spanish landscapes,[5] and portraits of Lorca, Machado, the sculptor Emiliano Barral and the Education Minister, Jesús Hernández.) It is worth noting, too, in the context of this book as a collaborative work between brothers, and not an enterprise controlled by the more famous of the two, that José's drawings for the most part are not determined by Antonio's written text, except in three instances: the portraits of Lorca, of Antonio himself and of Emiliano Barral. The book as an authentic collaboration between the two brothers gave, perhaps, whether consciously or not, an image opposed to the war of brother against brother and a vision of a new Spain, marked by the sign of cooperation, but based on a certain criterion of mutual independence. Examples of the

---

4   Compare, for example, a drawing of Miaja by Miguel Prieto in *Nueva Cultura*, of May 1937. Dressed in his greatcoat and general's cap, he presents a much more military bearing than in José Machado's portrait.

5   Rafael Ferreres ('Antonio Machado en Valencia', *Cuadernos Hispanoamericanos*, CCCIV-CCCVII [1975-1976], 374-85), has identified these landscapes as drawings of the environs of Villa Amparo in Rocafort about five miles from Valencia, where José and Antonio lived during 1937 and part of 1938.

latter are the portraits of Miaja and Jesús Hernández, since they are not referred to in the actual text of the book. It seems that both José and Antonio had almost complete freedom for the ordering of their work within the overall design of the book.

The work of the brothers Machado in *La Guerra*, both complementary and independent at the same time, projects a pluralist image of the threatened Republic. The independence of criterion is shown in the division of work in the book, as we have just noted. At times this independence creates some lack of equilibrium between what Antonio has written and José has drawn. Of the six landscape drawings, none is beside the only landscape piece of writing in the book: the verse section of 'Meditación del día'. Under the last portrait of the work, which immediately precedes the 'Discurso a las Juventudes Socialistas Unificadas', Jesús Hernández is described as the 'primer ministro de Instrucción Pública, comunista, de la República Española'. But in the piece itself Machado confesses: 'me falta simpatía por la idea central del marxismo: me resisto a creer que el factor económico, cuya enorme importancia no desconozco, sea el más esencial de la vida humana y el gran motor de la historia' (IV, 2191). The independent criterion of *La Guerra* can also be seen when Machado confesses that he has been deeply moved by aspects of the philosophy of Martin Heidegger, criticized at the time as a fascist by José Bergamín and other republicans. Machado uses Heidegger's philosophy to meditate on the situation of the militia, as we shall see. His defence of Unamuno in *La Guerra* is in contrast with Jesús Hernández's own description of Unamuno as a 'viejo escritor reaccionario'.[6] Also, the pluralism of *La Guerra* may be seen in the presence of the portraits of Miaja, a convinced Catholic, by all accounts, and the communist Hernández: an image of opposed ideologies united in defence of the Republic. These two portraits would also have represented the collaboration between arms and letters, symbolized by the general, and the minister responsible for cultural as well as educational matters.

The question of pluralism is an integral part of any discussion of culture and society in the Spanish Republic of the Civil War. The Republic's political roots lay in a liberal

---

6 *A los intelectuales de España* (Barcelona: Ediciones del Partido Comunista de España, 1937), 10 (a fifteen-page pamphlet).

parliamentary system, and while its hopes for survival in the war were initially connected with Soviet Russia, victory in the long run could not come about without the active assistance of at least one of the two principal European democracies, Britain and France. The identification of the vast majority of Spain's best-known artists and intellectuals with the cause of the Republic was itself an assurance of pluralism, because they could be relied upon to articulate the spread of views that a liberal democracy accepts as part of its ethos. If there could be said to have been a foreign cultural policy in the Republic during the Civil War, it was aimed at Britain and France, and attempted to demonstrate that these latter had much more in common with the Republic than with Franco's Spain, which had been recognized by the fascist dictatorships of Germany and Italy as early as November of 1936. As Georges Soria has observed: 'los intelectuales ... confirieron a la República popular pluralista una preciosa garantía de cara al exterior, en la medida en que se erigieron en fiadores, a los ojos del mundo, de aquel humanismo que el fascismo abominaba'.[7] Soria also observes that in the Republic 'los intelectuales constituyeron una especie de vínculo entre los diversos estratos de la población',[8] and writers' espousal of popular forms and themes certainly did help to build such bridges.

The Machados' book has also other physical or structural characteristics that can help us to place it within the Republic's artistic and political ideology. One of the first things about the 1937 edition of *La Guerra* that comes to the attention of the reader is its small amount of written text: not much more than about five thousand words. The one hundred and fifteen pages of the book are due in part to the forty-eight illustrations and also to the written text's typography, which is very large. José Machado called it a 'lujoso libro',[9] a rather misplaced description, although the quality of the paper is superior, unless he was referring here to his own pen and ink drawings in the book, meaning that it was 'lujosamente ilustrado'. If the book were destined for the trenches — and why not? — the

---

7 *Guerra y revolución en España (1936-1939)*, 5 vols (Barcelona: Ediciones Océano, 1978), V, 216-17.
8 *Op. cit.*, V, 216.
9 *Op. cit.*, 139.

combatants, less than half of them because of low standards of literacy in Garcilaso's situation, 'tomando ora la espada, ora la pluma', but all of them eager to receive views on the war, could peruse it in a short time before passing it on to a companion.[10] For those who found reading difficult, the large-faced, relatively brief text would facilitate at least some assimilation of its contents. If, however, for whatever circumstances, there was no time for other than a brief reading of Antonio's text, one or more of José's drawings might remain in the memory. Therefore, the conjunction of word and image could facilitate a fairly rapid assimilation of the book's contents; a conjunction that represented not only a work shared between brothers but also an art within the reach of all.

The inclusion of the portrait of Jesús Hernández means that it was very likely that *La Guerra* was supported financially by the Ministerio de Instrucción Pública. Unfortunately the archives of the book's publishers (Espasa-Calpe) for that period have been lost,[11] making it impossible to check the conditions of the book's publication and circulation. The reason for the inclusion of the portrait may, however, have been more altruistic. Hernández's work to bring about an authentic cultural revolution in Civil-War Republican Spain,[12] mainly through a sustained drive against illiteracy and the creation of thousands of new schools, was recognized by Machado, when he wrote to Tomás Navarro Tomás at the end of 1936: 'el Ministerio de Instrucción Pública ... aparece en España por primera vez a la altura de su misión' (IV, 2168). (Machado was one who chose his words carefully, and the quotation leads one to question what he may have thought of the Education Ministry that brought in the *Misiones Pedagógicas* in 1931.) Hernández was responsible for incorporating the *Milicias de la cultura*, formed in August 1936, into the military infrastructure

---

10 The journal *Armas y Letras* in its first number of 1 August 1937 stated that the organization *Milicias de la cultura* was aimed at 'analfabetos ... hombres de cultura media y otros que desconocen nuestro idioma'.

11 This information was communicated to me in 1989 by Sr Manuel Durán of Espasa-Calpe.

12 For a brief account of Jesús Hernández' educational and cultural initiatives during his time as Education Minister see Hipólito Escolar Sobrino, *La cultura durante la guerra civil* (Madrid: Alhambra, 1987), 80-92.

in January of 1937.[13] *Milicias de la cultura* in their turn were primarily responsible for raising literacy and cultural standards among the Republic's armed forces. A month after the foundation of the *Milicias de la cultura* Hernández, in a ministerial Order, gave effect to the creation of *brigadas volantes*, which were to pursue the same objectives among the civilian population, especially the *campesinos*.[14] The organization *Cultura Popular* dealt with the creation and servicing of a popular library system.[15] Vicente Salas Viu in his *Diario de guerra de un soldado* has evoked the setting of the Republic's battlefront in its basic cultural context:

> En la trinchera que ocupamos y que sólo unos metros separan de la del enemigo, los soldados han excavado el suelo con las bayonetas, para instalar en el hoyo un armarito lleno de libros, colocado ante un banco de arena, en el que se sientan para leer, y un tablón al que va fijado el periódico mural. Fotografías, lemas, artículos de líderes políticos que analizan la lucha que llevamos a cabo y las razones que la motivan.[16]

The written and visual texts that comprise *La Guerra* reflect in some degree these cultural initiatives, in their readily accessible format of short pieces of alternating prose and poetry, and proliferation of illustrative material. Of course the *Juan de Mairena* pieces of 1934 to 1936 had already moved firmly in the

---

13 Georges Soria gives details of this incorporation, *op. cit.*, V, 222. See also Juan Manuel Fernández Soria, *Educación y cultura*, who notes that the title 'Miliciano de la Cultura de Cuerpo de Ejército' became a military rank in the Republic's army in May 1937 (51).

14 For the text of this Order see *València, capital cultural de la República (1936-1937). Antologia de textos i documents* (Valencia: Generalitat Valenciana, 1986), 86-87. For its operation and extension into the countryside see Fernández Soria, *Educación y cultura*, 60-61. The journal *Armas y Letras* made the staggering claim in its issue of 1 August 1937 that 'El ochenta por ciento de los campesinos eran analfabetos' (3).

15 See Fernández Soria, *Educación y cultura*, 69-73. For a contemporary account of the work of *Cultura Popular* see the report by Teresa Andrés in 'Un año de labor cultural de la República Española (julio 1936—julio 1937)', *Tierra Firme, Revista de la Sección Hispanoamericana del Centro de Estudios Históricos*, III-IV (1936), 604-06. Rafael Abellá, *La vida cotidiana durante la guerra civil. La España republicana* (Barcelona: Planeta, 1975), makes the point that *Cultura Popular* was aimed at everybody, whereas the work of the *Milicias de la cultura* was mostly directed at the combatants (288).

16 Quoted by Georges Soria, *op. cit.*, V, 223.

direction of a wide accessibility, as we have discussed in the previous chapter. *La Guerra*, seen in the light of the very different circumstances of 1937, blends the contemplative, meditative elements of the historical, literary or philosophical text with what is effectively an *antología de urgencia*: the prose section of 'Meditación del día', the prose epitaphs for Emilio Barral and Lorca, and the speech to the Juventudes Socialistas Unificadas.

The seven pieces that make up the written text of *La Guerra* had mostly been published previously, between August 1936 and May 1937.[17] Of the five pieces published during that period, the newspaper *Ayuda* had published 'Los milicianos de 1936', 'El crimen fue en Granada' and 'Meditación del día' (and a few of the drawings used). The third piece, 'Apuntes', had appeared in *Madrid. Cuadernos de la Casa de la Cultura*, and the 'Carta a David Vigodsky. Leningrado' had come out as Machado's April contribution to *Hora de España*. The sixth piece, the poem to Emiliano Barral, had been published thirteen years before in *Nuevas canciones*; Machado added a footnote in *La Guerra* referring to Barral's death during the defence of Madrid. The final item, the 'Discurso a las Juventudes Socialistas Unificadas', must have received some form of previous newspaper publication, however truncated. It is also, however, the last item in the chronological sequence of the pieces and could have gone straight from delivery as a speech for May Day 1937 to publication in *La Guerra*. The chronological aspect of *La Guerra* is an important part of its structure, as we have suggested. Of the seven pieces, the first three, together with the verse section of 'Meditación del día' (that is, the first half of the book) are more muted and contemplative in tone, while the last three and a half sections include much more vigorous comment on the meaning of the war, as Machado saw it.

This contemplative 'backbone' of the first half of the book is a vital ingredient in the organization of Machado's view of the war. The contemplative aspect is most especially noticeable in

---

[17] For details of the first editions of all the pieces in *La Guerra* see Puértolas and Pérez Herrero, *ed. cit.*, 381-93 and 422. Our quotations from the texts that comprise *La Guerra* are taken from Macrì (Vol. II for poetry, Vol. IV for prose) unless otherwise stated.

the piece 'Los milicianos de 1936' (with its date and place given as 'Madrid, agosto 1936') where the reality of a city under siege must have been very different from the contemplative tone of the piece. A combination of illness and the dangerous state of Madrid may, of course, have prevented Machado from witnessing for himself the desolate scenes in the capital. Pablo de Azcárate has described in his Memoirs his reactions on seeing Madrid for the first time since the outbreak of war, at the beginning of September 1936, before taking up his post as the Republic's ambassador in London: 'El espectáculo de confusión y caos que ofrecía Madrid en aquellos días era indescriptible. El gobierno se había visto obligado a emplear hasta el último hombre y el último fusil de que disponía en un esfuerzo desesperado para contener el avance de las fuerzas franquistas en el Guardarrama y en las inmediaciones de Toledo',[18] with a concomitant breakdown of ordered life in the city. In the light of such a description Machado's emphasis on the serene contemplation of death seems calculated to achieve a stoical, steadying effect (the introductory epigraph is from Manrique's 'Coplas'). 'Los milicianos de 1936' was re-published in *Ayuda* under the title 'Divagaciones de actualidad' on 7 November, when the fighting in the *Casa de Campo* on the edge of Madrid's western suburbs was at its most critical.[19] In the context of the structure of *La Guerra*, however, coming as it does at the beginning of the book, 'Los milicianos de 1936' sounds the note of thought and reflection about the meaning of the war. In his interview of December 1936 Machado had cited the *Romancero de la guerra civil*, which came out of *romances* on the war published by *El Mono Azul*, as an example of what he called 'la militarización de los trabajadores del espíritu' (IV, 2170).[20] The

---

18 *Mi embajada en Londres durante la guerra civil española* (Esplugues de Llobregat [Barcelona]: Ariel, 1976), 26. The first air raids on Madrid took place on 28-29 August, after which Franz Borkenau, who was in Madrid, found that 'The atmosphere is lugubrious', *The Spanish Cockpit. An Eye-Witness Account of the Political and Social Conflicts of the Spanish Civil War* (London: Faber and Faber, 1937), 135.

19 For an account of the day's events see Gabriel Jackson, *The Spanish Republic and the Civil War 1931-1939* (Princeton: Princeton U. P., 1965), 324-27; and for its importance in the annals of the war see 'Antonio Machado habla del 7 de Noviembre', in *La Vanguardia*, 8 November 1938.

20 Machado's reference to the *Romancero de la guerra civil*, published

nouns in Machado's phrase sum up in lapidary form the desired alliance between the military, manual and intellectual sectors of society that was to be the mainstay of the Republic's fight for survival.

In this first text of *La Guerra* Machado chooses the *Poema de Mío Cid* to turn the usual perception of the Cid upside down, seeing in him, not an image of the traditionally heroic leader, but rather a working man, keen to show his family 'cómo se gana el pan' (IV, 2164). Nevertheless, the Cid, although seen as a humble worker, is also shown confronting King Alfonso, requiring proof of him that he is an honourable man, that is to say, proof of his capacity to govern. In other words, Machado appears to see in the attitude of the epic hero intimations — having due regard to medieval conventions — of how to treat a *caudillo*: more as a president of a Republic than as one who has absolute rights to rule. (In this context it may be helpful to remember Machado's words, perhaps among the last that he wrote, in his *Prólogo* to Manuel Azaña's *Los españoles en guerra*, referring to Azaña himself: 'España ... supo elegir su Presidente' [IV, 2304]. Or indeed we may remember Azaña's own words, in his speech of January 1937: 'nos batimos todos, el obrero y el intelectual, el profesor y el burgués — que también los burgueses se baten —, y los Sindicatos, y los partidos, y todos los españoles que están agrupados bajo la bandera republicana'.[21]) In this first section of *La Guerra* (they are not called chapters) the figure of the Cid as a worker is juxtaposed with the Republic's militia of 1936, who being in their vast majority from the working class and rank-and-file soldiers are, nevertheless, from a moral point of view considered to be 'capitanes' because of the look of concentration and reflection on their faces. (José Machado's illustrations capture this idea with

---

by the Ministerio de Instrucción Pública y Bellas Artes in November 1936, shows how carefully he chose his words. Two months before, he had written: 'La guerra civil, tan desigual éticamente, pero, al fin, entre españoles, ha terminado hace muchos meses. España ha sido vendida al extranjero por hombres que no pueden llamarse españoles' (IV, 2233).

21 *Hacia la Victoria. Por la Libertad y la Independencia de España* (Madrid: Consejo Nacional de Izquierda Republicana, 1937), 22. The address is subtitled 'Discurso pronunciado por S. E. el Presidente de la República D. Manuel Azaña, en el Ayuntamiento de Valencia, el día 21 de enero de 1937'.

only moderate success.[22]) If the famous first article of the Republic's constitution proclaimed Spain to be 'una República democrática de trabajadores de toda clase', Machado suggests, too, that during the Civil War divisions of social class are blotted out by the realization of the common destiny of death, something that is more acutely sensed in times of war. So also, Machado comments, the frivolous *señorito* has disappeared from the streets of Madrid. There are no militia, then, since all are captains; there are no *señoritos*: the phenomenon of *señoritismo* does, however, exist, but it has nothing to do with a showy way of dressing, rather it is a form of degraded manliness that may be seen in any social class (IV, 2163). In this way the boorish behaviour of the *Condes of Carrión* in the *Poema* represents 'el señoritismo leonés de aquella centuria' (IV, 2165).[23] Therefore, throughout 'Los milicianos de 1936' Machado expounds a series of variations on one of his favourite themes, expressed here in this text, as in various others, by the saying 'nadie es más que nadie'. The war, Machado suggests, underlines in a particular way the truth of this proverb.

The second prose text in the book is called 'Apuntes'. Done in the style of Mairena, Machado had published them previously as 'Notas de actualidad', but omitting in *La Guerra* the last

---

22 José's drawings did not meet with the approval of Antonio Sánchez Barbudo, who was Secretary to *Hora de España* during 1937. He has described them as 'deprimentes, pésimos' (16) in his *Ensayos y recuerdos* (Barcelona: Laia, 1980). Sánchez Barbudo recalls that Antonio showed him his brother's drawings with great eagerness, and suspected that he would have liked to have seen some of them published in *Hora de España* (16). It is probable that Antonio 'protected' his younger brother financially; the latter was married, with three young children at the outbreak of the war. (Machado was paid for his articles in *Hora de España*: *Ensayos y recuerdos* [13].) In this connection the postscript to the original letter to David Vigodsky is of interest. It was published in *Hora de España*, but omitted from *La Guerra*: 'P. D. Le envío a usted esos dibujos de mi hermano José para que vea algunos auténticos aspectos gráficos de nuestra España' (IV, 2183). Juan Gil-Albert, one of the four founder members of *Hora de España*, also remembers José as the 'hermano que dibujaba muy modestamente' (*Memorabilia* [Barcelona: Tusquets, 1975], 238). The only other book, apart from *La Guerra*, published by Machado during the Civil War was *La tierra de Alvargonzález y Canciones del Alto Duero* (Barcelona: Editorial Nuestro Pueblo, [1938?]). This book also contains six illustrations of *La tierra de Alvargonzález* by José Machado.

23 The original text in *La Guerra* has 'de aquellos tiempos'.

paragraph on Unamuno's sad final days in Salamanca. Since Machado was going to correct an error in the original text on Unamuno in the course of his 'Carta a David Vigodsky. Leningrado', which formed part of *La Guerra*, it is understandable that he should have taken the Unamuno paragraph out of the newly-named 'Apuntes'. With its omission, however, the brief text that remains is anything but a series of scattered notes; on the contrary, the four short paragraphs remaining comprise a deep meditation on the march of the people through time and the individual's march towards death. In spite of the reference to Juan de Mairena in the first line (he is, of course, supposedly dead for nearly thirty years) the image of Spain in this first sentence as 'este ancho promontorio de Europa' (*La Guerra*, 33)[24] strikes an up-to-date note. Spain is not only the 'rabo por desollar' of the European continent, as Machado had sometimes ironically described her, but is also of prominent strategic importance, now more than ever because of the Civil War, and is in the front line of the gravest decisions about the future of Europe itself. The text begins by maintaining a balance between past and future, although in the final analysis Mairena concludes that peoples are 'una empresa futura, un arco tendido hacia el mañana' (*La Guerra*, 33) and that as human beings 'vivimos hacia el futuro' (*La Guerra*, 39). But the balance between tradition and progress is an important part of the pluralism of the text, in which Machado suggests that there cannot be a future without a past, and that any programmatic view of the future must take into account the latter's 'infinita imprevisibilidad' (*La Guerra*, 39).

The introduction of Heidegger in the 'Apuntes' is another example of a pluralism that in this instance spans reflective and emotive modes of perception, and acts to form a link between the erudite and popular apprehension of things. One can see here, too, why Machado was generally attracted to the study of philosophy and to existentialist philosophy in particular. If popular wisdom explains its reasons in a direct, aphoristic way, philosophy with its systematic methodology can give a form and structure to such reasoning. The great attraction of Bergson's

---

[24] The quotations from 'Apuntes' are taken directly from the first edition of *La Guerra*, since the piece is missing from Macrì, either under that title or its original one, *Notas de actualidad*.

existentialism for Machado lay in the philosopher's attempt to get close to these 'immediate data of consciousness' in an effort to bring our daily experience of things close to some form of philosophical reasoning. The concomitance of the popular and the erudite is in Machado's work a complementary activity, that he summed up in the advice he gave in his *Cantar* LXXI of *Nuevas canciones*: 'Da doble luz a tu verso, / para leído de frente / y al sesgo'. In our text the 'doble luz' that Machado sheds on the noble expression of the militia is expressed by him 'a la manera popular', as he himself says, when he uses the direct aphoristic form: 'la muerte es cosa de hombres' (*La Guerra*, 41). Machado then gives us immediately the Heideggerian formula, with its philosophical language, in which the philosopher speaks of death as an essential, not accidental part of life; Machado quotes some words from the original German. There is thus intermingled in the text the existentialist philosophy of the intellectual and the 'profunda y contenida reflexión sobre la muerte' of the militia. These militia, 'vistos a la luz de la metafísica heideggeriana' (*La Guerra*, 43), become transformed through their intensified consciousness into the best examples of culture. They are, in effect, philosophers, who experience this philosophy intensely, through having to live so close to death. In this way Machado incorporates the militia into the cultural enterprise of the Republic, blotting out any essential division between the intellectual and the soldier. Each militiaman, therefore, is a Heidegger without knowing it, who will finish up, according to the Heideggerian scheme proposed by Machado, by triumphing over death through having looked at it face to face. As an example of the other pluralism — that of opinion — Machado's sympathetic reading of Heidegger may be compared with the piece by José Bergamín that we have mentioned. Written at almost the same time, Bergamín attacks Heidegger for his pessimism and labels him a 'filósofo fascista'.[25]

Machado's references to the intensified consciousness of the ordinary individual faced with extraordinary circumstances are very much of a piece with the political culture of the Republic in the Civil War, with its emphasis on a consciousness-raising ethos designed to inform and sustain the war effort. In his

---

[25] José Bergamín, 'Nuestra defensa de la cultura', in *Nueva Cultura*, III (1937), 4-5.

Civil-War speeches, especially in his panegyric of the Republic's army, Manuel Azaña was to make broadly similar points to Machado, although slanted from a more direct political point of view, and with the addition, perhaps, of a patronizing or at least paternalistic tone. In his speech of 18 July 1937 Azaña praised the Republic's soldiers for 'su concepto del deber, su descubrimiento terrible de que la vida es una cosa muy seria, de que nadie puede fiar nada a la improvisación, de que la vanidad es mala consejera y que no se logra nada con algarabías ni gritos, sino con esfuerzo silencioso, unas veces muscular y otras mental, y siempre de tensión moral'.[26] If it is the prerogative of Heads of State to use such language, Machado's position as 'un miliciano más' generally spared him from having to deliver direct exhortations to his fellow citizens, even in the elegant style of Azaña, with the exception of his speech to the Juventudes Socialistas Unificadas, which we will examine later in this chapter. In his Madrid speech later in 1937 Azaña remarked on 'la revolución interior moral operada en el combatiente cuando se ha dado cuenta de su enorme responsabilidad y de lo que iba jugado en la partida'.[27] Machado, although politically only 'un miliciano más', is in his writings an integral part of this effort to incorporate as many as possible into an intelligent, reflective view of the conflict. A further example from many years later, although from one who was in the thick of the battle to save Madrid for the Republic, comes from one of the volumes of Vicente Rojo's memoirs. Rojo organized the military aspects of the defence of Madrid, and understandably stressed the importance of the capital as a national example in the Civil War. Yet his mode of expressing this, his emphasis on the intelligent consciousness of the importance of Madrid on the part of the ordinary militia, is also of a piece with the observations of Machado and Azaña: 'en

---

26 *Al año de guerra. Por la libertad, por la República, por España* (Valencia: Ediciones Españolas, 1937), 24. The address is subtitled 'Discurso pronunciado por el Presidente de la República, Exmo. Sr. D. Manuel Azaña, en el Paraninfo de la Universidad de Valencia, el día 18 de julio de 1937'.

27 *Los españoles en guerra* (Barcelona: Editorial Crítica, 1977), 84. Azaña's four Civil-War speeches were about to be published under this title, but the fall of Barcelona in January 1939 prevented its circulation. Machado wrote the prologue for the book, which is included in this 1977 edition, and also in Macrì, IV, 2303-07.

Madrid era la conciencia nacional la que estaba presente en el hombre y en la masa, dominando sus acciones y reacciones, no se trataba de una pasión sectariamente ciega, ni de una obediencia servil, sino de la voluntad de acción, la de un pueblo cargado de historia y apasionado por su amor a la independencia y a la libertad'.[28] This broad coincidence of view between artist, politician and soldier gives a good pen-picture of the composition of mind of some representatives of the Republic's leadership, whether of arms or letters. Yet it would also be true to say that in their advocacy of the widest possible education in, and the fullest understanding of, the ethical and social issues at stake in the Spanish Civil War, Republicans, socialists, communists and anarchists would have found common cause together, however much their methods and conclusions might diverge.

Machado's representation of the militiaman as the 'hombre íntimamente humano, en cuanto ser consagrado a la muerte [y que] puede mirarla cara a cara' (*La Guerra*, 43) could also serve as a gloss on the poem that Machado wrote on the death of Lorca, which is the first text in verse in *La Guerra*. When the poem begins, the armed guards accompanying Lorca are presented as dehumanized entities, a little on the style of the opening verses of Lorca's own 'Romance de la guardia civil española': a thoughtful reminiscence by Machado of Lorca's poem. But the image also records Machado's view of the irreconcilable conflict between the humane poetic imagination and the dehumanized militaristic mentality that opposes it. When at the end of 1937 Machado, through Mairena, described war as 'el "crimen deshumanizado", la muerte entre ciegas máquinas, para permitirse el lujo de abreviar la vida de los mejores' (IV, 2434), it is likely that he was thinking of the death of Lorca. In the poem Lorca is seen walking, not between men but 'entre fusiles': the executioners have been transformed into their own instruments of death. Because they do not belong to 'el hombre íntimamente humano' they cannot look at the death they are bringing, so 'todos cerraron los ojos'. Machado must surely have remembered here Goya's painting *Los fusilamientos de la Moncloa*, a picture that received extensive publicity in the

---

28 *Así fue la defensa de Madrid [aportación a la historia de la guerra de España / 1936-39]* (Mexico: Ediciones Era, 1967), 236.

Republic during the Civil War. In the painting the principal figure in the white blouse who is facing death has opened his eyes as wide as he can, while the eyes of the undifferentiated line of soldiers (Machado's 'ciegas máquinas'?) cannot be seen. In his article 'El dos de mayo de 1808', written in 1938, Machado commented that 'en él [the Goya painting] se ve el vil asesinato de un pueblo inmortal por un sombrío pelotón de verdugos';[29] and he continues: 'Un pueblo inmortal asesinado. Perdonadme la expresión paradójica. La inmortalidad de un pueblo consiste precisamente en eso: en que no muera cuando se le asesina' (IV, 2255). And this is what happens in his Lorca poem. At the beginning of the second section, having been killed in the first, Lorca gets up and continues walking, on this occasion with death, to whom he talks, humanizing her as a flamenco gipsy.[30] Incidentally, the same and other effects are achieved in the last line of Machado's famous apostrophe to Madrid, '¡Madrid, Madrid! ¡Qué bien tu nombre suena!', which reads 'tú sonríes con plomo en las entrañas'. Here Machado uses the *tópico* of 'la sonrisa madrileña' to suggest the indomitable life of the city, renowned for its social life, its cafés and theatres, which will survive all military attempts to

---

29 Bernard Sesé describes the atmosphere of the first section of this poem as of 'un cuadro de Goya', in *Antonio Machado (1875-1939). El hombre. El poeta. El pensador* (Madrid: Gredos, 1980), 848.

30 Stephen M. Hart, 'War within a War: Poetry and the Spanish Civil War', in *'¡No pasarán!': Art, Literature and the Spanish Civil War*, ed. Stephen M. Hart (London: Tamesis, 1988), comments that 'The image of the resurrection, in particular, being a symbol of hope for the future, became a popular motif in the work of Republican poets' (108). And, we might add, not just in poetry: Rivera's story, in Azaña's *La velada en Benicarló* (written in 1937), of his escape from a death sentence by hiding for twenty-four days in a cemetery recess, is also part of the same idea, except that in the example from Azaña little hope ensues. Given the great ups and downs in the fortunes of the Republic during the first nine months of the Civil War, it is not surprising that the idea of resurrection should occupy the place that it did in the Republic's writings, although it is an old theme in Machado. We may remember his words written after the Great War of 1914-18: 'Cierto que la guerra no ha creado ideas nuevas — no pueden las ideas brotar de los puños —; pero ¿quién duda de que el árbol humano comienza a renovarse por la raíz, y de que una nueva oleada de vida camina hacia la luz, hacia la conciencia?' (III, 1603). Other famous poems with a similar theme to arise from the Civil War are Miguel Hernández's 'Caídos sí, no muertos' and Alberti's 'Vosotros no caísteis'.

extinguish it. The conceit, which the personification of Madrid allows, is a good example of the way that Machado was able to compress personal, social and political resonances into a single line of verse.

The popular flavour of Lorca's monologue with death, where he calls her 'compañera', 'gitana' and imagines her clapping her 'secas palmas', is Machado's way of suggesting in the poem what he declares in the 'Carta a David Vigodsky': Lorca's love for the ordinary people in the songs that he collected ('el pueblo que Federico amaba y cuyas canciones recogía' [IV, 2183]). As in the elegy for Francisco Giner de los Ríos, so here the bells of the church towers are silent when the new day breaks; only the repeated sound of the hammers on the anvil can now be heard, as through their work they toll for Lorca. Similarly the poet, even when dead, continues with his own work, composing verses, personifying death in the *cante jondo* style, and speaking of future poetic projects: 'te cantaré la carne que no tienes'. In these ways Machado is able to suggest the solidarity through their work between the true poet and the people, a central theme throughout *La Guerra*. Also, in Machado's imagination Lorca is not only one of the 'mejores' who can look at death face to face, but Lorca himself endows death with a face, with eyes, hair and lips, so that he can look at her and talk to her in a human fashion. Lorca is thus able to bring about that 'libertad para la muerte' of which Machado speaks in his 'Apuntes', and hence Machado links Lorca with the philosopher militia in their manner of triumphing over death, as he imagines him treating her familiarly and 'sin miedo', taking the initiative to speak to her ('ella escuchaba') and — at least metaphorically — embracing her, calling her 'muerte mía'.

Another strong current of thought running through this poem, and one that increases in strength as the texts of *La Guerra* unfold, is the duty of art and the artist to act as a faithful witness to events, and to point out evil wherever it is encountered. Hence the poem's title, which acts as a blunt piece of testimony: 'El crimen fue en Granada'. This, the plainest of titles, might appear too close to the point where, as Machado himself expressed in a similar context some eighteen months later, 'la verdad se come al arte' (IV, 2235). Machado, however, was able to use the plain ballad style here to full effect in the context of this poem as one of witness to a crime against art and against the ordinary people. Giving the poem 'a local habitation and a name' reinforces the accusatory element. Machado imagines that one (or more than one) person saw Lorca being marched to his death: each of the poem's three sections begins with the phrase 'Se le vio' (or 'Se les vio');[31] there was, too, ample opportunity to see and make a protest about Lorca's arrest: the procession of victim and executioners is imagined as moving 'por una calle larga'. But in Granada nobody speaks to denounce the crime. The first to give testimony in the poem is the narrator of Machado's ballad, when he says: 'Que fue en Granada el crimen, sabed'. Machado, by adding the word 'sabed' in a later version of the poem, may well have wished by so doing to reinforce the testimonial aspect of the poem, as well as its ballad atmosphere.[32]

Contemplating this time of the most cruel division of families, exemplified in Machado's case by his separation from Manuel, it is only natural for the critic to wonder whether any communication between them was possible. Gerardo Diego, who met the latter in Santander in 1938, describes how 'Manuel me contaba sus angustias y también sus esperanzas de reunirse con Antonio y las noticias que como todos los españoles recibía a través de misteriosas y precautorias mensajerías. Las versiones familiares de los sucesos y actitudes diferían no poco de las públicas y aireadas.'[33] The question is relevant with regard to the opening three words of Machado's poem — 'Se le vio' — and

---

31 In *La Guerra* the last section of the poem begins 'Se les vio caminar ...', which most of Machado's editors have taken to be a misprint for 'Se le vio caminar ...'. Yet the line in *La Guerra* may well be a reinforcement of the invitation, before the poem's end, to turn away from the circumstances of Lorca's death ('les' referring to the poet's dialogue with death) and concentrate now on the active commemoration of its meaning for humanity. For a full discussion of this variant see Antonio Fernández Ferrer, 'En busca del archilector imaginario', in *Antonio Machado hoy*, IV, 9-17. Bruce W. Wardropper's intelligent analysis of the poem is essential reading: see his article 'The Modern Spanish Elegy: Antonio Machado's Lament for Federico García Lorca', *Symposium*, XVI (1965), 162-70.

32 For the changes that Machado made in the first section of the poem, see the Catalogue for the exhibition *Los Machado y su tiempo* (Madrid: Fundación Antonio Machado, 1987), 125. Bernard Sesé has also seen 'ritmo y tonalidades de romance popular' in this section (*op. cit.*, 847).

33 *Manuel Machado, poeta* (Madrid: Editora Nacional, 1974), 58.

the links that we made earlier between the poem and Goya's *Los Fusilamientos de la Moncloa*. It surely cannot have been a coincidence that Manuel's earlier sonnet on this picture, and which bears its title, begins with the words 'Él lo vio', a reference to the legend that Goya may actually have witnessed the executions. The sonnet is mainly an atmospheric evocation of the dramatic qualities of the picture, but at the end there is a shift of focus when Manuel describes the fate of the ordinary people as 'la eterna carne de cañón'. It may have been this social comment, together with the testimonial opening, that Antonio has tuned into in his own first words.[34] Such an intertextual link would also reinforce the testimonial element in Antonio's poem, reaching out to his brother through what they shared in their view of the Goya picture. They are not in complete sympathy, we should add, because Manuel's interpretation emphasizes the immediate dramatic atmosphere of the picture, and is, moreover, irremediably pessimistic, seeing nothing hopeful in the slaughter depicted by Goya. (Thirty-five years after the publication of the sonnet Manuel wrote that in the picture 'predomina un acento dramático, trágico, ante la irremediable insensatez humana'.[35]) Antonio, on the other hand, looks beyond the moment of death to the inspiration and example of political martyrdom, as is also the case in his poem

---

34   The following is the text of Manuel's sonnet:

> Él lo vio ... Noche negra, luz de infierno ...
> Hedor de sangre y pólvora, gemidos ...
> Unos brazos abiertos, extendidos
> en ese gesto del dolor eterno.
> Una farola en tierra casi alumbra,
> con un halo amarillo que horripila,
> de los fusiles la uniforme fila,
> monótona y brutal en la penumbra.
> Maldiciones, quejidos ... Un instante
> primero que la voz de mando suene,
> un fraile muestra el implacable cielo.
> Y en convulso montón agonizante,
> a medio rematar, por tandas viene
> la eterna carne de cañón al suelo.

The text is from the first edition, *Apolo. Teatro pictórico* (Madrid: V. Prieto y Compañía, Editores, 1911), 109-10.

35   *Bicentenario de don Francisco Goya y Lucientes* (Madrid: Publicaciones del Instituto de España, 1946), 57.

on Lorca's death, especially in the last section.

In this final section Machado appears to leave aside the role of the anonymous balladeer, in order to speak in his own voice to his friends, asking them to bear witness to Lorca by constructing a memorial to his death. The artist, then, has a role of primary importance in the poem, using art as a witness to what has happened: the narrator of the ballad, the sculptor of the grave and the fountain, Machado himself, and also Lorca in his 'response' to his own death. The whole poem is a concentrated commentary on the testimonial role of art. The words that describe the monument to Lorca — 'piedra y sueño' — point to an opposition between the hard inertia of the stone and the dream of the poetic imagination. Machado's inclusion of his poem to Emiliano Barral later in *La Guerra* helps us to elaborate on this phrase. In this poem — to another artist who has also been the victim of the rebellion — Machado imagines the rock being used for the sculpture coming to life as a representation of himself, 'línea a línea, plano a plano', under the action of the sculptor's chisel. By using the very compressed phrase in the poem to Lorca, Machado has universalized the import of the creative act, because this is an art that is within the range of any person endowed with what Machado in *Soledades. Galerías. Otros poemas* had called the capacity to 'evocar los sueños' (II, 487). The universal import of the local circumstances of Lorca's death is also suggested in the way that these circumstances are raised to a higher and more significant plane. If the balladeer initially tells his story from a perspective that is one of pathos and intimacy, calling Lorca familiarly by his first name ('Federico ... Federico'), in the final section Machado gives Lorca his representative name, calling him 'poet'. (To some extent Lorca in the poem achieves this symbolic role from the moment of his death, because the second section of the poem is called 'El poeta y la muerte'.)

Machado's Civil-War poetry has been the subject of much negative criticism, mostly unjustified in my view, as we shall see when dealing with the poet's Civil-War sonnets. Aldo Garosci, who took part in the war on the side of the Republic, is particularly scathing about aspects of Machado's poem on Lorca. Garosci comments that the contrast between the public tone of section I of the poem and the (very effective) intimate one of section II redounds very much to the disadvantage of the first part, where the 'intentos de elocuencia política ... resultan fallidos, casi ridículos'.[36] The thrust of Garosci's argument is as follows: 'En este poema aparece muy clara la tentativa de conmover y conmoverse con el recuerdo natal de Federico y con las circunstancias de la ejecución: el "caminar entre fusiles" para "salir al campo frío", las "estrellas de la madrugada", "el pelotón de verdugos" que "no osa [sic] mirarle la cara" y, en fin, la insistencia casi lloriqueante (que además debía ser eternizada por el llanto de una fuente en la Alhambra) del estribillo'.[37] There is no legislating for taste, hence we will leave it to the reader's own experience of the poem to decide on the effectiveness or otherwise of the first section and its relationship with the rest of the poem. My own view of Garosci's negative criticism is that he cannot hope to prove his case by merely listing some of the elements of the poem's first section and then state that they fail in their 'aim' of arousing a sense of pathos in the reader. The anonymous editor or editors of *Poetas en la España leal*, published in the same year as *La Guerra*, offer what in my opinion is a more interesting view of the poem's contrasting moods, when they comment that Machado 'recoge como un eco toda su anterior melancolía andaluza templada por la serenidad de Castilla'.[38]

The poem's three sections are a compelling summary of Machado's view of the July military coup. The poem initially reflects what Machado in an interview called the 'impresión ... de estupor' (IV, 2173) produced by the rebellion, as Lorca is seen being marched to his death, but nothing is done to prevent it. Then in section II there is the sense of resurgence as the Republic responded, or as Machado graphically commented in the same interview: 'cuando pude ver la salida de aquellos primeros luchadores para el frente de la Sierra, sin más armamento que alguna escopeta de caza[,] tuve fe en la resurección de España'. In the final section Machado breaks away from the image of the poet in the company of death, to contemplate the abiding testimony, in the heart of Granada, of

---

[36] *Los intelectuales y la Guerra de España* (Madrid: Ediciones Júcar, 1981), 34.
[37] *Op. cit.*, 34-35.
[38] (Madrid/Valencia: Ediciones Españolas, 1937), 9.

the water rising from the stone monument; the kind of seemingly miraculous occurrence that Machado had seen in Soria — the water springing from the rock — and had written about before (in 'Pascua de Resurrección', for example). Now he uses the image to suggest the triumph of the creative Republic over the sterile force of nationalist Spain.

The poet's 'conciencia vigilante' acts as the centre for these testimonies. Perhaps the best example of Machado's poetic consciousness at work in *La Guerra* may be seen in 'Meditación del día', a blend of poetry and prose that forms the fourth section of the book. In the poem Machado describes the benign landscape and appears to be enjoying the perfectly calm weather. But the appearance of this beneficent landscape is undergoing a transformation in the poet's consciousness because of the war, which is imagined as a hurricane, with all the destructive consequences that it may be thought of as bringing in its wake. We have, therefore, two landscapes, one full of peace and abundance and the other in the grip of the hurricane, an example of Machado's poetic consciousness at work on two contrasting images: one seen at that moment in Valencia, the other remembered or imagined (Soria, Extremadura, Asturias, Cadiz/Sevilla). Seen in this light the poem is a portrait of the artist imagining a new reality through the landscape being contemplated. The poet is not deceived by this perceived landscape that is so apparently full of peace and abundance, because it is incomplete: it needs the poetic consciousness to grasp its true significance at present ('pienso en la guerra'). If, having read the poem, we go back and read the first complete sentence again, we notice that the subordinate clauses introduced by the relative pronouns and adverbs — 'que ... que ... mientras ... antes que' — need the final words 'pienso en la guerra' to complete the grammatical sense of the sentence. This primary clause is like a call to the consciousness of the poet not to become lost and absorbed in the beauty and fertility of the landscape around him. Speaking to Pascual Pla y Beltrán about his stay in Valencia, Machado commented: 'Estos campos ... esta hermosura materializa [sic] al hombre, lo vuelve en exceso terreno. Aquí, entre esta verdura, difícilmente se angustia uno con la muerte' (IV, 2208). The title of the piece indicates that this is a poem that is very much up-to-date. The poet's awareness of his duty means that he cannot lock himself away in his *torre valenciana*, and so he repeats the words 'la guerra. La guerra', to fix them firmly in his consciousness.

We can of course be certain that Machado did not need any reminder of the war that was raging. In the poetic economy of the piece, however, the beautiful landscape is not depicted for a kind of Wordsworthian celebration, or its fertility for the awareness of renewal that Machado himself received from his contemplation of the land. The image of the war as a hurricane is transcended through the poet's meditation on the reason for the conflict. The poem therefore ends with a view of the war, not as a natural phenomenon disturbing the peace, fertility and natural wealth of Spain, but as a visitation that has been caused by the greed of men. The poet's duty required him to make his landscape imagery correspond to the reality of the present, even to the point of finishing the poem on the hard and bitter note of imagining Spain as a country that is being sold off to foreign greed. Machado's use of landscape in this poem shows the kind of maturity of thought that we can expect from a poet of his class. The basic image is that the peace of the immediate landscape of Valencia is being threatened by a hurricane that has been destroying the length and breadth of Spain. The idea that emerges from the image, however, is that the hurricane is not a blind force, but is being fanned by foreign greed and expansionism. With such an economy of image Machado is able to insinuate into the poem the Republic's view of the Civil War: the destabilization of peaceful democratic Spain by the military insurgents, who are supported by Germany and Italy for their own expansionist ends. The linking of the political idea and the landscape image is also reinforced in summary form, in the two final verses of the poem: 'Pienso en España vendida toda / de río a río, de monte a monte, de mar a mar'. Antonio Sánchez Barbudo has remarked of Machado's articles in *La Vanguardia*, written in the last year of the war: 'No querría en esos escritos, naturalmente, parecer pesimista. Ello no estaba además permitido.'[39] Similarly with the verse section of 'Meditación del día', the ending would have been out of keeping with the general tone of hope and optimism that censorship, not to speak of

---

39 'Antonio Machado en los años de la Guerra Civil', in *Estudios sobre Antonio Machado*, ed. José Ángeles (Barcelona: Ariel, 1977), 259-96.

personal conviction, would have demanded. It is essential, however, to consider 'Meditación del día' as an indivisible piece of poetry and prose. The practice of editors who separate the two sections truncates the total sense of 'Meditación del día', in terms of the overall piece as an optimistic view of the war and in the solidarity between the artist and the people, both united in their complementary task of constant vigilance and in their faith in the final victory of this culture of critical consciousness. In order to understand the poetry and prose of 'Meditación del día' as the seamless piece that it is we should consider the cirumstances of its composition.

While Sánchez Barbudo is probably correct in speculating about the conjunction of poetry and prose, that the latter 'parece tener como propósito contrarrestar al lirismo de los versos primeros', he is on less sure ground in his opinion that Machado added the 'comentario en prosa en abril [de 1937]',[40] because he is going against the date that Machado put at the end of 'Meditación del día' in *La Guerra*: 'Valencia — Febrero 1937'. 'Meditación del día' was indeed first published in *Ayuda*, no. 50 on 11 April 1937. In this first version the piece was dedicated by Machado 'A mis amigos del S.R.I.', that is, *Socorro Rojo Internacional*. This charitable, left-wing organization published *Ayuda*, and on the night of 24 March 1937 it held a large international rally in the *Teatro de la Libertad* in Valencia, to celebrate the sixty-sixth anniversary of the Paris Commune of 1871. (If the anniversary did not actually celebrate a centenary or *cincuentenario* it would still have been of significance in Republican Spain as an example of the staying power of the French Republic, which had grown out of the Commune's barricades.) Reports of the meeting were given in the same issue (no. 50) in which Machado's piece appeared. It is possible that Machado may have been asked to read his piece for the commemoration. According to the same edition of *Ayuda*, Jacinto Benavente took part in it, composing a short piece of prose, followed by a sonnet, both of which were published in that number. Although published with the other speeches and compositions, there is no mention of Machado's piece having been read either by himself or by somebody else on that night.

---

40 *Los poemas de Antonio Machado* (Madrid: Editorial Lumen, 1967), 454.

The ending of the section in prose certainly makes it seem like a composition that was meant to be read aloud ('¡Viva España! ¡Viva el pueblo! ¡Viva el Socorro Rojo Internacional! ¡Viva la República Española!'). Other elements in the piece such as direct address tend to confirm the impression that this was meant to be delivered to a public meeting ('perdonadme ... si preguntáis ... os veríais ... yo os contestaría'). The optimistic trajectory of 'Meditación del día', taken as a whole, would also fit in perfectly with its being read at a rally of this kind. When Machado was collecting his texts for *La Guerra* he made some very slight changes to 'Meditación del día',[41] but kept the poem and the prose section together. To separate them would be to change the emotional structure of the piece as a whole, which unites the consciousness of the lyric poet in his 'jardín de paz' with the 'conciencia universal de los trabajadores' in the prose, where the solitude of the poet is complemented by the solidarity of the working people. The optimistic trajectory of 'Meditación del día' corresponds, too, to the overall structure of *La Guerra*, in which the harsh imperatives of war are overcome by the inextinguishable work of the artist in his position of solidarity with the people.

The five prose paragraphs of 'Meditación del día' are also interesting for the fact of their being linked to the poem. Already in the editions of his *Poesías completas* Machado had mixed poetry and prose: in 'La tierra de Alvargonzález' and in the sections devoted to the poetics of Abel Martín and Juan de Mairena. These are examples of Machado's desire, that we find too in *La Guerra*, to comment in a discursive and circumstantial way on the poems themselves. But in *La Guerra* Machado's comments are more extensive than in any other of his works, with the exception of his unpublished *Los complementarios*.[42] 'Meditación del día' is one example; the poem to Lorca is given a gloss in the 'Carta a David Vigodsky'; and after the poem to Emiliano Barral there is a note that seeks to integrate the life,

---

41 The changes made in *La Guerra* were: omission of the dedication, the addition of the place and date of composition, 'Valencia — Febrero 1937'; 'de pan llevar' becomes 'del pan llevar' (a printing error, perhaps); the phrase 'atentos a las aspiraciones' is preceded by 'y' in *La Guerra*.

42 The title *Los complementarios* may, in one of its meanings, respond to the complementary use of poetry and prose in the notebook.

work and death of the sculptor into the meaning of the conflict. In this pressing period of the Civil War Machado's lyrical reticence is made more sturdy by the words in prose, which may in part explain the overwhelming use of prose in the last five years of the poet's life, that is, after the bloody Asturias revolution of 1934. Machado was always concerned about the relationship between lyric poetry and a wider public, and the complementary use of poetry and prose in *La Guerra* is a response to this concern, and offers a solution. One of Machado's most repeated phrases in his prose work of 1934 to 1938 is 'todo hay que decirlo'. In *La Guerra* the phrase is used as a parenthetical justification for the highly critical remarks made by Machado about the inhabitants of Granada in connection with Lorca's death. One can see in the book, comparing the poetry and the prose, that the latter is much tougher and more plainly expressed than the poems: the crushing criticism of the aristocracy and bourgeoisie of Granada; the praise for Emiliano Barral 'defendiendo a su patria contra un ejército de traidores, de mercenarios y de extranjeros'; here in the prose section of 'Meditación del día' the comparison of the military rebels with Judas. Machado also talks in this prose piece of 'el análisis psicológico de las grandes traiciones' (IV, 2178), and of the need to find an historical pattern to explain the treachery of the insurgents. It would appear that for Machado the medium of prose offered a means of expression — critical, philosophical and historical — that offered a complementary outlet to his lyrical, intuitive nature.

In fact what Machado does in 'Meditación del día' is to reverse the conventional roles of the lyric and, in this case, the piece of political prose. In the verse section he plays down the emotive element, while in the prose the four *vivas* at the end raise the emotional temperature to a level that the poem never attains. Apart from the first word of the title of the piece, the repetition of the verb 'pienso' ('pienso en la guerra ... pienso en España') in the poem establishes a reflective atmosphere that is maintained throughout the piece as a whole. The peace and silence of the quiet Valencian evening not only serves as a contrast with the destructive image of the hurricane but it also suggests an ambience of serenity and seriousness that is conducive to reflection. This idea of reflection is developed in the prose, where the frivolity and stupidity of the insurgents is juxtaposed with the courteous, respectful and moderate behaviour of the Republic's Government that governs 'con un sentido de porvenir', whereas the rebels have not paused to measure the consequences of their actions (IV, 2178). In both the poem and the prose Machado considers the insurgents to be a moral hurricane ready to destroy the peaceful arts of the people of Valencia (that with their horticulture are 'trocando su río en rosas') and also the political arts of the Republican government that has been attentive to the needs of the people.

At the end of the penultimate paragraph of 'Meditación del día' Machado refers to the politics of the bourgeoisie being scrutinized by the workers. The complete sentence reads: 'Porque por encima y por debajo y a través de la truhanería inagotable de la política internacional burguesa, vigila la conciencia universal de los trabajadores' (IV, 2179). There is no doubt that Machado was influenced by the politics, if not of class struggle, at least by the role of the ordinary people in bringing about political change. Antonio Sánchez Barbudo, quoting the Machado sentence, describes it as an instance when Machado 'repetía clichés de la prensa que leía'.[43] If Machado did pick up part of this sentence from a press slogan, the complete phrase nevertheless bears the authentic stamp of Machado's own meditations on culture and on its relationship with the social and political conditions of his time. Machado's expression is typical of his reliance on the integrity and intelligence of the working class, and not on any physical or numerical superiority. The emphasis is far less on class struggle and conflict (although there is division) than on intelligent appraisal and a refusal to be either tricked or suborned. If there is a very peaceful version of the Marxist class struggle in the sentence quoted, it also crystallizes Machado's definition of culture at this time, in the February 1937 edition of *Hora de España*, the month in which, as we have seen, Machado dates 'Meditación del día'. In *Hora de España* he defines culture, not as a 'caudal, ni ... tesoro, ni ... depósito' but as 'el humano tesoro de conciencia vigilante' (IV, 2317). According to this definition both the thoughtful poet of the verse section of 'Meditación del día' and the vigilant workers in the prose part participate together in the work of culture,

---

43   *Art. cit.*, 280.

seeing the reality behind the appearances of the politics of the war.

'Meditación del día' ends with the four *vivas* mentioned earlier. (Machado left in the *viva* for *Socorro Rojo Internacional*, but omitted the dedication to them, which does not make sense in the context of the piece's inclusion in *La Guerra*.) It seems that this piece has suffered more than usually from editorial intrusions, because the 1983 editors of Machado's Civil-War writings have commented in a note that 'En ediciones posteriores a la guerra civil, los compiladores han considerado oportuno suprimir los cuatro vivas finales del texto'.[44] If, however, these *vivas* are omitted one loses not only the atmosphere of a discourse to a live audience but also the popular and emotive finale and its relationship with the previous sentence. If we compare the rather abstract language of the 'political' sentence (in spite of the image of the trickster) with the final *vivas* we have another example of the kind of stylistic pluralism to which we referred earlier, where the abstract and the conceptual can exist side by side with the energy and the immediate impact of popular language. Such a linguistic texture is a mirror, we have suggested, of the desired alliance between popular and intellectual interests in their common effort to win the war, defending their culture together.

As we have already indicated, the poem in the sixth section of *La Guerra* — to Emiliano Barral — does not belong chronologically to the period of the Civil War, having been written fifteen years before in Segovia, and published two years later in *Nuevas canciones*. With the two sentences on the death of Barral and the verses of Manrique that follow the poem we have another example in the book of elements of verse and prose forming a single composition. Yet the poem to Barral, with its emphasis on art as an inextinguishable act of creation, fits in perfectly with this theme, one that runs throughout *La Guerra*. The poem gives us a vision of the artist in the actual moment of creation. The suspension points with which it begins, the reiterated use of the copulative 'y', the image of the sculptor working 'línea a línea, plano a plano' give a dynamic sense of continuous creation: if not 'palabra' then certainly 'piedra en el tiempo'. As we noted in the Lorca poem, Machado here

---

44   Puértolas and Pérez Herrero, *op. cit.*, 391.

imagines how the sculpture of himself 'fue surgiendo de la roca'; that is, the image is of an imperishable art springing from the rock like a new biblical miracle. The prose sentences act as means of bringing up to date Barral's human and artistic example:

> Cayó Emiliano Barral, capitán de las milicias de Segovia, a las puertas de Madrid, defendiendo a su patria contra un ejército de traidores, de mercenarios y de extranjeros. Era tan gran escultor que hasta su muerte nos dejó esculpida en un gesto inmortal.

In death as in life the true artist knows how to respond to the immediate imperative and to go beyond it (Machado speaks of 'un ver lejano' in the poem): Barral, a *segoviano*, defends Madrid in order to defend his country, but in doing so he is also defending 'lo eterno humano' (III, 1594) that is art.

The two pieces of prose towards the end of the book present us with different images of Machado: the first underlines his 'destino cultural', while in the second the emphasis is on his role as 'un miliciano más'. In the 'Carta a David Vigodsky' he returns more closely than ever to literary themes, and by analogy to the work of culture that is to be promoted, whatever the circumstances. The requirements of the epistolary form — this letter is an answer to one received from the Russian Hispanist — means that Machado replies to various observations of Vigodsky, but the fact is that there are few pieces by the poet of similar length that contain so many literary judgements. In this letter Machado is on show as a literary critic and Hispanist, probably more than anywhere else in his published writings, keeping himself almost wholly within the literary application of his 'destino cultural'. For example, there is hardly any mention of the role of Soviet Russia as other than a cultural example to the Republic. The rhetoric of the letter is demonstrative of what these two inhabitants of their respective countries have in common: their work as Hispanists, for which work Machado thanks Vigodsky in the letter. Machado, indeed, confesses that he has been moved by some work done by Vigodsky's young son 'a la memoria del poeta querido' (Lorca, we assume): there is room for many kinds of endeavour in Machado's house of culture. If we take Machado's preferred definition of rhetoric — '[el] arte de conmover, deleitar y aun persuadir con palabras' (IV, 2399) — it will not surprise us that this letter to the Russian Hispanist is the most literary piece in the book, with its references to Cervantes, Calderón, Dostoievsky, Unamuno, Lorca, Alberti and María Teresa León.

In this letter Machado returns to a favourite subject, the essential Christianity of Russia, emphasizing how 'el alma rusa [es] maestra de cristianismo ... que ha sabido captar lo específicamente cristiano — el sentido fraterno del amor, emancipado de los vínculos de la sangre' (IV, 2181). It is in this fraternity that Machado sees Russia's Christian roots, which are implicitly contrasted in the letter with the lack of solidarity of the nationalist inhabitants of Granada with regard to the assasination of their famous poet. For Machado, of course, true Christianity knows no ideological frontiers: thus Vigodsky shows the catholic, that is non-sectarian, spirit of the Russian people by his translation of Calderón's *El mágico prodigioso*, described by Machado in the letter as 'la gran catedral estilo jesuita de nuestro barroco literario'. Immersed in literature as it is, Machado was able to use the letter to Vigodsky to suggest reassuring links of international solidarity. As well as this, by writing serenely to Vigodsky of these literary ideas Machado was responding in his own way to the spirit and goal of *Hora de España*, where the letter was first published (in April 1937): to keep alive the creation and criticism of culture during the conflictive circumstances of the war. But at the same time the letter lets the Spanish public know[45] — or any readers beyond the shores of Spain — that there is no red Soviet menace; rather, the letter offers an image of solidarity between two writers from the peoples of Spain and Russia as the pattern for a solidarity that is 'humana y universalmente cristiana' (*La Guerra*, 71).

The final piece by its hard, direct language acknowledges more than any other in the book the Civil War that is being fought throughout Spain. The rhetoric of the 'Discurso a las

---

45 Dionisio Ridruejo became Franco's 'jefe nacional de Propaganda' in February 1938 (see Hipólito Escolar, *op. cit.*, 246-48). Ridruejo recalls in his tortuous Preface to his edition of Machado's *Poesías completas* (Madrid: Espasa-Calpe, 1941): 'Cuando las revistas y los folletos [republicanos] llegaban a nuestras manos, allá, en Burgos, nos esforzábamos — y no pocas veces con harta razón — por encontrar nuestro y no rojo su [Machado's] mundo conceptual, los propios argumentos y tesis con que a los rojos creía servir' (XIII).

Juventudes Socialistas Unificadas' is also closely linked to the audience to which it is directed. Machado, therefore, sacrifices the more spacious and speculative literary references of the letter to David Vigodsky, and in the 'Discurso' addresses his audience in energetic prose. The 'Discurso' is composed around the base of the three words of the organization's name — *juventud, socialista* and *unificada* — but the main emphasis of the piece is on the first concept. Of the seven paragraphs, the first six deal with the idea of youth. Reflections on Marxism and socialism share almost the whole of the last paragraph,[46] and the reference to unification is left for the final valedictory phrase, demonstrating perhaps Machado's lack of sympathy for collectivist movements, both fascist and communist, even though an abyss would separate his preferences for one or other of these philosophies. With regard to collectivist solutions to contemporary social needs it is worth recalling Mairena's words in *Hora de España* of April 1938:

> La unión constituye la fuerza. Es una noción elementalísima de dinámica contra la cual nada tendríamos que oponer, si no hubiera tontos y pillos ... que pretenden acomodarla a sus propósitos, y que propugnan el acercamiento y la unión de elementos heterogéneos, dispares y contrapuestos, que sólo pueden unirse para estrangularse. (IV, 2378-79)

Not only does Machado devote almost no time to the idea of unification, but by also declaring in the 'Discurso' his reservations about Marxism (IV, 2191) he contributes to some extent to the divisions between the Republic's Marxists and socialists at a time when one of its most urgent problems was that of the unification of anti-nationalist forces. Poster art in the Republic of the Civil War, with the slogans 'Mando único' and 'La unión es fuerza' seem to have been plentiful, to judge by the space devoted to it in Josep Termes' book.[47] Machado's piece

---

46 Machado refers to both Marxism and socialism because the JSU were the result of the unification, in the spring of 1936, of the *Federación de Juventudes Socialistas* and the *Unión de Juventudes Comunistas de España*; see R. Viñas, *La formación de las Juventudes Socialistas Unificadas (1934-1936)* (Madrid: Siglo XXI de España, 1978).

47 See his *Carteles de la República y de la Guerra Civil* (Barcelona: Centre D'Estudis D'història Contemporània/Editorial La Gaya Ciencia, 1978), 172-85, for posters with this theme.

turns the requirements of the hour on its head by giving so much space to the idea of youth.

The 'Discurso' is of course only reflecting the cultural and political situation in the Republic by its oscillation between collectivist and individualist ideas. The latter, a legacy of nineteenth-century bourgeois thought, appears when Machado talks of 'mi ya larga vida' (IV, 2190): he was very conscious that his own existence had spanned two centuries.[48] He also confesses himself to be a descendant of the Romantics and blames 'una educación demasiado idealista' (IV, 2191) for his less than wholehearted sympathy to Marxism. At the same time throughout the 'Discurso' Machado stresses the need for the 'sacrificio de todo lo mezquinamente individual a las férreas normas colectivas que el ideal impone' (IV, 2190). The emphasis throughout, as one would expect, is on discipline and control but the integrity of the piece — its pluralist balance between individual and collective attitudes — comes through in Machado's main concern, expressed in his advice to the young people of the Republic to live their youth to the fullest extent.

Juventud is a word and concept that always fascinated Machado, doubtless because it is, in spite of its abstract quality, a 'palabra en el tiempo'. We could say that in the 'Discurso' Machado is again addressing his own youth, 'juventud nunca vivida', as he called it in Poem LXXXV of *Soledades. Galerías. Otros poemas*, a youth that is feverishly sought after in that collection, and dismissed so summarily in his 'Retrato' of *Campos de Castilla* ('mi juventud, veinte años en tierra de Castilla'). None the less, *juventud* is a concept with which Machado evidently felt at ease, and one can see this in his vigorous language as he attempts to give life and expressiveness to the idea for the young people who were listening to him. Speaking energetically of the value of a youth that is fully

---

48   In *Los complementarios* (the probable date is October 1917) Machado noted the following:

> Pero ¿no estamos en el siglo XX? ¿No se habla ya de novecentismo? ¿No hay quien pretende pisar la tierra firme de un siglo nuevo? Si esto fuera así — lo que yo no afirmo ni niego — dos bellas perspectivas se ofrecen a nuestra mirada. Una es el siglo que empieza y del cual aún no sabemos todo lo que lleva en el vientre; otra el siglo que se fue, y que ya podemos añorar. (III, 1197)

realized, denouncing the ageing Spain personified in the 'Discurso' by Alejandro Lerroux, then in his seventies, Machado's language professes a kind of strident certainty, a clear knowledge of things ('Yo las conozco bien', 'los conozco bien', 'vosotros sabéis', 'sabéis vosotros') that is absent when he speaks of the political questions that interest his audience. Thus in the midst of his references to Marxism, and when Machado remembers his own political formation — or lack of it — phrases such as 'es muy posible', 'acaso' and 'tal vez' return to the prose of the 'Discurso'.[49] If he expresses himself with more warmth and emphasis when speaking of socialism, he still only sees that political philosophy as 'una etapa' (although 'inexcusable') to achieve social justice, and he can only say that we should contribute to it 'de algún modo' (IV, 2192).

The 'Discurso', therefore, is an interesting mixture of individual doubts and uncertainties coupled with the recognition of the pressing collective demands of the hour. By emphasizing the idea of youth and drawing a contrast betwen the solidarity of a forward-looking Republic and the old Spain of egotism and hypocrisy Machado could draw together the ideas of a fulfilled youth within the 'férreas normas colectivas' of discipline, of obedience and respect ('sin sombra de adulación', he adds) for the Republic's leaders 'cuando están en sus puestos' (IV, 2190). In the 'Discurso' Machado gives his own example of the way the artist and intellectual should stay at his post. If he has to walk the tightrope between individual ideals and collective discipline, he nevertheless does not evade his duty to address the young people on the symbolic day of the worker, the first of May, the date on which Machado delivered his 'Discurso a las Juventudes Socialistas Unificadas'.

Machado's description of culture as 'el humano tesoro de conciencia vigilante' gives a characteristic tone to his work. The cultural treasury on display in *La Guerra* may be summed up as a presentation of culture as a consciousness that is alert to

---

[49] Machado also uses the words 'acaso' and 'tal vez' in the first paragraphs of the 'Discurso', but their dubitative connotations are counterbalanced by the presence of affirmative words such as 'siempre' (used four times in the first two paragraphs). For a detailed analysis of the rhetoric in the 'Discurso' see José María Nadal, 'Narratología y persuasión en el "Discurso a las Juventudes Socialistas Unificadas" ', in *Antonio Machado hoy*, IV, 357-68.

reflect the voice of a people, seen as 'una muchedumbre de hombres que temen, desean y esperan aproximadamente las mismas cosas' (*La Guerra*, 35). During the first months of the Civil War, when some of the early pieces in *La Guerra* were composed, Machado's meditations acquire a particular character, which is the ineluctable presence of death, reflected in the acutely sensitive consciousness of artists, intellectuals and militiamen. Their triumph over death is the triumph of 'los mejores' who, like Lorca, have known how to familiarize themselves with death beforehand. But this is also a triumph of the people that survives the death of the individual. A result of this enhanced consciousness and willingness to face death is Machado's serenity of spirit, 'al lado de la España joven y sana', in spite of the fact that he himself was 'viejo y enfermo' with his 'achaques habituales' complicated by an eye illness, as Machado portrays himself in the first lines of the letter to David Vigodsky. We note, however, in the next text, the final one in the book, that Machado seems to renew himself in order to express with unwonted energy his solidarity with the young socialists. The book thus ends in a kind of resurrection:[50] a Machado, young at heart, at his post, finding new reserves of energy to celebrate the first of May discoursing on the greatness of youth. The final image, therefore, is of the poet as a living emblem of a youthful Republic that will combat old privileges and will resist through word and work, in the solidarity of workers, soldiers, artists and intellectuals.

In this finale, with its incitement to united action, we have come a long way from the contemplative mood of the book's opening text. In fact, the two text types are meant to complement each other, as are others that we have noted: the poetry and prose of 'Meditación del día', the poem to Lorca and the comments on Granada in the letter to David Vigodsky, the Heideggerian meditation on death, and the artist's death in action, in the 'Apuntes' and the piece on Emiliano Barral respectively. Such complementarity, as well as offering an image of solidarity between workers and intellectuals, also gives

---

[50] Pont, *art. cit.*, 483, also quotes Aurora de Albornoz in this regard; for the latter critic the 'Discurso' 'es, en cierta forma, una afirmación de la vida sobre la muerte'; the quotation is from 'El libro último de Machado', in *Información de las Artes y las Letras*, Madrid, 24 July 1975.

a philosophical and ideological base to the defence of the Republic: that death and our awareness of it, are a necessary and ennobling part of life; that serious and thoughtful minds will listen to the people and hence govern wisely, something which is anathema to the mentality of *señoritismo* of the insurgents. *La Guerra*, which spans the meditative mood of August 1936 and the vigorous call to the Republican youth of May 1937, encapsulates in its texts the solidarity of thought and action, of principled ideology and stubborn resistance, that the Republic worked so desperately to harness to its cause. This alliance of intellect and action (and its ideological import) was the main theme of the *ponencia colectiva* given by the young Spanish artists and intellectuals who addressed the July 1937 meeting in Valencia of the *II Congreso Internacional de Escritores Antifascistas*:

> Hoy en España — y no es esta la victoria menos importante alcanzada sobre el fascismo —, nuestra lucha en todos sus matices, responde a un contenido de pensamiento con una expresión de voluntad. Los hechos, cada vez más, son asumidos y resumidos en formas coherentes de pensamiento. Se produce una poesía poética, absoluta, en cuanto a calidad, y una pintura y una creación intelectual, en suma, cada vez más apasionada y cada vez más inteligible.[51]

Machado's contribution in *La Guerra* belies its brevity and sets out parameters of deep, meditative principle allied to practical, vigorously expressed belief in the justice of his cause, not just for this first phase of the Civil War but for all his Civil-War writings through to his last, those of January 1939.

---

51 The *ponencia colectiva* was published in *Hora de España*, IX (September 1937), with thirteen signatories.

CHAPTER 3

'Deberes fraternos': Machado's Writings in the Early Issues of *Hora de España* (January-August 1937)

When towards the end of 1936 a group of young Republican intellectuals came together to create a broadly based journal (*Hora de España*) that would attempt to continue the work of the creation and criticism of culture that had been disrupted by the Civil War,[1] Machado, although of another generation, was an obvious choice as a contributor. *Hora de España* produced twenty-three numbers in monthly issues, dated January 1937 to November 1938.[2] Machado contributed to each number, for the most part continuing the type of *Juan de Mairena* format that he had begun in *Diario de Madrid* in November 1934. In an interview given about the same time that he was perhaps preparing his first contribution for *Hora de España* Machado was asked whether he planned to 'cantar esta maravillosa gesta que estamos viviendo'. He replied: 'Por ahora, no ... Estamos

---

   1   Francisco Caudet in his edition of *Hora de España (Antología)* (Madrid: Ediciones Turner, 1975), quotes a letter from Rafael Dieste, one of the founders of the journal, as follows: 'La revista nace, debe nacer — decíamos a los vacilantes — para que en ella tengan ocasión de expresarse los jóvenes y los mayores' (14). And in its opening *Propósito*, the founders of *Hora de España* spoke of their desire to show the world 'que España prosigue su vida intelectual o de creación artística en medio del conflicto gigantesco en que se debate'.
   2   For a brief account of the ethos of *Hora de España* see Francisco Caudet's *Antología*, referred to in the previous note; also Marisa Sotelo Vázquez, 'Las colaboraciones de Antonio Machado en *Hora de España*', in *Antonio Machado: el poeta y su doble* (Barcelona: Universitat de Barcelona, 1989), 227-47. Monique Roumette gives a useful summary of the contents of the journal, which had a very high print run, estimated by Roumette at between four thousand and five thousand copies per month, many of them distributed free by the government, especially abroad: see '*Hora de España*', in *Espagne/Écrivains. Guerre civile*, ed. Marc Hanrez (Paris: Les Dossiers H, 1975), 105-13.

demasiado cerca de ella ... Lo grandioso necesita de la pátina del tiempo para poder juzgarlo en todo su valor' (IV, 2174). Taken in conjunction with Mairena's repeated aphorism, 'toda visión requiere distancia', it may be no surprise that in spite of the 'fragores de lucha' to which he refers in one of his Civil-War sonnets, the *Mairena* sketches in *Hora de España* tend to continue the fiction of a teacher addressing his pupils at an unspecified period before 1909, the year of Mairena's death. The idea of continuity is, then, to an important degree central to the *Mairena* series, viewed in its totality from 1934 to 1938, and it may be closely linked to the idea of the continuity of the Republic, its legitimacy and its right to continue as the embodiment of the Spanish State. In this respect the fact that Machado continued with the *Mairena* series may be due, not to any lack of innovatory energy on his part, in spite of his rapidly failing health, but may have been a conscious decision to underline the legitimacy of the Republic through the continuity of the artist's work.

Given the prominence afforded to *Hora de España* (see note 2) Machado was about to assume a heavy responsibility, not only writing for every number but always occupying the front position in the journal (apart from a rare leading article). Thus Machado's first article, with its mixture of humour and solemnity, appears to be an attempt to bridge a gap in two directions: towards a sense of continuity with his past work in the *Mairena* series, and also towards an engagement with the needs of the present. (Needless to say, the different tones adopted in the pieces do not allow for an exclusive pigeonholing of one or the other into distinct categories such as 'past' or 'present'.) Another contributor, María Zambrano, when reviewing in *Hora de España* the hugely ambitious journal, *Madrid. Cuadernos de la Casa de la Cultura*, three numbers of which were produced by the Republic's artists and intellectuals during the Civil War, commented on the journal's tone and format in terms of 'Su serenidad, en que se muestra la continuidad de la vida intelectual española a través de tanta vicisitud', and noted the example that it gave 'en sus páginas cuidadas[,] tipográficamente impecables'. These comments were written in the August 1938 issue of *Hora de España*: after two years of war the idea of the right to continue the work interrupted by the insurgents is still expressed, even down to the detail of the importance of the production of 'impeccable' copy; in itself, one suspects, a desired image of a Republic that is far more sinned against than sinning. Other government-sponsored reports on pedagogical and cultural activities also laid stress on the fact that schools, libraries and research continued to function in the Republic and indeed, in the case of schools and libraries, were being greatly expanded during the conflict.

The shift in emphasis, therefore, between *Juan de Mairena* (1936) and Machado's articles in *Hora de España*, while significant, is not a radical one, in spite of the Civil War. In a sense this may seem contradictory in the light of Machado's impassioned interview from which we quoted at the beginning of chapter 2. This interview, and the one from which we have just quoted in this chapter, were given within the space of three weeks,[3] and while much depends on the style and tone of the interviewer, who is also responsible for its redaction, they suggest an oscillation between militant and meditative attitudes (although in the second interview, seemingly more bland in character, from which we have quoted in this chapter, Machado also urges a concentration on a single aim: 'aplastar al fascismo' [IV, 2174]). An important aspect of the policy of *Hora de España* was the continuity of the cultural work of the Republic, as well as allowing space for the expression and discussion of any radical change that the war would bring in its train. In general, however, the moderate tone of *Hora de España* may be seen in a leading article to commemorate its first anniversary in January 1938, when it described the expression of its ideas as follows: 'Hemos querido que todos nos oigan y para ello no hemos alzado la voz, sino que la hemos mantenido en su tono medio, en aquel que normalmente sirve al hombre para hacerse entender de sus semejantes'. In any case there is a consistent core of social thought in Machado's work, which in its ethical direction may be summed up by Machado's memory of hearing Pablo Iglesias speaking in about 1889 (Machado recalls this in August 1938) and his reaction to the words of the workers' leader: 'decididamente, el compañero Iglesias tenía razón ... La brevedad del camino [de la vida] en nada amengua el radio

---

3 Macrì gives the dates of the interviews as 29 November and 19 December (IV, 2172 and IV, 2175).

infinito de una injusticia. Allí donde ésta aparece, nuestro deber es combatirla' (IV, 2480). As in *La Guerra*, the main emphasis in Machado's writings in the early issues of *Hora de España* is on the desired solidarity between the artist and intellectual and the *pueblo*. It is the most distinguishing mark between the *Juan de Mairena* of 1936 and the *Juan de Mairena* pieces of January to August 1937. This latter issue of *Hora de España* was devoted to the *II Congreso Internacional de Escritores Antifascistas* held in Valencia in July 1937, and Machado took the opportunity to summarize his views on the issue of *cultura popular* for the foreign artists and intellectuals assembled there. When, therefore, we talk of a greater emphasis on solidarity with the *pueblo* in Machado's writings of the first year of the Civil War, it is only a change of emphasis, a logical evolution, and not a radical change in Machado's social commitment. Bernard Sesé aptly describes this change of emphasis as a 'revival': 'La guerra civil ha reavivado en el poeta su amor ardiente al pueblo'.[4]

If we are to judge by the way that Machado uses the word *pueblo* in the *Hora de España* writings under consideration, it is evident that he did not contemplate a fixed meaning for it, preferring to retain as all-inclusive a social and political resonance as possible. Indeed the phrase 'el radio infinito de una injusticia' just quoted is a very good example of how much Machado's language and thought tended to transcend everyday social issues. Just as in 'Los milicianos de 1936' he comments that the attitudes and activities of the *señorito* are to be found 'en individuos de diversas clases sociales' (IV, 2163), so Machado generally avoided using the word *pueblo* in a way that was connected with class struggle (with a couple of possible exceptions, to be noted later), and rather allowed the word to encompass a notion of the spirit of democracy, of the freely-expressed will of the people. Indeed he was to make his position very clear in his radio broadcast, published in *La Vanguardia* (22 November 1938): 'la palabra pueblo no tiene para mí una marcada significación de clase: del pueblo español forman parte todos los españoles' (IV, 2291). This is the case in the prose section of 'Meditación del día' (which, as we saw, Machado dates 'febrero, 1937' in *La Guerra*). In it he describes

---

4   *Op. cit.*, 838.

the Government of the *Frente Popular* at the time of the rebellion of the generals as 'un gobierno de hombres honrados, atentos a las aspiraciones más justas del pueblo, cuya voluntad legítima representaban' (IV, 2178). In general, the word 'trabajadores' did not form part of Machado's social and political vocabulary, possibly because of the social divisiveness to which it could give rise, its use as a slogan, and its association with the word 'masas', a word that he disliked, as we shall have occasion to examine. Hence he preferred the vaguer and more inclusive word 'pueblo' when considering ideas that broached sociopolitical themes. Thus, when he writes in his 'Carta a David Vigodsky' in the *Hora de España* issue of April 1937, that he is 'de todo corazón al lado del pueblo' and that 'En España lo mejor es el pueblo' he is content to allow these simple aphoristic forms to convey the meaning of popular resistance against oppression and invasion. That Machado was prepared to contemplate different political meanings for the word *pueblo* can also be seen in the letter to Vigodsky, when he remarks in connection with Lorca's death that 'el pueblo que Federico amaba y cuyas canciones recogía no era precisamente el que canta la Internacional' (IV, 2183).

The political thrust of Machado's language during the first year of the war is mainly of this inclusive variety, embracing as it does a pluralism of styles, breaking down the barriers between so-called 'elevated' and 'low' styles, between supposedly noble and plebeian states, and generally through his language turning upside down the notion that the *pueblo* is in any way inferior to what might be conventionally thought of as a socially superior position. The aphoristic phrases just quoted from the Vigodsky letter are by their very form an expression of solidarity with, and respect for, the *pueblo*. In the paragraph in which these phrases occur one notices, too, how the gap between rhetoric and action is exposed: the phrase 'invocar la patria' for all its high-sounding rhetoric, is very much inferior to the attitude of the *pueblo*, whose integrity is shown in its deeds, not in any rhetorical flourish:

> En España lo mejor es el pueblo. Por eso la heroica y abnegada defensa de Madrid, que ha asombrado al mundo, a mí me conmueve, pero no me sorprende. Siempre ha sido lo mismo. En los trances duros, los señoritos — nuestros *barinas* — invocan la

patria y la venden; el pueblo no la nombra siquiera, pero la compra con su sangre y la salva. En España, no hay modo de ser persona bien nacida sin amar al pueblo. La demofilia es entre nosotros un deber elementalísimo de gratitud. (IV, 2180)

Alberto Gil Novales has commented on the use of the word *demofilia* here: 'Al pronto nos sorprende esta palabra, demofilia, que parece demasiado culta',[5] and relates its use to the pen-name of Machado's father, *Demófilo*. Rather than the fact that the word is 'culta' one might express surprise that the word here seems redundant, coming immediately, as it does, after the previous three words that say the same thing. However, the use of the learned form makes an important social point: the phrases 'amar al pueblo' and 'la demofilia' are not merely stylistic variations by Machado to make his prose more readable, but are meant to be inclusive of so-called high and low styles, where the popular and the learned co-exist and are fused into each other in mutual recognition. This stylistic trait of inclusiveness is an expressive mode to which Machado was particularly drawn during his early Civil-War writings. The war, of course, created further division in society, by imposing military regulation on the normal divisions based on economic interests. Thomas J. Hamilton has summed up this aspect of the Spanish Civil War as follows:

> In Spain the class issue split every section — except perhaps mediaeval Navarre — and military capacity, rather than the views of the people, determined which side held a particular area. Andalucia, for example, stayed with Franco because of the superb audacity of Lieutenant-General Queipo de Llano, who held Seville with 200 men. Yet the workmen of Seville, and the discontented peasants on the neighbouring estates, were Republican sympathizers.[6]

Machado generally avoids a view of this division based on social class, by suggesting that the division is between the *señoritos* and the *pueblo*, preferring to allow the diminutive and isolated connotation of the former to act as a contrast with the solidarity and integrity of the latter, rather than draw any overt political conclusions. In the first issue of *Hora de España* the

---

5 *Antonio Machado* (Barcelona: Fontanella, 1966), 145.
6 *Appeasement's Child. The Franco Régime in Spain* (London: Victor Gollancz, 1943), 31.

word *pueblo* has as broad a meaning as in the following sentence: 'Escribir para el pueblo es escribir para el hombre de nuestra raza, de nuestra tierra, de nuestra habla' (IV, 2315-16). (Machado was to universalize this idea in his revised version of the passage that he delivered to the International Writers' Conference in Valencia.[7]) Are the insurgent generals, then, part of the *pueblo*? The question raised by the *Hora de España* definition is answered by implication in the paragraph from the Vigodsky letter that we have quoted, and also in section 10 of the March issue of *Hora de España*. The generals are part of the mentality of *señoritismo* in Spain: they have divorced themselves from the *pueblo* by selling their country to foreign powers. We find another very broad definition of the *pueblo* in *Hora de España*, March 1937, section 8. Here, the *pueblo* or at least 'el alma del pueblo' is identified with 'la conciencia del hombre, impregnada de cristianismo' (IV, 2325). The breadth of this concept of the *pueblo* cannot be contained within the boundaries of nationality or of the class struggle: its humanism transcends the divisions, within western civilization at least. Rather than seeking to emphasize division because, as he comments in 'Los milicianos de 1936', 'no me gusta denigrar al adversario' (IV, 2165), Machado attempts to make a case for the essential nobility of the human person, which he sees epitomized in what he calls in the final section of his speech to the International Writers' Conference 'un hombre del pueblo, que es, en España al menos, el hombre elemental y fundamental y el que está más cerca del hombre universal y eterno' (IV, 2204). Here is another definition of the *pueblo* that transcends considerations of social class and position.

There are moments, however, in these early issues of *Hora*

---

7   Machado 'internationalized' the last section of the January piece in *Hora de España* when he re-used it for his July *Discurso*, including in the latter such phrases as 'escribir para el pueblo nos obliga a rebasar las fronteras de nuestra patria; es escribir también para los hombres de otras razas, de otras tierras y de otras lenguas' (IV, 2198), which did not appear in the January article. While this may have been a natural addition in the context of delivery to an international audience, it is also an 'internationalist' concept, responding in all likelihood to the socialist ethos of the *Congreso* and reacting against the nationalist ethos of the insurgent *Movimiento*. (The additions or changes in Machado's *Discurso* to pieces written earlier in the war would make an interesting study in themselves.)

de España when Machado does allow the word *pueblo* to take on overtones of the Marxist class struggle. Nothing can better illustrate the tensions within the position of an artist and intellectual like Machado who, while confessing that he is an old Republican rather than a true socialist, nevertheless is drawn into taking sides in the political cockpit of the war. (The actual idea of taking sides was an issue that concerned Machado, both before and during the Civil War, as we will discuss later, in chapter 4.) In the March issue of *Hora de España* (section 11) the word *pueblo* has an immediately obvious meaning of 'the working class', when Mairena advises his pupils: 'Si algún día tuviereis que tomar parte en una lucha de clases, no vaciléis en poneros del lado del pueblo, que es el lado de España, aunque las banderas populares ostenten los lemas más abstractos' (IV, 2326). We could (and perhaps should) draw attention again to the perspectivist framework of the *Mairena* classroom scene, set probably in the Spain of 1909. It is nevertheless a clear direction from Mairena to his young aspiring artists and intellectuals, in the face of their possible uncertainty — 'no vaciléis' — to take the side of the 'banderas populares'. Yet even here, there is enough of the sense of a popular democratic mass movement in the latter phrase to suggest that taking the side that Mairena recommends in such a class struggle is to obey the will of the people. A train of thought, however, that could lend itself to a Marxist interpretation is in evidence in section 2 of Machado's February 1937 contribution to *Hora de España*, where Mairena rejects the then current idea of 'revolución desde arriba' in favour of its opposite: 'revolución desde abajo, me suena mejor' (IV, 2326), he comments. However, the image used in connection with both phrases — that of renewing a tree through its crown or its roots — tends to dissipate the socio-political element in Mairena's discussion of the topic of revolution in this section.

The young Spanish artists and intellectuals who signed the *ponencia colectiva* given to the International Writers' Conference identified the year 1917 (the year of Spain's first general strike) as the beginning of a revolutionary process that had led to the outbreak of hostilities in 1936.[8] In Machado's case, too, any change of direction after 1936 is part of a process

---

8   *Hora de España*, IX (1937), 86.

of the refinement of his thought rather than a root-and-branch change of heart, following the outbreak of the Civil War. The war, however, inevitably makes its impact on Machado's writings, even in *Hora de España,* in spite of his continued use of the *Mairena* format, with its anachronistic time-frame and ironic, apocryphal, perspectivism. Examples of some ways in which the war gave Machado the opportunity to deepen the import of his thought can be seen from time to time throughout *Hora de España*. Machado himself realized this and commented on it in section 3 of his August 1938 contribution, which we will examine in detail in chapter 4; but it is interesting to note in passing that he uses the word 'hondo' (or its variations) four times in that brief passage to denote, as he was to write two months later in *La Vanguardia,* that the war was 'un tema cordial esencialísimo' (IV, 2475).

An example of how the war occasioned a change towards a 'tema esencialísimo' is to be found in Machado's care to distinguish the concept of the *pueblo,* for all its resonance of the will of the majority and of *vox populi,* from that of *las masas,* in his February 1937 contribution to *Hora de España,* having already dealt with this idea in his *Mairena* article of 24 October 1935. Machado warned in the Civil-War article that the phrase 'las masas' was used by 'Muchas gentes de buena fe, nuestros mejores amigos' (IV, 2319) and when, in the light of Machado's remark, one reads texts by other representatives of the liberal or socialist intelligentsia in the Spain of the Civil War, one is indeed struck by the number of references to 'las masas' and the dehumanizing resonance that results from its use. (It must be said that even Machado himself used the phrase 'las masas combatientes', in an article published in August 1938 [IV, 2274]; but, then, his view of war was that it turned people into 'masses': fodder for the enemy cannon that awaited them.) In the texts under consideration the difference between the sections is a telling one, coming in the brief penultimate sentence of the Civil-War piece. It would require a very close acquaintance with both the 1935 and the 1937 texts to tell which of the following quotations belongs to Machado's writing before or during the Civil War:

> Imaginad lo que podría ser una pedagogía para las masas. ¡La educación del niño-masa! (IV, 2059)

and

> De modo que, en estricta lógica, las masas humanas ni pueden salvarse, ni ser educadas. (IV, 2320)

(They are in fact in chronological order.) Here, however, are the sentences following the respective quotations:

> Ella [la educación] sería, en verdad, la pedagogía del mismo Herodes, algo monstruoso.

and

> En cambio, siempre se podrá disparar sobre ellas [las masas].

Both these latter sentences draw similarly sombre conclusions from the devaluation of the individuality of human beings. Yet the first, with its Swift-like satire, is an altogether more convoluted image, its impact coming through the black humour, following on from the witty neologism *niño-masa*. The Civil-War sentence is more direct and sober, reflecting the deadly seriousness of the thoughtless use of a cliché such as 'las masas'.

Very early in his *Hora de España* writings — the third section of the first number — Machado re-introduced the subject of 'deberes fraternos', in the context of the Christian belief in the brotherhood of humanity under the fatherhood of God. These 'deberes fraternos' had already been subjected to a more extended gloss in the final section of the *Mairena* article of 28 November 1934, although in this latter piece the expression used is the less urgently phrased 'virtudes fraternas'; also, in XV, 5 of *Juan de Mairena* (1936) Mairena had discussed the twin imperatives: 'el amor de radio infinito hacia el padre de todos' and the 'virtudes y deberes fraternos' (IV, 1969). The difference in emphasis between the two periods is highlighted by a comparison of a similar *Mairena* piece from 22 December 1935, with the passage from the first number of *Hora de España*. The context, it should be noted, is that Mairena is quoting his teacher Abel Martín in both pieces. Martín, by and large, is more interested in philosophy and theology than sociology, and this predominance of interest comes through in the December 1935 piece:

> El Cristo — decía mi maestro — predicó la humildad a los poderosos. Cuando vuelva predicará el orgullo a los humildes. De

sabios es mudar de consejo. No os estrepitéis. Si el Cristo vuelve, sus palabras serán aproximadamente las mismas que ya conocéis: 'Acordaos de que sois hijos de Dios; que por parte de padre sois alguien, niños.' Mas si dudáis de una divinidad que cambia de propósito y de conducta, os diré que estáis envenenados por la lógica y que carecéis de sentido teológico. (IV, 2073-74)

Cuando el Cristo vuelva — decía mi maestro —, predicará el orgullo a los humildes, como ayer predicaba la humildad a los poderosos. Y sus palabras serán, aproximadamente, las mismas: 'Recordad que vuestro padre está en los cielos; tan alta es vuestra alcurnia por parte de padre. Sobre la tierra sólo hay ya para vosotros deberes fraternos, independientes de los vínculos de la sangre. Licenciad de una vez para siempre al bíblico semental humano'. (IV, 2311)

In spite of the overwhelming verbal similarities between the passages, one can immediately perceive the difference brought about by the inclusion of the penultimate sentence in the Civil-War piece. Even more interesting, however, is how in this latter piece the perspective is clearer and more direct: although Mairena is here attributing the ideas to Abel Martín, there is a fairly clear transfer of the thoughts from Martín to Mairena. In the earlier passage, because it is set in Mairena's classroom, and the class have presumably reacted with derision to the idea of the Divinity having a change of heart, Mairena intervenes to calm things down. The reader is therefore unsure whether the ideas that follow Mairena's intervention belong to Mairena or to Martín. What the earlier passage gains in atmosphere, in its incorporation of the *palabra hablada*, in perspectivist ambiguity, it loses in directness to the 1937 piece. Also, whereas the earlier piece dealt with two quite separate ideas (the fatherhood of God and the infallibility of God), in the section from *Hora de España* there is a much more direct link between the first idea (pride in our spiritual origins) and the second (the fatherhood of God and the brotherhood of humanity). A comparison between the passage in *Hora de España* and the other pieces in the 1936 book mentioned above would also show the more direct impact of the later piece.

There is a passage of similar import in Machado's *Mairena* contribution of 1 December 1935, in which the metaphysical rather than the social consequences of Mairena's brand of

Christianity (heavily dependent on Abel Martín) is brought to the fore. Addressing his class, Mairena puts forward his idea that

> Si todos somos hijos de Dios — hijosdalgo, por ende, y ésta es la razón del orgullo modesto a que he aludido más de una vez —, ¿cómo he de atreverme, dentro de esta fe cristiana, a degradar a mi prójimo tan profunda y sustancialmente que le arrebate el ser en sí para convertirlo en una mera representación, en un puro fantasma mío? (IV, 2071)

One notices that the question uppermost in Mairena's mind here concerns the ontological status of one's neighbour, the relationship between the one and other being summed up at the end of the piece in Martín's phrase 'la esencial heterogeneidad del ser'. The issue is left like that 'para tratarlo más largamente en otra ocasión' (IV, 2072). The early *Mairena* articles in *Hora de España* offered a means of dealing with the social consequences of these ideas.

Another comparison between a *Mairena* passage published on 19 November 1934 and section 17 of the article of January 1937 in *Hora de España* may be illuminating in any consideration of the degree of radicalization of Machado's thought in the wake of the outbreak of the Civil War. It is in this section 17 of the Civil-War piece that Machado derives the most direct consequences from the Christian ethic of the brotherhood of humanity. This single paragraph, although loosely set within the classroom framework of the *Mairena* series, bears all the stamp of the revolutionary thrust of the Spanish Republic during the first year of the Civil War. At least there is nothing in Machado's pre-Civil-War writings to compare with it, in its radical proposal that predominantly physical or repetitive work should be shared among the whole community. Although Mairena is speaking as usual some time before or during the year 1909, Machado is here unquestionably writing from within the collectivist revolution that took place in Republican Spain during the first year of the Civil War, the importance of which has been summarized by Gabriel Jackson as 'the most profound social revolution since the fifteenth century'.[9]

---

9   *Op. cit.*, 277.

There are no verbal similarities between the January piece from *Hora de España* and the earlier passage, but their subjects are broadly similar: attitudes to work. The 1934 piece is in the form of a dialogue between Mairena and a student; the first part of the passage is as follows:

> La sociedad burguesa de que formamos parte — habla Mairena a sus alumnos — tiende a dignificar el trabajo. Que no sea el trabajo la dura ley a que Dios somete al hombre después del pecado. Más que un castigo, hemos de ver en él una bendición del cielo. Sin embargo, nunca se ha dicho tanto como ahora: 'el que no trabaje que no coma.' Esta frase, perfectamente bíblica, encierra un odio inexplicable a los holgazanes, que nos proporcionan con su holganza el medio de acrecentar nuestra felicidad y de trabajar más de la cuenta. Uno de los discípulos de Mairena hizo la siguiente observación al maestro:
> — El trabajador no odia al holgazán porque la holganza aumente el trabajo de los laboriosos, sino porque les merma su ganancia, y porque no es justo que el ocioso participe, como el trabajador, de los frutos de su trabajo.
> — Muy bien, señor Martínez ... Pero aquellos bienes de la tierra que da Dios de balde, ¿por qué no han de repartirse entre trabajadores y holgazanes, mejorando un poco al pobrecito holgazán, para indemnizarle de la tristeza de su holganza?
> (IV, 1922)

Even in this truncated version of the section, one can immediately sense the atmosphere of the semi-informal debating chamber that constitutes Mairena's 'pre-Civil-War' classroom. It is no coincidence that this piece contains another student 'interruption': in general, this type of dialogue is much more prevalent in *Juan de Mairena* (1936) than in the *Hora de España* series. (The dialogue in the passage just quoted continues to about double the length given here.) The idea that workers and idlers should share the fruits of the former's labour is put forward as a question for debate, and expressed in a semi-humorous way, in the reference to the 'pobrecito holgazán', not to mention Mairena's highly ironic tone throughout.

This playful tone of Mairena is a startling contrast to the purposeful tone of the January 1937 passage. There is a weight and solemnity in the latter, absent from the earlier piece, in the phrasing of a sentence such as: 'Hemos llegado ya a una plena conciencia de la dignidad esencial, de la suprema aristocracia del hombre; y de todo privilegio de clase pensamos que no podrá sostenerse en lo futuro'. This sentence, with its plural form,[10] its sense of having arrived at a definite conclusion, does not admit debate, let alone denial. There are many other examples of the solemn tone of the piece in this paragraph from *Hora de España*:

> el aventajamiento de un grupo social sobre otro carece de fundamento moral; Para nosotros es esto éticamente imposible; nada nos autoriza ya a arrojar sobre las espaldas de nuestro prójimo las faenas de pan llevar; es este trabajo necesario que, lejos de enaltecer al hombre, le humilla, y aun pudiera degradarle, el que debe repartirse por igual entre todos. (IV, 2315)

This tone is in keeping with an addition to the title of the January 1937 contribution, which did not feature in the subtitle of *Juan de Mairena* (1936) or in any of the thirty-four headings to the individual articles that comprise it. The word 'consejos' ('counsels'), added to the January 1937 title, gives us a leading hint of the more solemn tone of the *Hora de España* series.

It is also wholly in keeping with Mairena's profession to consider the *pueblo* in terms of educational attainment, as he had done in section 3 of the *Diario de Madrid* article of 21 January 1935. In this section Mairena speculates that 'Es muy posible que, entre nosotros, el saber universitario no pueda competir con el *folklore*, con el saber popular' (IV, 1954).[11] (In 'Meditación del día' of February 1937, as we have seen, Machado contrasts the short-sighted and self-interested folly of the insurgent generals with the integrity and intelligence of the workers.) On a theological level, too, the *pueblo* is observed to be more clear-sighted than the academically privileged, its quickness and generosity of mind and action being demonstrated in a willingness to put into practice the fraternal virtues of Christianity. In the section (17) of the January piece in *Hora de España* that we have been discussing, Machado

---

10 Paul Aubert (*art. cit.*, 31) makes the point that, after the outbreak of the Civil War, Machado 'No se expresa en solitario — notemos el empleo de la segunda persona del plural en sus declaraciones — sino que alcanza el conocimiento de una conciencia colectiva'.

11 Macrì follows the first edition, using 'puede' instead of 'pueda'. For this latter reading I have followed Fernández Ferrer, *Juan de Mairena*, I, 134.

implies that the practical outcome of Christian thought has already been anticipated by the *pueblo* in the Republic's social revolution: 'De la gran experiencia cristiana todavía en curso, es ésta [la ética popular] una consecuencia ineludible, a la cual ha llegado el pueblo, como de costumbre, antes que nuestros doctores' (IV, 2315). In the 1935 article Mairena goes on to contrast the stale method of rote learning and hand-me-down *recetas* of the university of his time, with the concentration and commitment of the artisan, making a guitar or a shoe. Again the difference between the 1935 and 1937 remarks is a telling one: the individual artist/artisan of 1935 has been replaced by the 'grupo social' of 1937, which demonstrates its integrity and ethical superiority by communal action.

The reference to 'nuestros doctores' in the 1937 piece, however, is not aimed solely at the inadequacy of theoreticians in the working out of practical ethical imperatives. We are also aware that although Mairena is teaching young boys of secondary-school age, his concern is not with curricular requirements (his classes are 'libres') but with preparing his young volunteers for some role, however minimal, as artists (in his classes of *retórica* and *poética*) and intellectuals (in his classes of *sofística*) in their society. This section 17 is a meditation on the position of artists and intellectuals in society in general, but the background is likely to have been the decision of the Republic's government some weeks earlier to evacuate leading artists and intellectuals from Madrid to the relative safety and comfort of Valencia. Machado had confessed that he wanted to remain in Madrid, and he must have been concerned at the potential wedge being driven between the country's best-known artists and intellectuals on the one hand, and the great bulk of the Republic's population on the other. As we have seen from his interview in Valencia, in November 1936, Machado stresses the existence of the close links between the intellectual and the *pueblo*, describing the publication of the *Romancero de la Guerra Civil* as a splendid example of 'la militarización de los trabajadores del espíritu' (IV, 2170), and he continues, in that interview, in his simplest and plainest style: 'Junto al pueblo ha de estar el intelectual' (IV, 2170). Rather than a discussion of the precise mechanisms of how any division of labour is to be achieved, the January 1937 piece is concerned with establishing the principle of the active, practical solidarity of the intellectual with those who perform the 'faenas ... tan embrutecedoras' in society, and the conviction that this work 'debe repartirse por igual entre todos'.

Machado's speech delivered to the *II Congreso Internacional de Escritores Antifascistas*, is in the main a collection of previous Civil-War writings grouped together, with pieces of connecting prose, in which he uses the latter to clarify the sense of these pieces, as he sees them. (*Hora de España* published his conference speech in its August issue.) According to at least one eye-witness Machado looked seriously ill at the final session, in which he delivered his address,[12] and it is possible that delivering an anthology of pieces written on other occasions may have been dictated by considerations of health, since the kind of sustained piece of work required for a closing *Discurso* (which he delivered) may well have been beyond Machado's physical capacities at this juncture. In any case it was a good opportunity for Machado to gather together the briefest of anthologies of his Civil-War writings, with which foreign delegates would not have been familiar, and to which we could loosely give the title *cultura popular*, with its central idea of solidarity between artists and intellectuals and the *pueblo*. Machado includes his earliest Civil-War piece, 'Los milicianos de 1936' (dated August 1936) in which the dignity and intelligence of the ordinary militiaman are contrasted with the servility and superficiality of the *señorito*. In his clarifying remarks to 'Los milicianos de 1936' in *Hora de España*, Machado writes that the piece represents 'mi fe democrática, mi creencia en la superioridad del pueblo sobre las clases privilegiadas' (IV, 2199). In fact, it is the first phrase of this quotation that more closely represents 'Los milicianos de 1936', unless we understand 'las clases privilegiadas' as encompassing anyone, irrespective of social class, who seeks privilege over others. Machado in the same piece, as we have seen, describes *señoritismo* as a form of

---

12 Arturo Serrano Plaja who brought Machado from Rocafort to the *Congreso* has recorded his impression on seeing him: 'le vi una cara tan gris, tan de cansancio', he writes, that he asked Machado if he was all right. Machado then asked Serrano Plaja to get him a 'copa de coñac' (quoted in M. Aznar Soler, *Pensamiento literario y compromiso antifascista*, 239). José Machado watched his brother wasting away in Rocafort, commenting that 'Cada día su gabán parecía mayor y él más pequeño' (*op. cit.*, 138).

'hombría degradada ... que puede observarse a veces en individuos de diversas clases sociales'. Indeed, in the August 1936 piece he introduced the sections on *señoritismo* with the comment that the *señorito* had disappeared from Madrid, having been absorbed by the surrounding human tragedy of the war.

The two pieces in the August issue of *Hora de España* that 'sandwich' 'Los milicianos de 1936' are concerned with the writer, and the writer's audience. They may be summed up in Machado's simply expressed faith that to write for ordinary people is to be the best kind of writer (Cervantes, Shakespeare, Tolstoy) because 'escribiendo para el pueblo se escribe para los mejores' (IV, 2202). As to why the *pueblo* should represent 'los mejores', we have already commented on how Machado, rather than dwell on aspects of social division, preferred to stress the intelligence and integrity of the *pueblo*. In sections 8, 9 and 10 of the July *Discurso*, he examines different attitudes to culture and its diffusion. Francisco Zaragoza Such makes an interesting observation on Machado's phrase 'aumentar en el mundo el humano tesoro de conciencia vigilante' used in section 9, when he comments: 'Defender la cultura es difundir la cultura, pero esto [Machado's phrase just quoted] es mucho más, y otra cosa, que transmitir saberes: es aumentar la conciencia vigilante'.[13] Mere transmission is insufficient: the encounter with culture should result in an enlargement of our perception, through greater participation with 'la comunidad de los hombres'.[14] Mairena's description, in section 9, of culture as 'el humano tesoro de conciencia vigilante', in its insistence on culture as a product of intelligent consciousness, links culture with the *pueblo* rather than with those who see it as a treasury of valuable merchandise which is to be preserved for the privilege of the few. This latter view, Mairena argues, turning the tables on conventional notions of education, is culture being seen 'desde la ignorancia o, también, desde la pedantería' (IV, 2203). The highly radical nature of Machado's view of culture

---

[13] *Lectura ética de Antonio Machado* (Murcia: Editora Regional de Murcia, 1982), 241.

[14] See P. Cerezo Galán, *Palabra en el tiempo. Poesía y filosofía en Antonio Machado* (Madrid: Gredos, 1975), 601, who underlines the expression of this aspect of Machado's thought.

may be illustrated by a quotation from an anarchist-inspired publication of 1938. In it the author describes the politics of culture very much in terms of Machado's own definition, just given: 'La cultura no reconoce clases: es cultura. Cultura de clase, es cultura monopolizada, corrompida'.[15]

The final section of the *Discurso* returns to the theme of the diffusion of culture, through a related idea that surfaces from time to time in the *Mairena* prose: that of mass culture. In his opposing emphasis on the individual, Machado was to find himself very much in accord with the young artists and intellectuals who had given the *ponencia colectiva* earlier in the conference: they may even have inspired Machado's choice of his previously written texts for the closing *Discurso*. They too sought to get away from over-theorized abstractions, and maintain the ideology of the revolution within the realm of the everyday hopes and fears of every single citizen of the Republic. In the *ponencia* they defended an art that responded to such an individualistic view, as follows: 'Los obreros son algo más que buenos, fuertes etc. Son hombres con pasiones, con sufrimientos, con alegrías mucho más complejas que las que esas fáciles interpretaciones mecánicas desearían'. And they continued, towards the end of the *ponencia*: 'El humanismo que defendemos ... Porque vive de realidades y no de supuestos ... depende de la existencia del hombre como hombre, esto es, liberado de todo cuanto no sea una confección del mundo en que el hombre es, ciertamente, el valor esencial'.[16] Reading such quotations in the light of one of Mairena's pre-Civil-War pieces in *El Sol* one can realize that even in statements without any overt political content, Machado's consistent humanism, the supreme value that he apportions to the treasury of the individual human consciousness, placed him close to the Civil-War culture that formed around him in the cities of Madrid, Valencia and Barcelona, a culture that Juan Manuel Fernández Soria has described as 'el protagonismo que se le

---

15 J. Peirats, *Los intelectuales en la revolución* (Barcelona: Ediciones 'Tierra y Libertad', 1938), 79.

16 *Hora de España*, IX (1937), 88-89 and 93.

concede al ciudadano de la República'.[17] In his *Mairena* piece of 5 April 1936 Machado takes Galileo to task for his excessively technological vision of the world ('El [Galileo] hablaba a los astrónomos, a los geómetras, a los inventores de máquinas'.) And he replies: 'Nosotros, que hablamos al hombre, también sabemos lo que decimos' (IV, 2105). The short section ends there, and Mairena then turns to an anecdote about his childhood in Seville; the latter subject is still about our inadequate vision of things, but it effectively leaves the Galileo piece in an embryonic state, lacking an illustration of Mairena's objection to Galileo's mathematical view of phenomena. In his closing *Discurso* to the conference Machado chooses as his example 'un hombre del pueblo' who cannot be reduced to what 'el hombre tiene de común con los objetos del mundo físico' and who is part of 'esos millones de conciencias humanas, esparcidas por el mundo entero, y que luchan — como en España — heroica y denodadamente por destruir cuantos obstáculos se oponen a su hombría integral' (IV, 2204-05). Mairena's reference to Spain, although expressed as an aside, brings the argument up to date, but it is the revolutionary solidarity of millions of 'consciousnesses' that constitutes the reply to Galileo's mathematical view of the world. In the example taken from the July *Discurso*, and others quoted earlier, it is evident that the Civil War extended Machado's response, to encompass areas of experience that he might have left without overt analysis and expression. Machado himself expressed it in October of 1938 in one of his simplest and clearest aphorisms: 'hay cosas que sólo la guerra nos hace ver claras' (IV, 2475).

One final example may be chosen to illustrate the relevance of this aphorism in Machado's case, this time involving an addition that Machado made to part of his February 1937 article in *Hora de España*, when he re-cast it for his July *Discurso*. Machado incorporates part of the earlier piece on the danger of using the cliché 'las masas', and concludes in the *Discurso* that

---

17 'La asistencia cultural de la República en guerra', in *València, capital cultural de la República (1936-1937)*, 46. During the course of his essay Fernández Soria makes the related point that while the *Misiones Pedagógicas* of the pre-war Republic were aimed at the *pueblo*, or at a *población*, the Civil War's *Milicias de la cultura* targeted the individual soldier.

to write for the masses is to write for nobody, because 'el hombre, el *cada hombre* que os escuche no se sentirá aludido y necesariamente os volverá la espalda' (IV, 2205). There is an interesting clarification in this final section (11) of the *Discurso*, with regard to Mairena's remark that the cliché *las masas* 'proviene del campo enemigo'. Where there was a full stop after 'enemigo' in the February piece, Machado now places a colon and identifies the enemy: 'de la burguesía capitalista que explota al hombre y necesita degradarlo'. When we recall Mairena's whimsical praises of the bourgeoisie in the article of 13 November 1934: 'la burguesía, con su liberalismo, su individualismo, su organización capitalista, su ciencia positiva, su florecimiento industrial, mecánico, técnico ... no es una clase tan despreciable' (IV, 1914), we become aware that alongside Machado's unwillingness to draw rigid lines that would divide humanity by social class, there are rare occasions when there is a perceptible hardening of tone, and a readiness to spell out the consequences of what was up to then not a fully articulated view of society.[18]

In general, however, the note of fraternalism prevails, rather than emphasis on division, whether in Mairena's classroom or in attitudes to the issues of the hour, such as work, education, or the links between the *pueblo* and intellectuals. The war, indeed, gave an urgency and prominence to issues such as these in *Hora de España* that was less visible in earlier writings, perhaps, but always ready to surface: the emphasis on dialogue, on the extension of culture is an essential part of *Juan de Mairena* (1936), for example. Reflected, too, in a general way in these early issues of *Hora de España* is Machado's support for the revolutionary aspect of the Civil War, as the former affected collectivist movements in the Republic, although Machado never involves himself in any specific political mechanisms that might bring about egalitarian directions in society. Alberto Gil Novales sums up the poet's humanism in this period of strife,

---

[18] Without giving examples José Luis Cano, referring to the *Mairena* writings of the Civil War, also remarks that 'al escepticismo inicial sucede una actitud firme frente a la sublevación militar y frente a la guerra', *Antonio Machado* (Barcelona: Bruguera, 1982), 72. Rodríguez Puértolas and Pérez Herrero, *op. cit.*, 25-26, give examples of Machado's tougher use of language during the Civil War.

when he comments on the essence of Machado's view of the *pueblo*: for Machado, he writes, 'Cualquier hombre puede ser un gran hombre'.[19] In these first months of *Hora de España* Machado contented himself with such simple reminders, through Mairena, of the dignity of the individual and of the 'deberes fraternos' that follow from such a conviction.

---

19 *Op. cit.*, 128.

CHAPTER 4

'Sobre la guerra y la paz': Machado's Writings in *Hora de España* (1937-1938)

While Machado's articles in *Diario de Madrid* and *El Sol* from November 1934 to June 1936 were completely devoted to the teachings of Juan de Mairena, his twenty-three articles in *Hora de España*, although dominated by the *Mairena* format, contain three complete, or almost complete, interruptions to it, with the publication of 'Carta a David Vigodsky. Leningrado', 'Sobre la Rusia actual' and 'Nueve sonetos y una cuarteta' in the journal.[1] The remaining twenty contributions contain one hundred and seventy-one sections, an average of between eight and nine sections per piece (consistent with the original fifty *Juan de Mairena* articles, that had yielded their average crop of over eight sections per contribution, out of a total of four hundred and twenty-two sections). From these one hundred and seventy-one sections, not many more than thirty deal specifically with issues of war and peace, and even then the overwhelming majority of these sections are set within Mairena's own lifespan, with 1909 (the date of his death) as its upper limit, or more rarely are 'prophecies' (Machado usually preferred the biblical word to the more scientific 'pronóstico') about an unspecified time in the future. We should remember also that Machado began to write his (mainly) political articles for *La Vanguardia* at the end of March 1938, so that there is an overlap affecting the last eight numbers of *Hora de España* (the issues published from April to November 1938) when Machado would have had ample opportunity to exercise his concern about the present state of Europe in the articles for the Barcelona newspaper. Taking the series of contributions to *Hora de*

---

1 In the 'Carta a David Vigodsky. Leningrado', the paragraph dealing with the death of Unamuno is attributed to Mairena, so that part of this piece belongs to the *Mairena* format.

España as a whole, there is a notable lack of reference to the Spanish Civil War, as distinct from general issues of war and peace. The Civil War itself is only referred to substantially on about half a dozen occasions throughout the *Mairena* series in *Hora de España*.[2]

In the first issue of *Hora de España*, only one of the eighteen sections (number 8) deals with war. The subject here is, characteristically, the related issues of rhetoric and propaganda, and their significance in time of war. (None, suggests Mairena, who nevertheless finds use in a later class for what Machado terms 'retórica peleona' in section 2 of his *Hora de España* contribution of September 1938.) In the February 1937 contribution none of the six sections contains any mention of war or peace, unless we wish to argue that the reference to 'nuestros adversarios' in the very last sentence of the piece, and Mairena's accompanying label of himself and his students as 'demócratas incorregibles' (IV, 2320), are pointing us towards a view of the cause and effect of the Spanish conflict. In the March contribution any reference to the war is confined to the last of the ten sections that comprise it (and to its last sentence). Here, however, although expressed as a piece of advice from Mairena to his students about their conduct in the future, it is directed both towards a potential civil war that is the outcome of a class struggle, and towards the possible involvement of Russia in such a war. Yet we should not forget that this is just one piece — and one of the shortest — out of ten in that month's contribution. While Machado may have deemed it more effective to place his rather oblique comments on the Spanish conflict right at the end of the February and March pieces in *Hora de España*, it is more likely that at this stage they are meant to be just one strand in his many-sided meditations on culture, of what he called 'este continuo abigarrado de que somos parte' (IV, 2347). As we have seen from his Valencia interview, Machado was under no illusions as to the nature of

---

2 The *subliminal* presence of the Civil War may be found much more extensively throughout Machado's contributions to *Hora de España*. Francisco Caudet, for instance, finds that in the opening *sentencia* of the first article ('Nunca peguéis con lacre las hojas secas de los árboles para fatigar al viento') Machado is 'denunciando los errores del bando rebelde', where the wind symbolizes time and the revolution; in 'Juan de Mairena durante la guerra', *Antonio Machado hoy*, I, 267-85.

the conflict, yet he was obviously reluctant to allow the war radically to affect the continuity of his cultural work.

This pattern is to some extent maintained in Machado's next contribution to *Hora de España*, which is the text of an actual letter sent in February to the Russian Hispanist, David Vigodsky. Here too the assessment of the literary work of Unamuno, Lorca and Alberti takes precedence over their respective political positions and fortunes during the Civil War. Machado's assessment of Unamuno is a case in point. The paragraph is written as if spoken by Mairena, which has the effect of distancing it from the present. Most of the brief necrology (Unamuno had died a few weeks earlier in nationalist Salamanca) is devoted to Unamuno's status as a philosopher, leaving his political position during the first months of the Civil War until the end of the paragraph. On the death of Lorca, Machado's way of commenting on it is through a re-reading of his own poem ('cosa rara en mí', he says) written some months earlier to mark the event. In these early contributions to *Hora de España*, therefore, the continuity of the cultural task is uppermost in Machado's mind. His May 1937 contribution continues the pattern. Of the thirteen sections, the last ('*Lo que hubiera dicho Mairena el 14 de abril de 1937*') is the only one that mentions the present, and then in only one sentence out of the four paragraphs. (The rest of the section is an evocation of the early days of the Second Republic in 1931.)

In the *Hora de España* articles it is not until June 1937 that we come to the first substantial meditation on war and peace: *Sobre la Alemania guerrera*. Although typical of the earlier *Mairena* pieces by coming at the end of that month's contribution of ten sections, it is the most substantial part of the June piece, being nearly as long as the other nine together. The section is built around the image of Germany as a conscientiously logical teacher, applying intellect, philosophy, popular wisdom, and all the national culture generally, to the service of militarism. The other image used is that of wholeness, completeness and perfection, the pursuit of which in this case is empty and hollow because devoid of any meaning other than a search for such completion and fulfilment. The piece is not just a satire on Germany and a brief exposition of how a country with Germany's intellectual and philosophical tradition turned to militarism. It is also a criticism of intellectual pursuits that are divorced from the concerns of humanity at large and a demonstration of the sterility of such pursuits.

If we look back briefly to the attack on logic in the *Mairena* article of 5 January 1936, we become aware again that in the intervening year and a half, while the concern — the absurdity of logic — is the same, the issue as portrayed in *Sobre la Alemania guerrera* has taken on menacing proportions for humanity, something quite different from the example chosen in the earlier piece. In January 1936 the exercise of logic produces a remote and solipsistic God 'arriba ... pensándose a sí mismo' (IV, 2081). Mairena's remark that 'Todo esto es perfectamente lógico' anticipates the similar attack on logic in the later piece. In the latter, however, Machado spells out the dangers for humanity of the pursuit of intellectual goals that result in one's becoming isolated from one's fellow human beings. On this global scale, as well as in the more intimate surroundings of his voluntary classes, Mairena's philosophy is the same, as he expressed it in the last specifically classroom scene in *Hora de España*. Explaining to the students why he uses only verbal persuasion in his classes, he comments: 'de ningún modo conviene que enturbiemos con amenazas el ambiente benévolo, fuera del cual no hay manera de aprender algo que vale la pena de ser sabido' (IV, 2395). The corollary is the need for dialogue and solidarity in any intellectual enterprise, and Machado's concern, as he expressed it in 'Sobre la Rusia actual', for what he called 'el total destino del hombre' (IV, 2219). P. Cerezo Galán has similarly remarked, as we noted in our previous chapter, in connection with Machado's attitude to peace: 'No es, pues, la paz un fin en sí, sino la comunidad de los hombres, y en consecuencia sólo serán realmente pacíficos los actos que crean vínculos de solidaridad'.[3] In *Sobre la Alemania guerrera* Germany drives a wedge between itself and three-quarters of humanity. Mairena comments that on conscientiously pursuing militaristic ends by setting out to lay siege to a town, a million people spring up to defend the town. The image throughout the piece is of an inhuman dedication to a hollow, senseless efficiency.

---

3   *Op. cit.*, 601.

As in *Juan de Mairena* (1936), so also in *Hora de España* the critical examination of clichés, *tópicos* and *refranes* forms an important part of the *Mairena* series. Machado's contribution to the February 1937 number of *Hora de España* is devoted almost entirely to this subject, in which the phrases 'revolución desde arriba', 'la cultura' and 'las masas' are given close scrutiny, the concern there being to bring to the surface 'la malicia que lleva implícita la falsedad de un tópico' (IV, 2320). In *Sobre la Alemania guerrera* a variation on the Latin phrase *si vis pacem para bellum* is subjected to the first of several examinations throughout the Civil War. Antonio Fernández Ferrer[4] has pointed out that the original phrase was 'Qui desiderat pacem, praeparet bellum'. Machado makes the original more succinct, incisive and direct, more memorable, in a word, creating a new aphorism, the examination of which reveals a wealth of meditation on the negative aspects of the influence of Darwinism, of the Nietzschean will-to-power and of the competitive, activist climate of Western civilization.

From a perspectivist point of view the examination of what Machado here calls '[el] lenguaje de Pero Grullo' (IV, 2337) is a useful stance by Machado to distance himself from too uncritical an acceptance of the products of popular wisdom, such as proverbs and aphorisms. (Raimundo Lida overstates the case, in my view, when he asserts that 'Le exaspera [a Mairena] el lugar común tomado por sentido común'.)[5] In this context the examination in *Sobre la Alemania guerrera* is of 'toda una aforística guerrera'. Once again a comparison between *Juan de Mairena* (1936) and *Hora de España* is revealing in this respect. In the section of the article of 23 March 1935 in which 'tópicos, lugares comunes y frases más o menos mostrencas de ... nuestra lengua' (IV, 1982) are discussed, the example picked is an innocuous piece of threadbare rhetoric: 'Porque las canas siempre venerables ...'. Mairena, as we saw in an earlier chapter, rings the changes on the cliché, humorously demonstrating to his students the way that they can follow his advice: 'que adoptéis ante ellas [the *frases hechas*] una actitud interrogadora y reflexiva'. With the intervention of the war, the phrases for examination are not chosen at random (as

---

4   *Ed. cit.*, II, 46.
5   *Art. cit.*, 366.

apparently with the 1935 example) but with deadly earnest concentration. 'Si vis pacem [or as in the *Alemania guerrera* piece, 'si vis bellum'] para bellum' is exposed as summing up within its few words a whole culture of belligerence that extends back to the Roman Empire and through to contemporary political ambitions in Western Europe. To make this point Machado juxtaposes his version of the Latin phrase with Nietzsche's advice, 'vivid en peligro' (IV, 2337).

Machado's next contribution to *Hora de España* (the July 1937 number) also contains a long section (out of a total of six) on issues related to war and peace, and is entitled *Sobre el pacifismo*. It is as if with the continuation of the war his intervention on these issues in the *Mairena* series is becoming more substantial (although this section is still placed second last in the article). The robust tone of this piece makes one suspect a sub-theme of *anti-derrotismo* throughout, possibly in connection with the fall of Bilbao in June, which was a major blow to the Republic. Mairena's objection to contemporary manifestations of pacifism is that in the overwhelmingly belligerent atmosphere of Europe, in the social and moral climate of Europe and North America, the absence of a 'metafísica de la paz' (IV, 2341) and of 'una forma de conciencia de sentido amoroso' relieves Mairena and his students of any moral obligation to be pacifists, although he confesses that his own intellectual temperament leads him towards numbering himself among the latter.

This divorce between theory and practice is very evident in the section. Certainly if we were to judge Machado's position on the issue of pacifism by this one section alone, we should have to conclude that the argument for not being a pacifist because everyone is at war, is a pragmatic view that is unworthy of the poet's humanism. Machado was aware, of course, of the potential replies to such a position: the last sentence of the section in which Mairena describes his argument as having been put 'en la forma menos ventajosa para mi tesis' is in part a negative critique of it. No replies, however, are allowed to surface here: Mairena is addressing his students, but they do not contribute to the question. So the section is allowed to end with the view that while the theory of pacifism may be attractive to the individual, 'mi posición personal ante esta grave cuestión, que acaso divida al mundo en días no lejanos, importa poco' (IV, 2340-41) because the practice of pacifism in the present cultural climate of Western civilization is futile and will be swept away. The implication of the rhetorical question in the second-last sentence of the section — '¿creéis que hay motivo alguno que nos obligue a ser pacifistas?' — is that there is no overriding imperative for choosing pacifism in such a belligerent climate. The pragmatic fact, of course, was that to be a pacifist was to desert the Republic, in the short term; as Machado often remarked, there was no option to remain *au dessus de la mêlée*. In *Sobre el pacifismo* Machado views the practice of pacifism in a way that appears to offer no hope for the future, because the Western world is drowned in a sea of aggression. This negative moment of pessimism (we shall encounter it a year later in the Guiomar sonnet) is very unusual in Machado's work. In the next *Mairena* piece properly so-called, written for the October issue of *Hora de España*, and to which Machado gave the title 'Algunas ideas de Juan de Mairena sobre la guerra y la paz', Mairena sweeps back with a number of propositions for peace; not, however, 'peace for our time': the propositions are a listing of the necessary conditions for peace in the future. In this second half of the October article (which begins: 'Los futuros maestros de la paz ...') Machado reverses the negative emphasis of *Sobre el pacifismo* and offers a testament of peace, based on the primacy of spiritual and intellectual values, as opposed to the pragmatism and competitiveness of Western society.

In the interval between the July and October issues of *Hora de España*, which both form part of the *Mairena* series, Machado continued to meditate on the issues of war and peace, as can be seen in his September contribution, 'Sobre la Rusia actual'. This break with the *Mairena* series may well have been prompted by the publication of the *Carta colectiva* of the Spanish bishops, dated July 1937, in which their central thesis is that the rebellion of the generals had thwarted a communist, atheist, Russian-inspired revolution in Spain.[6] This possibility

---

6 See, for example, sections 4, 5 and 6 of the *Carta colectiva del Episcopado español sobre la guerra*, of 1 July 1937 (quoted in *La guerra de España en sus documentos*, ed. Fernando Díaz-Plaja [Madrid: Sarpe, 1986], 267-73). The full title of this document in its English translation (London:

is reinforced by another coincidence earlier in the year, with the publication in April 1937 of Machado's letter to the Russian Hispanist, David Vigodsky, which we examined in chapter 2. In the previous month of March, Pius XI's encyclical letter *Divini Redemptoris* had been published. The Pope's letter, mainly an attack on Communist Russia, contained a paragraph referring to 'El azote comunista y la guerra de España' (I quote from a Spanish translation) and accuses the Spanish Republic of allowing destruction of churches and mass assasinations of 'buenos cristianos' to be conducted with a barbarity unimaginable in the twentieth century.[7] The July *Carta colectiva* of the Spanish bishops, published simultaneously in Spanish, French and English and devoted exclusively to the origins and progress of the Civil War, was a major propaganda coup for the insurgents, depicting nationalist Spain as leading a tranquil and ordered existence and labelling the revolution in the Republic as 'anticristiana'. In 'Sobre la Rusia actual' Machado focuses on the essentially Christian nature of what he calls 'el alma rusa' and contrasts the writings of the great nineteenth-century Russian writers with those of Nietzsche, the latter seen as a representation of the materialism and cynicism of Western society. With breathtaking compression Machado delivers his verdict on nineteenth-century Western European culture, in a ferocious attack on Nietzsche and what he represents:

> En los momentos de mayor auge de la literatura rusa, hondamente cristiana, el semental humano de la Europa central lanza por boca de Nietzsche, su bramido de alarma, su terrible invectivo contra el Cristo viviente en el alma rusa, su crítica corrupta y corrosiva de las virtudes específicamente cristianas. Bajo un disfraz romántico, a la germánica, aquel pobre borracho de darwinismo, escupe al Cristo vivo, al ladrón de energías, al enemigo, según él, del porvenir zoológico de la especie humana, toda una filosofía tejida de blasfemias y contradicciones. (IV, 2220)

As so often in Machado's late writings, these two sentences are

---

Catholic Truth Society, 1937), gives a good idea of its importance in the conflict: *Joint Letter of the Spanish Bishops to the Bishops of the Whole World concerning the War in Spain*.

7   Pius XI, *Divini Redemptoris*, ed. Ignacio Segarra Bañares (Madrid: Mundo Cristiano, 1977), 24-25.

packed with years of meditation, years of notes committed to *Los complementarios* and doubtless to many other notebooks besides, in which it is no exaggeration to say that there is a lifetime's thought and feeling. Given compressed language and sentiment of such power and range, it was inevitable that Machado should return at greater length to the subject of the aggressive mentality of Western civilization, and this he did in the October issue of *Hora de España*.

It is perhaps important, in the context of the *Mairena* series in *Hora de España*, and of any relationship between the various contributions, to open a parenthesis here and to remind ourselves of the obvious fact that Machado was writing isolated pieces each month for the journal. Of necessity he did not have the time, the facilities or, as the events of the war carried everything before them, and Machado's health declined irremediably, the opportunity to order the overall shape of his Civil-War writings, once committed to print. With *Juan de Mairena* (1936) Machado did take the opportunity to change the structure of some of the chapters, making them different from the grouping of the sections, as they had appeared in *Diario de Madrid* and *El Sol*.[8] It is impossible to know how Machado would have edited his contributions to *Hora de España*, if he had lived to be able to do so. We can reasonably speculate, however, that the three non-*Mairena* pieces would not have appeared where they did in *Hora de España*.[9] (Some of the *La*

---

8 José María Valverde, *Antonio Machado* (Madrid: Siglo Veintiuno, 1975) writes that the text of *Juan de Mairena* (1936) 'modifica el de las entregas periodísticas sólo en quitar epígrafes y números romanos, y en corregir algunos errores' (278). However, in his Cátedra edition Fernández Ferrer lists seven of the fifty sections of the book (IX, X, XI, XII, XVIII, XIX) whose sections do not completely correspond with its equivalent newspaper article (231-32).

9 Oreste Macrì, Machado's most important editor to-date, has proceeded along these lines, devoting sub-section 1 of section VII of his edition of Machado's *Poesía y prosa* to *Juan de Mairena póstumo [en] Hora de España*, omitting the three non-*Mairena* pieces that featured in *Hora de España*, and including these latter in his section VI, *Prosas sueltas de la guerra*. Macrì, however, also omits from his section VII, sub-section 1 (by placing it in section VI) Machado's *Discurso* to the *Segundo Congreso Internacional de Escritores Antifascistas*, in spite of the fact that there are four quotations, or interventions, from Juan de Mairena in the *Discurso*, a piece of posthumous editing that illustrates the difficulties of such an

Vanguardia pieces might also have been slotted in chronologically to a second *Mairena* volume.) The August 1937 contribution, being almost totally an anthology of earlier Civil-War pieces, would have to have been omitted, to avoid repetitions. After the August piece comes 'Sobre la Rusia actual', which also breaks the *Mairena* cycle. This may have been an article that was directly commissioned as a response to the Bishops' *Carta colectiva*. If such were the case, then the October 1937 issue of *Hora de España*, in which the section 'Los futuros maestros de la paz' appears, would have been the next opportunity that Machado had, using the *Mairena* format, to return to the general issues of war and peace. In any subsequent rearranging of the *Mairena* series, parts of the July and October contributions may well have ended up side by side in the same chapter, as had happened with different newspaper contributions in *Juan de Mairena* (1936). One of Machado's editors, Antonio Fernández Ferrer, is also of the opinion that Machado might have re-ordered his *Mairena* Civil-War texts, had the opportunity presented itself, when he writes: 'Resulta vano conjeturar cuál habría sido finalmente la futura ordenación elegida por Machado, pero no me parece un disparate imaginar para los apócrifos un ciclo diferenciado con ordenación específica'.[10] In speculating on what might have been, had Machado lived on in a victorious Republic or away from a defeated one, is it too much to imagine these pieces, *Sobre el pacifismo* and 'Los futuros maestros de la paz ...', appearing side by side in a second volume of *Juan de Mairena*, published in 1940, or whenever the vicissitudes of war permitted? The conjunction of the July and October pieces would have illustrated the dilemma of an artist and intellectual such as Machado, faced with the immediate imperatives of involvement in war.

If we examine again in more detail the long penultimate sentence from *Sobre el pacifismo*, from which we have only quoted extracts, and study it from the perspective of the piece 'Los futuros maestros de la paz ...', we can see in it seeds of the later piece, but sown here in a negative mood:

---

undertaking.
   10 *Art. cit.*, 11.

Sin que germine, o se restaure, una forma de conciencia religiosa de sentimiento amoroso; sin una metafísica de la paz, como la intentada por mi maestro, que nos lleve a una total idea del mundo esencialmente armónica, y en la cual los supremos valores se revelen en la contemplación, y de ningún modo sean un producto de actividades cinéticas; sin una ciencia positiva que no acepte como verdad averiguada la virtud del asesinato para el mejoramiento de la especie humana, ¿creéis que hay motivo alguno que nos obligue a ser pacifistas? (IV, 2341)

The spiritual and intellectual values propounded here ('conciencia religiosa de sentido amoroso'; 'la contemplación') also form the essence of the October piece. Yet in this quotation these values are subordinate (grammatically as well) to a series of negatives ('sin ... sin ... de ningún modo ... sin ...') that results in the concluding pragmatic rhetorical question and in what appears to be the exclusion of any idealistic means or motivation in the search for peace. The harmonic ideal of Abel Martín's Krausist world-view[11] seems very ineffectual compared to the activist 'ambiente de belicosos y beligerantes' (IV, 2341) that dominates the section.[12]

Not merely because Machado's October 1937 piece, 'Algunas ideas de Juan de Mairena sobre la guerra y la paz', reverses the negative emphasis of *Sobre el pacifismo* has this his tenth contribution to *Hora de España* claims to be called a key piece of writing in the series. It is the only one that is completely devoted to the issues of war and peace. In proposing a programme of peace to his students Mairena is aware of the

---

[11] Eugenio D'Ors commented in 1949 that 'el libro de Juan de Mairena [es] como *el único épitome donde se conservan lecciones de lo que ha sido el krausismo español*', 'Carta de Octavio de Romeu al Profesor Juan de Mairena', *Cuadernos Hispanoamericanos*, XI-XII (1949), 289-300. The quotation (the italics are the author's own) is from p. 295.

[12] Francisco Zaragoza Such, *Lectura ética de Antonio Machado*, sees the 'Sin que germine ...' quotation as an illustration that for Machado 'la verdadera paz humana es siempre una paz comprometida éticamente' (290-91), which, while true of the section 'Los futuros maestros de la paz ...' (from which he goes on to quote) goes against the sense of the 'Sin que germine ...' passage, where the negative emphasis is so strong. Rafael A. González, 'Las ideas políticas de Antonio Machado', *La Torre*, XLV-XLVI (1964), 151-70, devotes a section of his article ('La guerra y la paz', 162-67) to Machado's view of the peace beyond the frontiers of the Spanish Civil War, which González characterizes as a 'paz agresiva' (165).

enormity of what he sees as nineteenth-century Western Europe's exaltation of strife and power. The ideas devoted to war lay the blame for the war-like environment of Europe at the door of England and Germany, in very different proportions and for different reasons. Mairena is especially critical of Germany's single-minded pursuit of the will-to-power, as against the more sporting, liberal attitude of what he calls 'el mero campeonismo inglés' (IV, 2345). Once again Darwin and Nietzsche are the thinkers who are singled out for having given new impetus to the aggressive mentality of Western culture. Yet the whole history of Western philosophy, from Plato to Kant, is also included for its negative contribution to peace, through not doubting sufficiently the validity of its own thought processes. Descartes is held up for special scrutiny in this regard because of his claim — falsely made, says Mairena — to have incorporated a methodology of doubt into his thought.

As the vast chronological perspectivism of the example from the history of Western philosophy makes clear, Mairena's series of propositions for political peace is not strictly a programme for peace as such, but rather a call for the creation of a culture from which peace will necessarily emerge; not a 'paz vacía ... hueca, horra de todo contenido religioso, metafísico, ético', but one that will offer its own challenges in these spheres of human speculation and action. The seven propositions for peace are in fact Machado's own 'Notes towards the Definition of Culture', having regard to the conflictive circumstances of this period of Spanish and European history. They are also an extended gloss on his description of culture (in the February and August issues of *Hora de España*) as 'el humano tesoro de conciencia vigilante'. So, contemplation, meditation, study and critical judgment are the four cornerstones of Machado's heptagonal house of culture. This metaphysical foundation is to be completed by a trio of ethical propositions: detachment from material things, the reduction to its proper proportion of work done for the acquisition of only such things as are materially necessary, and finally the expansion of the principle 'love your neighbour as yourself' to become 'un amor que exceda un poco al que os profesáis a vosotros mismos, que pudiera ser insuficiente' (IV, 2349). Rodríguez Puértolas' and Pérez Herrero's summary of Machado's war writings is apt, in this regard: 'un pensamiento mucho más cargado de criterios morales y éticos que de concretos análisis políticos'.[13] Such consistent reference to moral and ethical imperatives on Machado's part is indeed the measure of the integrity of his writings on war and peace. Even in the *La Vanguardia* writings, with their contemporary political analysis and consideration of European *realpolitik*, these latter are always subordinate to the call to examine the fundamental imperatives of right thinking and virtuous action.

The last ethical proposition involves, of course, the kind of imperative that covers an infinity of potential programmes for practical action, offering a critical (and humorous) refinement of the Judaeo-Christian imperative of love of one's neighbour as one's self: even the most hallowed (if theoretical) maxim of the Christian era — 'love your neighbour as yourself' — is not free from Mairena's ironic yet affectionate scrutiny. Ricardo Gullón, picking up, perhaps, the challenge to our own society contained in the adjective '*futuros* maestros de la paz', frankly declares that the word he would associate with the seven propositions is 'anacrónico', because the critical, ascetic quietism advocated by Mairena is hopelessly at odds with the conformist activism of modern (i.e. Gullón's) society.[14] Indeed the lack of any specific link between the ideas of peace and justice is a notable omission from the seven propositions. (Machado was to rectify this omission in his next contribution to *Hora de España*, as we shall see.) In the last year of the war the non-interventionist attitude of Britain and France effectively sentenced the Republic to death. Machado's thoughts (coinciding with his *La Vanguardia* articles) then turned increasingly to the idea of a search for peace that could only rest on the premise of justice, rather than on the doctrine of the survival of the fittest, as Machado saw confirmed in the attitude of the League of Nations at that time (see IV, 2459). In the circumstances of the Republic's last year of existence, the ethical issues concerning war and peace are more often expressed by Machado in variations of the aphorism 'o cruzarnos de brazos ante la iniquidad, o guerrear por la justicia' (*Hora de España*, April 1938) rather than in any of the more metaphysical terms of the seven propositions for peace, of

---

13 *Ed. cit.*, 25-26.
14 *Espacios poéticos de Antonio Machado* (Madrid: Fundación March/Cátedra, 1987), 102.

October 1937. This is not to suggest, of course, that before 1938 Machado did not see social and political justice as a precondition for peace in the world. Yet as an emphasis in his writings it is evident that Machado became increasingly aware, in the Spanish situation, of the injustice of an attitude that always sought to avoid war because peace was perceived as an ethically more desirable goal.

The scene for these weighty, transcendental propositions of peace is the classroom in Mairena's *Instituto*. Mairena makes his points with all the energy and urgency of his brisk, schoolmasterly tone (taking into account that his pupils are always, as here, 'amigos míos'). After each of the seven propositions or teachings, the hope of peace is repeated. Machado may well have been remembering the July piece *Sobre el pacifismo* and its predominantly negative tone, as we outlined in our examination. Here, in 'Los futuros maestros de la paz ...', Mairena addresses his class with another rhetorical question, that is the opposite of the one in *Sobre el pacifismo*: '¿Pensáis vosotros que de una *clase* como ésta puede salir nadie dispuesto a pelearse con su vecino, y mucho menos por motivos triviales?' (IV, 2347). The Latin tag, cut down, as we noted earlier, and made more concise in the lapidary form 'si vis pacem para bellum' is again turned around, but in the act of its examination and rejection becoming a succint summary of the seven propositions: 'si quieres paz, prepárate a vivir en paz con todo el mundo' (IV, 2349).

Given, however, the conflictive circumstances of the hour, Machado confronts the question of active participation in the war: Mairena answers an imaginary question from the students about taking part in an armed conflict. If we compare Mairena's answer here with the discussion in *Juan de Mairena* (1936) on a similar topic, we become aware of the necessary shift in Machado's perspective and judgement on the question. In his *Diario de Madrid* article of 13 December 1934 Mairena attacks the idea of taking sides in 'tiempos de lucha' (IV, 1933). One of the students, Rodríguez, replies: 'hay que tomar partido, seguir un estandarte, alistarse bajo una bandera, para pelear. La vida es lucha, antes que diálogo amoroso y hay que vivir' (IV, 1934). For Mairena life is not worth living in such a conflictive ambience, hence his reply to the student's last sentence: 'Nous n'en voyons pas la necessité [de vivir]'. Nearly two years later, in the middle of the Civil War Machado has Mairena tell his students in the most positive tone that they should take sides in war, because having been 'preparados para la paz' (IV, 2349) they will only take the part of those who like themselves would never provoke war. They will then know how to die 'con una elegancia de que nunca serán capaces los hombres de vocación batallona' (IV, 2349). It is interesting to note that Machado does not spell out here in *Hora de España* the consequences of war for all sides, as he had done in the article of 13 December 1934: 'Tomar partido es no sólo renunciar a las razones de vuestros adversarios, sino también a las vuestras; abolir el diálogo, renunciar, en suma, a la razón humana. Si lo miráis despacio, comprenderéis el arduo problema de vuestro porvenir: habéis de retroceder a la barbarie, cargados de razón' (IV, 1933). Machado's decision in the October 1937 contribution of the *Mairena* series to face the reality of involvement in the war also makes this article one of the most important pieces of writing in the *Hora de España* series. Here one can detect the beginnings of the formulation of a view of the war, that while not at all a positive one, at least seeks a reason for taking part in it, and by analogy a positive view of the Republic's participation in the Civil War.

Ramón Gaya's drawing that heads Machado's October 1937 contribution to the *Hora de España* sums up with stunning simplicity the dilemma of those who sought an honourable peace: the drawing is of a dove with its olive branch; the dove is perched on the barrel of a rifle, the barrel and the olive branch pointing in the same direction. In Machado's October text there is no reference to killing the enemy, but the rejection of 'la paz como un fin deseable sobre todas las cosas' in the preamble to the seven propositions for peace would appear to carry with it the logic of killing in self-defence, although as we have seen, all the emphasis is placed on the manner of dying rather than the requirement of killing. I say 'would appear' because in the next sentence but one that follows the reference to 'peace before everything else', when Mairena speaks of the idea of the just war, all the perspectivism and distancing instincts of Machado come to the fore, creating a philosophical and ethical position that demands the most discriminating of responses from the reader. Here is the sentence in question, describing the attitude of the 'futuros maestros de la paz' to war: 'Pero serán maestros cuyo consejo, cuyo ejemplo y cuya enseñanza no podrán impulsarnos a pelear sino por causas justas, si estas causas existen, lo que esos maestros siempre pondrán en duda' (IV, 2346).

Who are these teachers, we might ask? The actual teaching that they do is relegated to third place of importance in their work: they teach by offering advice, by the example of their own lives, and only thirdly by the formal act of teaching itself. The reference to 'impulsarnos a pelear' is probably best understood in the context of the last sentence of the article, where Mairena describes 'los mejores' as those who will never have provoked war. In this context the phrase 'impulsarnos a pelear' appears to mean 'to provoke war'. The reference to the just war is also phrased in such a way as to cause ambiguity, particularly the last four words of the sentence. We may assume that these teachers who will discuss such concepts as the just war are philosophers by inclination, if not by profession (as was relatively the case of Machado himself). If this is so, then the phrase referring to the idea that these teachers 'pondrán en duda' the concept of the just war is an ambiguous one. It means either that they will doubt to the extent of denying any justification for the concept (this would be the layman's interpretation of 'pondrán en duda') or they will doubt philosophically, that is, debate the logical and ethical validity of the idea. The time-layering of the sentence (and the section) is another potent force for ambiguity, or at least uncertainty. Machado in 1937 is writing about Mairena, speaking before or during 1909 about future teacher/philosophers, who may or may not exist ('Los futuros maestros de la paz, si algún día aparecen'). The October contribution as a whole illustrates that the concepts of both war and peace were equally problematical for Machado: war because of its dominance of so many areas of life, 'apoyada en una religión y una metafísica y una moral' (IV, 2344), as Mairena comments at the beginning of the article, and as the *Carta colectiva* of the Spanish Bishops had recently confirmed; peace, because it seemed such a distant dream, however vividly pictured in 'Los futuros maestros de la paz ...'. Machado's conclusion is that participation in the war is justified for those who have not provoked it. Is it a coincidence that this advice of Mairena is relegated to the final sentence of the October contribution? Indeed, to judge by the first ten contributions to *Hora de España* Machado was reluctant to confront the terrible issues of war, such as killing in self-defence. (Two months later, however, he did tackle the latter issue in an article which although not in *Hora de España* will have to be examined in conjunction with that journal's *Mairena* series.)

The first section of Machado's November 1937 article in *Hora de España* is entitled '(*Sobre la guerra*)'. This piece, along with the rest of that month's contribution, is not a classroom scene, but is made up of 'Apuntes y recuerdos de Juan de Mairena', as the article's subtitle states. The 'recuerdos' are most likely Mairena's memories of Abel Martín, whose words are called to mind in sections 4, 5, 6 and 7 of the article. The 'apuntes' include the first section on war (and peace): as if this were a private postscript consigned to Mairena's notebook, following the extended exhortation to his students ('Los futuros maestros de la paz ...') in the previous piece. (Here is another example of sections in separate contributions to *Hora de España* that might easily have been grouped together in any re-ordering of these writings, had Machado lived to be able to do so.) Machado's aphoristic version of the Latin phrase (*si vis pacem para bellum*) is again examined, as it had been in the final paragraph of the previous article, and Mairena offers three more homespun replies to it. This examination of classical phrases or sayings hallowed by time and use, begun in *Juan de Mairena* (1936), and continued, as we noted, in the February 1937 number of *Hora de España*, is not used as extensively in the later series. When such a revaluation occurs, however, in the context of the Civil War, the result is a broad, simply expressed ethical vision. In the context of his reply to the original Latin tag, what could be more endowed with such a simple, yet universal ethic than the Mairena aphorism: 'si quieres la paz ... *procura tratar a tus vecinos con amor y justicia*' (IV, 2350)'? Here is another example of the way in which Machado was able to use a subsequent piece of writing in order to illuminate, refine and even rectify something that he had written before. In this connection it is useful to remember Mairena's description of himself in *Juan de Mairena* (1936) as 'un alma siempre en borrador, llena de tachones, de vacilaciones y de arrepentimientos' (IV, 1933). We have mentioned the predominantly metaphysical and ethical nature of the seven propositions for peace in 'Los futuros maestros de la paz ...'. In this subsequent aphorism the socio-political implications of the foundations for peace are adumbrated as entailing the need to 'tratar a tus vecinos ... con justicia'.

In this section Mairena attacks the Latin phrase as a dangerous legacy for modern Europe, particularly the Roman Church, having been adapted, Mairena writes, by 'los filisteos y los sacristanes ... para bendecir los cañones, las bombas incendiarias, y hasta los gases homicidas' (IV, 2350). There is also, in the section, both a reflection of and a reflection upon Mairena's (and Machado's, we assume) position as a writer in times of conflict: a critique of his own effectiveness as an artist and intellectual. Here, the critique involves an awareness that words, no matter how highly motivated and well put together, may not lead to desired results, because the gap between thought and action cannot be bridged, as least as far as the attainment of peace is concerned: 'Comprendo también que las sentencias más discretas y mejor intencionadas pudieran no llevarnos inevitablemente a la paz' (IV, 2350). Whether intentional or not, this reflection, consigned to the privacy of his notebook, bears all the hallmarks of a poignant postscript to Mairena's discourse on peace to the students, in which he had used all the resources of his rhetoric to plead for peace. As a critique of his own rhetoric it is an ironic commentary by Mairena: the blessing of the machines of war seems a more effective use of rhetoric. Machado, too, may have had the immediate situation in mind; the Spanish Bishops' *Carta colectiva* had referred benevolently to the symbolic aspect of this Church practice: that 'la Iglesia, aun siendo hija del Príncipe de la Paz, bendice los emblemas de la guerra'.[15] In general, these two sections, 'Los futuros maestros de la paz ...' and '(*Sobre la guerra*)', taken together may be viewed as an extended gloss on Mairena's aphorism, enunciated in the first issue of *Hora de España*: that as far as bringing about peace is concerned, 'Cuando los hombres acuden a las armas, la retórica ha

---

15 Díaz-Plaja, *ed. cit.*, 264.

terminado su misión' (IV, 2312).

The article, 'Notas del tiempo. Voces de calidad', which Machado published in December 1937, in the government's *Servicio Español de Información. Textos y Documentos* (No. 333), is included for discussion here because of the light that it throws on Machado's view of the Civil War, in the context of the *Mairena* series in *Hora de España*. The article is partly contemporary (section 1 deals with the position of Thomas Mann in Nazi Germany) and partly a *Mairena* piece (sections 2 and 3). These latter might well have been given a place chronologically with the *Hora de España* series in any subsequent collection of Machado's writings, had the author lived to be able to do so. The first section comments on Thomas Mann's loss of his Honorary Doctorate in the University of Bonn, and his reply to the official who had notified him of the decision. (Mann's letter had been translated in the *Hora de España* issue of September 1937.) In his letter Mann addresses himself to this official, to reply to a decision against which he has no appeal, since it is consequent upon an earlier decision by the Hitler régime to strip Mann of his German citizenship. Arising, perhaps, from the Thomas Mann issue Machado begins the second section of the article with a comment by Mairena on the general question of the rights of the individual. On the issue of the precedence of the individual over 'el complejo social o agregado de hombres' (IV, 2433) Mairena adds his typical 'sin embargo' and recognizes that there is food for much discussion here. However, on the question of the extent of the individual's ultimate rights *vis-à-vis* another individual, Mairena is adamant about the limitations of such rights: 'Pero lo verdaderamente inaceptable es que el hombre mate a su prójimo, es decir, que "disponga de su muerte". Esto es lo verdaderamente criminal y lo absurdo' (IV, 2433). The repetition of the adverb in these sentences suggests Machado's belief in a fundamental truth, which the Spanish Civil War cannot shake.

Machado approaches the issue mainly from the point of view of the article that he had either just completed or was writing for the January 1938 issue of *Hora de España*: Heidegger's 'interpretación existencial de la muerte — la muerte como un límite, nada en sí mismo —, de donde hemos de sacar ánimo para afrontarla' (IV, 2364). In the 'Notas del tiempo' article, Machado (through Mairena) argues for this right to confront death in a reasoned, philosophical way: those who have provoked and prepared war violate this right, because they have introduced 'la muerte entre ciegas máquinas, para permitirse el lujo de abreviar la muerte de los mejores'. The image of the blind machines acts as a contrast to the reasoned and enlightened preparation for death on the part of the philosopher. A good proportion of the Republic's poster art of the Civil War shows the human figure, strong and sinewy, defying the machines of war. Here Machado shifts the emphasis from the essentially physical impact of such posters (although this is not to deny their deep psychological resonances) and places it on the intelligent apprehension of and preparation for death, denied to the individual by the weapons of mass destruction. It is a shift, typical of Machado, towards reflection and enhanced conciousness, while at the same time maintaining an acute awareness of the brutal realities of war. Violent death, and war, above all, Machado suggests, threatens or denies Heidegger's *Freiheit zum Tode*, which Machado translates as 'libertad para la muerte' (and quotes in his *Hora de España* article of December 1937). In the 'Notas del tiempo' piece, the adaptation of Heidegger as a means of looking afresh at the commandment 'Thou shalt not kill' recalls Machado's use of Heidegger earlier in the war, in the pieces 'Los milicianos de 1936', and 'Notas de actualidad', the latter first published in February 1937. Here, at the end of 1937, we can detect a significant shift in mood. In the earlier pieces, which are understandably more optimistic, Machado, while not exalting the war, had already commented on 'el signo de resignación y triunfo de aquella *libertad para la muerte*' on the faces of the Republic's militiamen.[16] The war had brought about a Heideggerian meditation on death, because of the more immediate presence of death 'en los umbrales de la conciencia humana'. Now, at the year's end, Machado sees only the stupidity and waste of war. The exaltation of war as a way of life, Mairena comments, will lead to a new species of human

---

16 Since the piece 'Notas de actualidad' is not in Macrì, this quotation and the one that follows are taken from Puértolas and Pérez Herrero, *ed. cit.*, 88-89.

being: 'un "Homo stupidus", que va a adueñarse de los destinos del hombre' (IV, 2434). This is the strongest statement against war that Machado makes throughout the Civil War: war simply threatens the species *Homo sapiens* with extinction, just as the militaristic Hitler régime threatens to wipe out artists and intellectuals such as Thomas Mann. Machado, however, reserves his toughest words for those who have provoked and prepared for war: those who have been its instigators cannot receive any pardon for their actions. The implication therefore is that the Republic, having been drawn into a war that was not of its making, although it has killed its fellow human beings, has the hope of peace and pardon in the future, because the Republic has not wanted or started the war. For the warlike mentality of the nationalist generals there can be no peace or pardon, because they have provoked and prepared for the war, 'el crimen deshumanizado' (IV, 2434). They are part of a dehumanized machine that cuts down the life of 'los mejores' before their time to die. This clarification, appearing in the last sentence of the section — that there is no pardon for the instigators of war — is a vital insight into Machado's organization of his thought in the matter. On an ethical scale, killing a fellow human is 'verdaderamente criminal', but Mairena reserves his absolute condemnation for war itself and by extension for its promoters, as a stupid and brutalizing crime against humanity.

Another element introduced in the 'Notas del tiempo' piece serves to act as a commentary on an aspect of the expression of Machado's thought in 'Los futuros maestros de la paz ...' of the previous October. This type of retrospective review may have been a compensatory mechanism whereby Machado could refine or explain ideas that he had already consigned to print, perhaps meeting a pressing deadline that the war made even more imperative. We remember that in the October piece Mairena had assured his students that by being on the side of 'los mejores' — that is, those who had not sought or provoked war — 'sabréis morir con una elegancia de que nunca serán capaces los hombres de vocación batallona' (IV, 2349). The October piece ends with this reassurance, a rather slender thread of consolation, one would have thought, for those readers of Machado who faced the prospect of death in battle during the war: that they would at least die in an elegant manner. Not, perhaps, the most felicitous expression that Machado might have chosen, the phrase 'con ... elegancia' was evidently meant to contrast with the mechanized and individually insignificant death of the ordinary soldier that is brought about as a result of military strategy, and hence may have been deemed more suitable than a phrase such as 'con dignidad'. In 'Notas del tiempo' Machado elaborates on the meaning of this phrase when he argues, through Mairena, that since we must all die, 'Muera cada cual de "sa belle mort", que dicen los franceses, con tiempo para meditar sobre ella y para resignarse a lo irremediable; véala venir como cosa de Dios, o como engendrada en las mismas entrañas de la vida' (IV, 2434). To live in this state of vigilant preparedness is an assurance of dying elegantly ('sa belle mort') and such a person will concede the possibility of the same to others, by never being the first to set in motion the blind machines of war.

When Machado wrote his section '(*Sobre la guerra*)' in the November issue of *Hora de España*, he did not return in a direct way to the subject of war and peace in the journal until his contribution of March 1938: that month's article is entitled 'Alemania o la exageración'. However, within the context of our study of the issues of war and peace in *Hora de España*, it is worth examining one of the sections (6) of Machado's contribution to the February 1938 issue of *Hora de España*, together with other related texts, as a demonstration of the way that he used his reading of literature to meditate on the nature of true heroism in times of conflict. The piece is a commentary on the episode of the lions in Part II, chapter XVII of *Don Quixote*, 'el capítulo más original del *Quijote*' (IV, 2371), according to Mairena. The scene recalled is the one where the knight, having faced the lions but without engaging them in battle, makes his claim, quoted by Mairena, that the enchanters may rob him of success but not of his strength of spirit. One of Machado's *coplas*, 'Sobre la maleza', published in 1938 (see Macrì: I, 265) is closely connected with the February 1938 piece, and is also relevant to the way that Machado could use a literary text for a political purpose:

> Sobre la maleza,
> las brujas de Macbeth
> danzan en corro y gritan:
> ¡tú serás rey!
> (thou shalt be king, all hail!)
> Y en el ancho llano:
> 'Me quitarán la ventura
> — dice el viejo hidalgo —,
> me quitarán la ventura,
> no el corazón esforzado.'
> Con el sol que luce
> más allá del tiempo
> (¿quién ve la corona
> de Macbeth sangriento?)
> los encantadores
> del buen caballero
> bruñen los mohosos
> harapos de hierro. (II, 831)

The 'maleza' is the 'blasted heath' of *Macbeth*, and the second stanza refers to the episode of the lions in *Don Quixote*. The whole of section 6 of the article in *Hora de España* is effectively a prose commentary on this particular poem, and while it is sometimes unwise to speculate about the chronology of later Machado writings on the basis of their close relationship of ideas, section 6 and the *copla* are so kindred in thought that we would be justified on those grounds in assigning a date early in 1938 to 'Sobre la maleza'.

In the last stanza of the poem Machado takes the perspective on the two heroes 'más allá del tiempo' and suggests that where lasting virtue is concerned Don Quixote has the advantage over Macbeth, inasmuch as their deeds were so differently motivated, Macbeth's for power, Quixote's in order to prove his greatness of soul. Hence, without any effective arms, he defeats the enchanters (or at least wins them over to his side: they are busy polishing his rusty armour at the end of the poem) whereas Macbeth begins and ends being defeated by them. In his brief reference to the poem, whose meaning he calls 'oscura', Sánchez Barbudo remarks that 'Al parecer alude a la guerra y la situación política ... ¿Quiénes son esos "encantadores" que impiden vencer a don Quijote? ¿Las democracias extranjeras?'.[17] Rodríguez Puértolas and Pérez Herrero state more forthrightly that 'La cita del *Macbeth* de Shakespeare alude, sin duda, a la traición y ambiciones de los sublevados de 1936'.[18] This latter interpretation seems well judged, especially if we see the reference to the *maleza* as an analogy or portent of what the insurgents (like Macbeth in Scotland) are doing, or will do to Spain: turn it into a 'blasted heath'. (From the various references to it in Machado's later works, it is certain that he knew the play well.) We can take the political comparison a step further and suggest that Machado is using the *Macbeth* analogy to express his conviction that the short-term future for Franco, given the promise of pomp and power by the rhetoric of the Axis dictators, can only be bloody destruction, and in the long term is doomed to oblivion, while the Spanish people will survive their present devastation and emerge as victors. Machado had made the link between Don Quixote and the Spanish people in his February 1938 article, when he wrote: 'Es muy posible que un pueblo que tenga algo de Don Quijote no sea siempre lo que se llama un pueblo próspero. Que sea un pueblo inferior: he aquí lo que yo no concederé nunca' (IV, 2371). Section 6 of the February piece may also have been aimed (in a very indirect way) at Chamberlain's policy of appeasement, if, or as Machado suggests, when, he has to face up to the might of a fully militarized Germany: 'Porque algún día habrá que retar a los leones, con armas totalmente inadecuadas para luchar con ellos. Y hará falta un loco que intente la aventura'; or in other words: Spain will be an ally that can offer the kind of sublime Quixotic inspiration, a quality lacking in what Mairena had called earlier in the section '[el] pragmatista, [el] hombre que hace del éxito, de la ventura, la vara con que se mide la virtud y la verdad'.

By the time he came to write his last piece for *Hora de España*, composed perhaps around Christmas of 1938 when he knew that Barcelona must fall, Machado understandably saw only the desperate courage of Macbeth's final battle with Macduff, as the former learns that he is fighting against hopeless odds. Macbeth, therefore, in Machado's eyes, has

---

17   *Los poemas*, 456.
18   *Ed. cit.*, 386.

taken on something of the quality of Don Quixote, and Mairena invites his students to meditate on the last words of Macbeth, '[el] gigantesco Macbeth, cuando se decide a afrontar su lucha con un adversario invencible' (IV, 2413). The lesson for Machado here is learnt not only from a benevolent soul such as Don Blas Zambrano (to whom he had devoted a long portion of this last article) but also from a more hard-boiled adventurer such as Macbeth, with his capacity to draw on reserves of pride and courage in the final trial. If identifying with such a dubious hero as Macbeth may seem ethically ambiguous, Macbeth's last sentence — 'Lay on Macduff / And damn'd be him that first cries, "Hold, enough!" ' — appears to have held out the hope, in Machado's view, of some kind of salvation, at least in Macbeth's own mind: each of Shakespeare's characters, including Macbeth to whom he had just referred, 'ha de bastarse a sí mismo', Machado wrote in his February article in *Hora de España* (IV, 2372).

We will also encounter references to *Macbeth* in Machado's *La Vanguardia* articles. From the evidence of what we have just outlined, Machado's view of Macbeth is a response to the dual character of the play's protagonist: initially, his naive yet none the less bloody pursuit of power (in Machado's *copla*), an idea that may be linked to the actions of the nationalist generals by Machado's comments on 'la trágica frivolidad' of the insurgents in 'Meditación del día' (IV, 2178). Then in the final article of *Hora de España* Macbeth becomes an example for the Republic in the way that he faces the end and redeems something of the past. For the supporters of the Republic the implication may be that since their hands are not culpably bloodstained like Macbeth's, they have every hope to be redeemed and to redeem others, present and future, through their exemplary courage; or, as Machado expressed it in the last sentence of his last *La Vanguardia* article: 'habrán salvado, con el honor de la Europa occidental, la razón de nuestra continuidad en la Historia'.[19]

We saw in the pre-Civil-War *Mairena* series how the teacher encouraged his students to consider critically all writings, no matter how hallowed by tradition. Shakespeare, referred to on

---

[19] This article is not in Macrì; our quotation is from *La Vanguardia*, 6 January 1939, 3.

occasions in the same sentence as Cervantes and Tolstoy, is generally assigned the status of universal genius by Machado. As we have seen, however, in Machado's characterization of Macbeth, the emphasis on self is given a good deal of prominence. In the February 1938 article Machado also suggests a correspondence between Shakespeare and his characters, based on the ingenious though debatable theory that if Hamlet and Macbeth, since they are both opposites, agree on something then it must be Shakespeare's view too, the view in this particular instance being that 'El pensamiento marchita y deslustra la acción' (IV, 2371). There is so much emphasis on the alert consciousness in Machado's prose writings that the reference to the primacy accorded to action in two of Shakespeare's major works must have a negative resonance. Likewise at the end of the paragraph when Mairena says that 'En verdad, los personajes del gran Will dialogan consigo mismos', the implication in spite of the affectionate reference is again negative. Indeed, the negative resonance becomes more evident in the following paragraph when Cervantes' use of dialogue between Don Quixote and Sancho is praised for its inexhaustible depth of meaning for human existence.

Reading these two paragraphs of 1938, especially through the focus suggested by the Spanish Civil War, it is impossible not to discern in this seemingly mild piece of literary criticism an implied rebuke for Britain's self-centredness, on two counts. First, that pragmatic considerations of successful action take precedence over thought-out principles of conduct. Second, that Britain's concern with herself prevents her from reaching out to other nations in a true spirit of dialogue. In his political articles for *La Vanguardia* Machado was to denounce in a forthright way what he saw as the isolationist attitude of the British government towards Spain and Europe; here in *Hora de España* such questions, being confined to what would be conventionally thought of as literary criticism or, at most, to meditations on the national spirit, are almost always deflected away from direct political comment.

In the first section of 'Alemania o la exageración' (*Hora de España*, March 1938) Machado uses the same basic idea as in '(*Sobre la Alemania guerrera*)' in *Hora de España* of June 1937: that the Germans are utterly serious in their commitment to war, preparing a perfect war machine with all the conscientiousness that the logic of their 'ímpetu peleón' demands, accompanied by all the battery of their culture. Although this first section is ostensibly about pre-1914 Germany and Europe, the Spanish Civil War is never far from the surface. The war had been in progress for nearly two years (*Hora de España* was running two or three months late by now); hence the question of Mairena to his students in section I: '¿qué pensáis vosotros de la guerra, cuando nadie puede ganarla?' (IV, 2373). The last sentence of the section is an interesting example of how the *Mairena* format can deepen the reader's appreciation of current events. In this sentence Mairena is predicting Europe's loss of world leadership in the wake of the 1914 war: 'El resultado será que Alemania no ganará la guerra; pero Europa perderá la paz y, con ella, su hegemonía en el mundo' (IV, 2374). Machado can use what he called 'el arte de profetizar el pasado' (IV, 2005) as a *nota de actualidad* to underline the consequences of another European conflict. Mairena's predictions here could equally have been read as a prediction made in 1938, and is as much directed by Machado against contemporary Britain and France as is Mairena's criticism of the 1914-18 allies. The subject of Europe's loss of influence and leadership is one to which Machado increasingly turned in his *La Vanguardia* articles, which he was beginning to publish at this time (the first is dated 27 March 1938). The European dimension of the Spanish conflict is, broadly speaking, Machado's theme in these final months, and is mainly reserved for the newspaper pieces. After the April issue of *Hora de España* there is a transfer of interest in the issues of war and peace from the intellectual journal to the Barcelona newspaper, certainly as far as their European resonances are concerned.

Machado's contribution to the April 1938 issue of *Hora de España* contains sixteen brief sections, eight of them notes on peace and war. Three of the sections (IV, IX and X: they are numbered in Roman) are developed at greater length (and with greater clarity) in Machado's *La Vanguardia* article of 3 May 1938. This latter article is an interesting facet of the way Machado adjusted his prose style to suit his reading public. Although Machado remarks in an early *La Vanguardia* article that he is 'el primer convencido de mi insignificancia como escritor político' (IV, 2452), it cannot be a coincidence that for the last year of the war (or for the last nine or ten months of it that he remained in Spain) Machado turned increasingly away from the compressed gnomic form to a more explanatory and discursive form of writing. Exaggeratedly so in some instances: the article in *La Vanguardia* from which our last quotation was taken contains one paragraph of well over a thousand words.[20] In the April 1938 issue of *Hora de España*, section III gives us a good idea of the difficulties that can arise with the use of an over-compressed aphorism, expressed in the form of a paradox: 'Si la vida es la guerra, ¿por qué tanto mimo en la paz?' (IV, 2379). The first half of the aphorism compresses Machado's criticism of the competitive, aggressive instincts of Western culture, with its militaristic overtones, which he sees as a product of a philosophical and political culture that flourished in nineteenth-century Europe, and continues into the twentieth (hence Mairena's use of the present tense). The phrase 'mimo en la paz', as well as being a criticism of Western acquisitiveness, also suggests a note of anti-pacifism and anti-defeatism. Only Machado's regular readership in *Hora de España* could have been expected to focus on implications such as these, which had emerged in one form or another throughout his previous fifteen contributions to the journal.

Another way in which Machado is able to use the *Mairena* format (here, the teacher's 'Notas y recuerdos') to reflect on and summarize a major aspect of the Spanish Civil War, may be seen in the brief section IV of this April 1938 issue of *Hora de España*. In the piece, Machado's misgivings about the *masificación* of human beings, which he particularly associated with war, are expressed with a brevity that shows how these individuals are devalued and dehumanized by war: 'No parece que a la vida de esos miles de hombres que llenan los cuarteles — decía Juan de Mairena — y que mañana serán lanzados a la muerte, se le conceda mucha importancia. Sin embargo, cada

---

20 Machado's recent editors have not followed the original structure of the paragraphs of this article of 2 June 1938 which contained just two paragraphs, the second consisting merely of the last two sentences. Rodríguez Puértolas/Pérez Herrero, and Macrì, create three new (i.e. different) paragraphs, while Fernández Ferrer, *ed. cit.*, II, 189-92, reproduces the article as one single paragraph.

uno de ellos tiene un padre y una madre para él solo' (IV, 2379). In the image used, these individual human beings are literally cannon fodder: 'lanzados a la muerte' like shells. Mairena's humanism, expressed in his concern for the value of each soldier as an individual, was being mirrored in aspects of the life of the Republic at war which, as we have seen, under its energetic young Education Minister, Jesús Hernández, had begun in early 1937 an extensive programme of education, under the title *Milicias de la cultura*, aimed primarily at soldiers who were illiterate or semi-literate. The journal *Armas y Letras* set the idea in its political framework, as follows: 'La República será tanto más gloriosa cuanto prefiera asentarse sobre la voluntad libre de unos ciudadanos conscientes a imponerse por la fuerza a unas masas aborregadas y abúlicas'.[21] Machado preferred a less political and more universal connotation for the value of the individual human person: it is simply enough that each one should have had a mother and a father. It is interesting, too, to note that Machado avoids the more romantic image of the soldier separated from girl-friend or wife (an image, for example, to which Miguel Hernández was understandably drawn) in favour of the more universal picture of the soldier as a son. In this way, no soldier is excluded from Machado's condemnation of the waste of war; as he analogously expressed it in the first article in *Hora de España*: everybody belongs to the proletariat because we are all 'la prole de Adán' (IV, 2313). Machado, who was sixty-four towards the end of the war, was able to voice the concern of an earlier generation, without turning his back on this universal aspect of war as a disruption of the family of humankind itself.[22]

---

[21] Quoted in *València, capital cultural de la República (1936-1937)*, 81-82.

[22] The nearest Hernández came to expressing the universal loss and disruption caused by war is in his ballad 'Llamo a la juventud' (*Viento del pueblo* [Valencia, Ediciones Socorro Rojo, 1937]):

> Pero en los negros rincones,
> en los más negros, se tienden
> a llorar por los caídos
> madres que les dieron leche,
> hermanas que los lavaron,
> novias que han sido de nieve ...
> desconcertadas vïudas

Given that the Spanish Civil War was a war that the Republic did not want, it is nevertheless no surprise that Machado spent little time bemoaning the fact of the war and preferred instead to show how war can concentrate the mind on important issues. We have seen how in his first published piece after the outbreak of the Civil War, 'Los milicianos de 1936', Machado sees in the faces of the Republic's militiamen the concentrated look of men who have been made more intensely aware of life through the proximity of death, brought about by the war. In sections IX and X of the April 1938 article the emphasis shifts from the war itself to the peace that had preceded it, peace seen here as 'algo más terrible todavía' (IV, 2380). The two sections comprise only five sentences between them, and the compression makes it difficult to imagine the response of any contemporary reader of *Hora de España* to their contents, unless they had read Machado's article of 3 May 1938 in *La Vanguardia* (which would have been published before the April issue of *Hora de España*). What would his readers have made of the phrase in section 10: 'esta tregua de la paz que llamamos *la guerra*'? The paradox seems over-compressed.

We will deal later with the newspaper article and with Machado's idea that a certain kind of war is preferable to a certain kind of peace. The article of 3 May was the first to have the title 'Desde el mirador de la guerra' and in the *Hora de España* piece Machado uses the perspective of war as a vantage point from which to view the peace that had preceded it: 'Lo más terrible de la guerra es que, desde ella, se ve la paz, la paz que se ha perdido, como algo más terrible todavía. Cuando el guerrero lleva este pensamiento entre ceja y ceja, su semblante adquiere una cierta expresión de santidad' (IV, 2380). If we compare these sentences with the picture of the militiamen of

---

        desparramadas mujeres,
        cartas y fotografías
        donde los expresan fielmente,
        donde los ojos se rompen
        de tanto ver y no verles.

The absence of the father of any of these soldiers in the dramatic scene depicted by Hernández is an interesting contrast with Machado's much more sober version of war and its consequences. (Hernández was to write memorable poetry after the war's end, from the perspective of a father separated from his children through absence and death.)

August 1936 going to the front or waiting to be called to it, we can see that the look of the philosopher has changed to become the look of a saint: from August 1936 to April 1938 the stakes have been raised from an intellectual understanding of the impact of the war to a quasi-mystical belief in its necessity and, indeed, validity. Machado, having lived through the intervening twenty-one months of war, has necessarily come much closer to it, from what he was later to call 'distancia' to 'vivencia' (IV, 2394); from intellectual awareness as exemplified in the dignity and thoughtfulness of the *miliciano* of 1936 to the idea of what he described in his sonnet to Líster as a 'lucha santa sobre la tierra ibera', and what he calls the 'contenido espiritual' (IV, 2382) of the war, at the end of this April article in *Hora de España*. Antonio Sánchez Barbudo's negative interpretation of the two sentences from *Hora de España* cannot be justified, when he comments: 'Escribe [Machado] entonces, en días de desaliento, cuando ya se adivina cuál sería el triste final de la guerra, después de tanto sacrificio: "Lo más terrible ..." ' etc.[23] There is no dejection about the course of the Civil War in Machado's lines; rather the opposite: his view that an unprovoked war in defence of basic human rights may be ethically superior to a peace that denies them. What is interesting from the point of view of the essentially cultural and artistic role that *Hora de España* played in the Civil War is that Machado leaves the political implications of his remarks (in particular his references to the mass unemployment and inadequate social welfare of his time) to be spelt out in his *La Vanguardia* article. We should add, too, as a relevant comment on the kind of compression that characterizes some of Machado's writing in *Hora de España*, that if Sánchez Barbudo, who was Secretary to the journal during most of 1937 (before being called to active military service), can misinterpret one of the little sections in this way, then such compression may well have left less gifted or privileged readers with even greater interpretative difficulties.

The final sections (XIII-XVI) of the April piece for *Hora de España* continue and reinforce the strong anti-pacifist note that runs throughout those parts of the complete article that deal with war and peace. The references to the positive value of

---

[23] *Art. cit.*, 280.

desperate courage for a future Spain, to Numancia, the use of the *refrán* 'de cobardes no se ha escrito nada' (IV, 2382), the presentation of the stark choice 'o cruzarnos de brazos ante la iniquidad, o guerrear por la justicia' (IV, 2382); all these combine to overwhelm Mairena's remark to his pupils in the final section that he has spoken out and will continue to speak out against war. Machado had already summed up the dilemma of the intellectual in the *forma refranera* of section VI of this article: 'Es más difícil estar a la altura de las circunstancias que *au dessus de la mêlée*' (IV, 2379). As Antonio Fernández Ferrer suggests in a note, the use of the French phrase is perhaps a reply to Romain Rolland's book with that title, published in connection with the hostilities of 1914.[24] (It could not, in that context, of course, with any verisimilitude have formed part of Mairena's 'Notas y recuerdos'.) The French phrase may be more immediately aimed at French involvement in the Non-Intervention Committee, the deliberations of which were probably the principal reasons for the Republic's eventual collapse and defeat. The use of Spanish and French together suggests the distance between the two concepts, not just linguistically but also from the national and international political perspective. Yet if the French phrase is self-explanatory, the Spanish is much less so, because 'rising to the occasion' implies a level of involvement that is not easily encapsulated within the form of a proverb or axiom. An interesting indication of the tensions that could arise within the Republic's intellectual and artistic elite may be gleaned from a quotation in *Hora de España*, attributed to a professor of molecular physics, who describes how some researchers remained behind in Madrid after the evacuation of November 1936 and were able to continue there with their research 'manteniendo incólume su espíritu au dessus de la melée [*sic*]'.[25] Machado could not have sympathized with the form of expression used here, however well intentioned the professor's motives might have been. Two issues later in *Hora de España* Machado had Mairena confess 'mi poca simpatía' for those who 'en tiempos de combate se dicen siempre *au dessus de la mêlée*' (IV, 2334).

---

24 *Ed. cit.*, II, 42.
25 *Hora de España*, IV (1937), 58.

In an interview, given in October of 1938, reflecting perhaps on these *La Vanguardia* articles, Machado made his often-quoted comment: 'De ser un espectador de la política he pasado bruscamente a ser un actor apasionado' (IV, 2280). In the August 1938 issue of *Hora de España* he devotes the third section of that month's contribution to the role of the intellectual in the war, constructing the piece around this *espectador/actor* dichotomy. The brief section, which is about three hundred words in length, is worthy of a prominent place in any anthology on the subject. It is one of the very few pieces in *Hora de España* when Machado drops the perspectivist mask afforded by the *Mairena* framework. (He had used the mask in section 2 and picks it up again in the three that follow section 3.) The result of this direct intervention, *voce propria*, coming in the midst of the *Mairena* format, is highly effective, with its startling opening sentence, urgent and direct, which is without parallel in the *Mairena* writings: 'Tiempo es ya, tiempo es acaso todavía, de que los españoles intentemos los más hondos análisis de conciencia' (IV, 2393). The piece is centred on an implied revaluation of one of Machado's favourite aphorisms: 'toda visión requiere distancia'. It is no small part of Machado's integrity as an artist and intellectual that on this occasion he was prepared to submit one of his dearly-held views, expressed in the aphorism, to scrutiny and revision (or literally 're-vision'), and hence to an implicit questioning of the aphorism as a philosophical answer to taking sides in the Civil War. Here, the use of a non-*Mairena* format for such a re-examination means that Machado in this instance is replacing the concept of 'distancia' (the Mairena mask) with the idea of 'vivencia ... que toda honda visión implica' (IV, 2394). The form of this piece (direct intervention by Machado) is therefore an integral part of the idea of *vivencia* for which the piece argues. The last sentence of the piece, too, is as much about Machado's own re-adjustment from spectator (*Hora de España*) to actor (*La Vanguardia*) as about any criticism of other artists and intellectuals at home and abroad who wished to remain *au dessus de la mêlée*: 'Si [la guerra] nos coge totalmente desprevenidos de categorías para pensarla, esto quiere decir mucho en contra de nuestras meditaciones, y en pro de nuestro deber de revisarlas y de arrojar no pocas al cesto de los papeles inservibles' (IV, 2394).

A central point in Ortega y Gasset's essay 'En cuanto al pacifismo' of 1937 is that the momentous political and military events of the previous three or four years in Europe have taken British opinion by surprise. One of Ortega's remedies, typical of his interest in identifying major social constituencies of influence, is to suggest 'una profunda reforma de la fauna periodística',[26] by requiring journalists to study history as well as contemporary events. Although there are several references to the Spanish Civil War in Ortega's essay, the tone is one of detachment, the general character of which is captured in one of his concluding sentences: 'El "totalitarismo" salvará al "liberalismo", destiñendo sobre él, depurándolo, y gracias a ello veremos pronto a un nuevo liberalismo templar los regímenes autoritarios'. Ortega's article was first published in January of 1937[27] and it is possible that Machado might have read it by the time he sat down to write for the August 1938 issue of *Hora de España*. Machado's abrupt call for a deep analysis of the motivation behind the current strife, including his own motivation, is in any event a stark contrast with Ortega's distant-seeming view of 'Europa ... desocializada' or lacking in 'principios de convivencia': his *España invertebrada* thesis brought up to date in a European context. It may also not be coincidental in this regard that although Machado did not entirely turn his back on using Mairena in a contemporary, that is, a pre-1909 time-frame, his remaining contributions to *Hora de España* result in some weakening of the original *Mairena* format, through the use of the 'Mairena póstumo' formula (which is also the title for each of his last three articles in *Hora de España*).

The rhetorical, contextual impact of this little piece should not be underestimated. Although the previous two sections were devoted to a brief commentary on an article by the Catalan intellectual Joaquín Xirau, published only a few months

---

26 *La rebelión de las masas. Epílogo para ingleses* (Madrid: Espasa-Calpe, 1976), 234. The quotations from 'En cuanto al pacifismo' that follow are from 239 and 227.

27 Vicente Romano García gives this date in his detailed 'Índice cronológico de la producción de Ortega', in *José Ortega y Gasset publicista* (Madrid: Akal Editor, 1976), 330.

earlier,[28] the use of the *Mairena* formula and the choice of subject ('Charity') distance these sections from the immediate concerns of the war. Machado's abrupt return to the war in the following section, is not a criticism of Xirau's subject matter, but rather a self-consciously critical meditation on the place and function of intellectual culture in times of war. What makes this piece stand out in the total context of the one hundred and seventy-one sections that comprise the *Mairena* articles in *Hora de España*, is the way that Machado uses the concept of *vivencia* to involve himself and all Spaniards, not just in the war effort ('un deber imperioso ... de morir al lado de los mejores', as he expresses it in the passage) but also to call to mind the reasons for their involvement in it in the first place. Although Machado avoids going into any detail on this latter issue, his invitation to search in the depths of one's own conscience is an essential part of the profundity of vision that he seeks. The concept of *distancia*, however, is not rejected entirely: Mairena continues speaking to his pupils in the next section, and Machado, in the one being discussed, talks of 'esta *exigencia* de distancia para la visión' [our italics], a word that like its English counterpart 'requirement' falls somewhere between the meanings of 'necessity' and 'demand', between the objective and subjective resonances that these two words respectively embody.

In the next section we are back again in Mairena's classroom. We get here a fascinating insight into Machado's 'técnica psicológica' (his own words in this piece) through the use of the *Mairena* format. Mairena's subject here is confession, but the brief meditation also ends with a telling reference to artists and intellectuals, albeit of the worst kind. Machado, in asking his compatriots in the previous section to accept their share of responsibility for the war, has gone as far as he could go in the circumstances. This following piece, on confession, is a gloss on the previous idea of accepting responsibility, but done here in an oblique, distancing way, using Mairena's advice, as he tells his pupils: 'el hombre se hace tanto más fuerte, tanto más se ennudece y tonifica, cuanto más es capaz de esgrimir el látigo contra sí mismo. Todo, amigos, antes que engolados abogadetes

---

[28] Xirau's article was published in *Madrid. Cuadernos de la Casa de la Cultura*, III (1938). (Machado's poem 'Ya va subiendo la luna' was published in the same volume.)

de vuestras personillas — dejad que se las coman las ratas — porque daréis en literatos de la peor laya, ateneístas en el impeorable sentido de la palabra' (IV, 2395). By switching the perspective from direct address to his fellow Spaniards, to the framing device of the teacher addressing his pupils, Machado is able to reinforce his previous point about the recognition and acceptance of our mistakes, and incidentally illustrates thereby the different validities of an approach to a subject that enshrines both the concepts of *vivencia* (section 3) and *distancia* (section 4).

In the following month's contribution to *Hora de España* Machado uses a similar structure to his August piece. He begins with a brief review of a contemporary piece of writing (Bataillon's *Erasme et l'Espagne*) followed by a meditation on an event of more immediate relevance to Spain and the war: the *Fiesta de la Raza* of 12 October 1938. This latter piece partially recalls (as does Machado himself during it) the paragraphs on the Cid, written in 'Los milicianos de 1936'. On a first reading the *Fiesta de la Raza* passage appears to be in Machado's voice, until the last three lines of text are reached. Not only does it begin as a contemporary piece, but it continues throughout its extended length in this voice (it is one of the longest sections of Machado's contributions to *Hora de España*). There then follows the final three-line paragraph which switches the narrative voice from Machado to Mairena: 'Así hablaría Juan de Mairena en nuestros días, sin más objeto que el de iniciar a sus alumnos en lo que él llamaba *retórica peleona* o arte de descalabrar al prójimo con palabras' (IV, 2401). Indeed with the technique of the abrupt opening reference to the war ('Es la tercera Fiesta de la Raza que celebramos en plena guerra') the reader who might have remembered Machado's comments on the Cid in 'Los milicianos de 1936' might feel somewhat disconcerted at the end of this one, because Machado refers to these comments here as 'razones expuestas hace más de dos años', that is, in August 1936, the date of 'Los milicianos de 1936'. The result is that Mairena is claiming authorship of that piece of writing: the only occasion, to my knowledge, where Machado confuses himself and his 'yo filosófico'.

What is more interesting, however, than a small *lapsus calami* by Machado is his return at this late stage in the war to an idea expressed at the beginning of it. A comparison between the two pieces reveals significant shifts in attitude. There is, no doubt, a distinct hardening of Machado's attitude towards 'nuestros adversarios' (IV, 2399) in the 1938 article. Indeed in the August 1936 piece, as we have seen, Machado refuses to be drawn into the kind of derogatory analogies that he was to make in the 1938 *Fiesta de la Raza* piece, because as he wrote in 1936, 'no me gusta denigrar al adversario' (IV, 2165). We must recall, of course, the difference in perspective between the pieces: the 1936 one is in the narrative voice of Machado, while, perhaps as a perspectivist afterthought (the *Mairena* formula usually comes at the beginning) the 1938 passage is given the *Mairena* tag at the end. There is also another perspectivist framework in the later piece, in which Machado draws the reader's attention to the act of writing (or, at the end, speaking) as a rhetorical art. The rhetoric, Machado/Mairena writes, comes from both sides, and hence should be subjected to critical scrutiny, albeit on this occasion it will be an 'examen ligero' of nationalist rhetoric. (The implied invitation to scrutinize Machado's/Mairena's rhetoric comes in the short, single-sentence last paragraph quoted earlier.)

In both the 1936 and the 1938 pieces Machado takes two features from the life and legend of the Cid: the *Jura de Santa Gadea*, and the characters of the *Infantes de Carrión*. The former episode results in the Cid being exiled for requiring King Alfonso to swear that he has not gained the throne by means of fratricide. In the 1936 article Machado is content to use this incident as an example of the Cid's 'hombría', with inklings, perhaps, in the episode, of 'una democracia naciente': the Cid faces the King 'de hombre a hombre'. However, in the later piece the same example is used to show the Cid as 'un campeón de la ética universal' and a 'modelo de lealtad a su patria, al pueblo burgalés, cuyo mandato supo cumplir a costa del destierro' (IV, 2400). The second reference is aimed at the nationalist insurgents who, in Machado's words of 1937, 'volvieron contra el pueblo todas las armas que el pueblo había puesto en sus manos para defender a la nación' (IV, 2186). The other reference is more obscure because of its generalized and compressed form. Perhaps it was deliberately left so by Machado, due to the delicate question that it raised. The phrase 'campeón de la ética universal' could refer to the Cid's readiness to denounce the crime of fratricide at great personal cost to himself; or it could mean, more simply, 'champion of the universal commandment: "Thou shalt not kill" '. In either case the phrase was a reminder, however compressed, to all Spaniards, of a fundamental ethical obligation, that the Civil War was violating.

The two pieces being considered are roughly the same length. In the later one, however, Machado devotes much more space to the unflattering analogies between the Francoists and the episode of the *Jura de Santa Gadea*. In the 1938 piece the Francoists are 'los perjuros por excelencia y los desleales por antonomasia' (IV, 2400) because, even worse than King Alfonso, they have tried to exile loyalty itself from the territory that they hold, that is, to 'la España leal' or the Spanish Republic. One notices, too, that the idea of loyalty in the 1936 article is a question of personal integrity. The Cid, Machado suggests there, is exiled for being loyal to a higher ethical responsibility than obedience to a King: the episode serves to prove the 'hombría' of the Cid; whereas in the 1938 version of the episode the Cid's civic example is also stressed. Here, he is 'un modelo de lealtad a su patria'. The kind of loyalty envisaged in the later piece has been coloured by the intervention of Germany and Italy on the nationalist side in the Civil War: loyalty to one's country now takes predecence over questions of personal integrity, although both still come second (and third) to 'en primer lugar ... la ética universal' (IV, 2400).

The other feature of the *Poema de Mío Cid* referred to both in the 1936 and 1938 articles is the representation of the characters of the Condes de Carrión. In 'Los milicianos de 1936' Machado refuses to be drawn into making any analogy between their criminal boorishness in the Robledo de Corpes and the 'ejércitos facciosos' of General Franco: 'no afirmaré tanto, porque no me gusta denigrar al adversario', he had commented. By 1938, however, Machado concludes that 'esos nietos de Campeador [the Francoists], se parecen demasiado a los yernos del mismo, nos evocan demasiado la fechoría del Robledo de Corpes, para que nos obliguen a pensar en las virtudes y en el valor de su ilustre abuelo' (IV, 2400). One can see how in the 1938 piece the progress of the war has caused Machado to expand his idea of loyalty and integrity, from that of personal *hombría* to *lealtad a la patria*. The progress of the war pushed Machado into political considerations that he was unwilling to contemplate at the beginning of it.[29] The lack of chivalry of the Condes in treating the women in the way that they did, and the analogy with the nationalist bombings of undefended civilian populations may also be hinted at here. If so, Machado left the analogy in this very muted form. He goes on to draw two other examples from the actions of the Spanish aristocracy of the past: that of the Conde de Benavente, who set fire to his palace because it had been occupied by a French nobleman who changed his allegiance from the King of France to the Emperor Charles V; and that of the Conde Don Julián, assigned the responsibility in legend for the Moorish invasion of Spain. Machado's theme in these two illustrations is again that of loyalty to one's principles, in the context of one's position in the body politic. The Conde de Benavente by his gesture places 'la lealtad a la patria por encima del interés y del éxito' (IV, 2400). The example of Don Julián illustrates a kind of fidelity, but it is a narrow one that could not transcend his sense of personal grievance over the loss of his daughter's honour: the result was betrayal and invasion. Machado may have been led to the latter example as a contrast with his earlier remarks on the Cid, who shows true statesmanship in the way that he deals with his own grievance against the Infantes de Carrión over their conduct towards his daughters. At the end of the section Machado describes what he sees as the ideal embodiment of 'las virtudes tradicionales de [la] raza', and the piece as a whole is an attempt to order the degrees of these virtues — essentially one: that of loyalty, in its personal and civic ramifications — as well as assessing in what way the virtue of loyalty is lacking in nationalist Spain. In the final analysis, for Machado the gesture of the Conde de Benavente, while an authentic gesture of *españolismo*, is based more on fine-sounding rhetoric and falls

---

29 In his radio broadcast for 'La voz de España' on 22 November 1938 Machado also drew a clear distinction between the domestic aspects of the war and the defence of Spain against invasion: 'En el trance trágico y decisivo que hoy vivimos, no puede haber dudas ni vacilaciones para un español. Ya no les es dado elegir bando ni bandera: ha de estar necesariamente con España y en contra de los invasores' (IV, 2292-93).

short of that of the ordinary Republican militiaman 'que no invoca ninguna de las virtudes tradicionales de su raza; se limita — sencillamente — a tenerlas' (IV, 2401).

In this last sustained reflection on contemporary issues related to the war that was to appear in *Hora de España* it seems appropriate that Machado's final example of true *Hispanidad* should be concerned with the Spanish language, which he calls 'la lengua de Cervantes'. In commenting on its defence by the ordinary people of Spain against the insurgent generals, Machado may have had two things in mind. It is worth noting that Machado twice uses the phrase 'la lengua de Cervantes', because he always sees Cervantes as the supreme promotor of dialogue, in the creation of Don Quixote and Sancho Panza, in whose make-up there are no essential divisions of social class: they represent, as he expressed it in February 1938, 'el diálogo entre dos mónadas autosuficientes y, no obstante, afanosas de complementariedad' (IV, 2372).[30] The implication is that if the nationalist generals win the war, this kind of dialogue will perish and with it, if not the language of Spain, then certainly the language of Cervantes, thus conceived. Another, more simple explanation of the reiterated phrase 'la lengua de Cervantes' is that if the Axis powers help the nationalists to win the war they will destroy Hispanic culture by the imposition of their own. As already noted, Machado finishes this paragraph by bringing all the aristocracies, more or less ancient, back to the present position of the ordinary Republican *miliciano*, who represents a truer aristocracy, defending the virtues of the race simply and unrhetorically by embodying them and by dying for them.

The fact that Machado was slow to address issues immediately connected with war and peace in *Hora de España* may be due to a combination of factors: the specific artistic and cultural ethos of the journal, with its objective of renewing as far as possible during the Civil War the task of the creation and

---

30 See also Carlos Barbachano and Agustín Sánchez Vidal, 'Tres pilares del diálogo en la prosa de Antonio Machado: Sócrates, Cristo y Cervantes', *Cuadernos Hispanoamericanos*, CCCIV-CCCVII (1975-1976), 614-24, who make the interesting but necessarily undeveloped comment in a note (624), that 'sería muy prolijo mostrar punto por punto la coincidencia de los mecanismos machadianos empleados en Juan de Mairena [*sic*] con sus homólogos cervantinos'.

criticism of artistic culture, which the war had disrupted. Machado's own inclination, too, expressed in his aphorism 'toda visión requiere distancia', meant that he was philosophically disposed to allow the events of the war to settle, until they had acquired what he called 'la pátina del tiempo' before he was prepared to comment on them in any depth or detail, even if then. Continuing with Mairena into a new series was one of Machado's ways of expressing the need for continuity as well as distance, in order to achieve clarity of vision (and thought). Whether he was able to achieve such clarity of vision in the midst of the tragic turbulence of the Civil War is a question that will exercise the minds of scholars for a long time to come. Antonio Sánchez Barbudo sees Machado's use of distancing modes of expression as a sign of uncertainty rather than clarity: '[Machado] expone lo que muchas veces es en verdad apasionado pensamiento, con cierta frialdad, con ironía, como si contemplara esas afirmaciones a distancia, inseguro de sí, dudando de sus propias ideas y emociones'.[31] One can see such a dilemma summed up in Machado's writings on war and peace in *Hora de España*: the imperative need to face the immediate reality of the war, coupled with the equally imperative if inevitably future need in those present circumstances of espousing the victory of peaceful politics. The use of the *Mairena* time-scale gave Machado some opportunity to express this dilemma of present and future needs, as well as enabling him to develop a temporal perspective that sought the causes for contemporary Western belligerence largely in the cultural conditions of Mairena's lifetime. There is no doubt, however, that in *Hora de España* Machado directly confronted the general issue of war and, although to a much lesser extent, the particular issue of the Spanish Civil War. His approach is two-pronged. In the pieces on militarism, especially German militarism, there is a straightforward condemnation of the war machine, of militarism as a way of life, of the stupidity and waste of war, and, by implication, of the insurgent Spanish generals. On the other hand, faced with the reality of the Civil War, Machado drew from it whatever positive meaning he could, from the philosophical reflections of the early days of the war (seeing the faces of the militiamen) to the 'lucha santa sobre

---

31 *Art. cit.*, 282.

la tierra ibera' of his sonnet to Líster.

If we are surprised by the relative lack of references to the Civil War in *Hora de España*, we should remember, too, that even in the *La Vanguardia* articles the Civil War itself was not the essential subject of Machado's pen. The principal title which he gave them, 'Desde el mirador de la guerra', makes it clear that the war is not to be the subject of the articles, but rather a vantage point from which to view distant, if contemporary, events in Europe. The Civil War, of course, inevitably makes an impact in the *Hora de España* series, in the various ways that we hope to have shown in this chapter. What interests Machado most in these writings, in the context of the Spanish conflict, are the origins of the belligerent climate of contemporary Western civilization, and what role the pursuit of peace can play in such a climate. If, as Ricardo Gullón suggests, Machado's 'espacio mental pertenece al ayer', it also belongs, as that critic goes on to say, to 'un ayer abierto, liberal, progresista'.[32] Machado's conclusions, if understandably bleak in the short run, are mixed with hope for a more distant future, when the teachings of Mairena, and especially of his 'futuros maestros de la paz', having achieved some contemporaneous exposure in the guise of Machado's *consejos* to his readers in *Hora de España*, may become contemporary realities for the generations that follow.

---

32 *Op. cit.*, 102.

CHAPTER 5

'Más fuerte que la guerra'
Machado's Civil-War Sonnets (1938)

Machado's nine Civil-War sonnets first published together in the June 1938 edition (number XIX) of *Hora de España*, have attracted little detailed attention from critics, and most of the comment is lukewarm or negative. Johannes Lechner's general remark about Machado's Civil-War poetry sums up the reception that the sonnets themselves have received: 'Como versos de guerra, estos poemas de Machado, significativos acaso en su propia trayectoria, no son de los más interesantes'.[1] Concha Zardoya's comments on the poems of the period are in a similar vein: 'La mayoría de estos poemas son circunstanciales'.[2] José María Valverde virtually dismisses the poems of the period, with the comment that 'por lo que toca a su calidad añade poco al conjunto anterior'.[3] He does remark of the sonnets that in these poems there is 'un peculiar desajuste ... entre formas estilísticas y sentido total; desajuste en que las formas visiblemente insuficientes, llegan a ser supremamente expresivas por ello mismo'. Valverde, however, does not attempt to solve this paradox by giving any examples of what he means. Carl W. Cobb in his Twayne volume on Machado does not devote any space whatsoever to his Civil-War writings.[4] In his article on Machado's sonnets Gerardo Diego completely ignores those composed during the Civil War.[5]

---

    1   *El compromiso en la poesía española del siglo XX*, 2 vols (Leiden: Univ. Pers Leiden, 1968), I, 159.
    2   'Los autorretratos de Antonio Machado', in *Estudios*, ed. José Ángeles, *op. cit.*, 309-53.
    3   *Antonio Machado* (Madrid: Siglo Veintiuno de España Editores, 1975), 299-300.
    4   *Antonio Machado* (New York: Twayne Publishers, 1971).
    5   'Antonio Machado y el soneto', in *La Torre*, XLV-XLVI (1964), 443-54.

Bernard Sesé and Antonio Sánchez Barbudo, while finding some good things to say about individual verses of the sonnets, criticize respectively 'el tono de énfasis declamatorio'[6] and 'el tono clamante decimonónico'[7] of the last three sonnets. Fernando Lázaro Carreter's judgment is the most damning, all the more so because it was delivered on the occasion of an *homenaje* for the poet's centenary. This critic sees Machado's poetry of the Civil-War period as mere tired pastiches of an earlier, more vigorously creative era: 'Antonio Machado — ¿cómo no iba a ocurrir? — está en estos pocos versos últimos, pero sin progreso, antes bien, recurriendo a la memoria para ser, para seguir siendo poeta'. Lázaro Carreter's conclusion is that 'el último Machado' was left with 'un ímpetu político y bélico al que ya no puede corresponder del modo que, como artista, sabe que debería hacerlo'.[8]

These, in summary, are the main criticisms levelled at the sonnets: that they depend on and hence add little to Machado's earlier poetry, and that some of them suffer from overblown rhetoric. This chapter, while accepting the strong presence of the past in the sonnets, will conclude that in them Machado does indeed engage with the needs of the day. With regard to the second criticism, Machado himself was conscious of the problems for him of writing verse during such an intensely conflictive period. He also published the first four sonnets in the *Boletín* of the Republican Government's *Servicio Español de Información*, and in a note to the editor, Juan José Domenchina, he commented: 'Le envío esos cuatro sonetos de circunstancias, que quisieran estar a la altura de las circunstancias. Creo que dentro del molde barroco del soneto, contienen alguna emoción que no suelen tener los sonetos. De todos modos, en estos momentos de angustia en que la verdad se come al arte, no es fácil hacer otra cosa' (IV, 2174). One can see from this brief description that Machado wanted his poems to rise to the occasion that the Civil War presented. Yet the rather guarded reference to 'alguna emoción' suggests that he wished to avoid the emotional rhetoric that the war demanded.

---

6   *Op. cit.*, 848.
7   *Los poemas*, 464.
8   'El último Machado', in *Curso en homenaje a Antonio Machado*, ed. Eugenio de Bustos (Salamanca: Univ. de Salamanca, 1975), 119-34.

In this context, too, his reference to the overtly formal characteristics ('el molde barroco') of the sonnet points towards one way of understanding why Machado may have chosen such an unlikely poetic form at this time. Machado's concern with the relationship between the writing of verse and the war, what he called the effort to 'acercar la poesía a la guerra, que es lo vital de nuestros días' (IV, 2301), is most evident in an article that he published about the same time as these sonnets: 'El influjo de la guerra sobre la poesía joven española. El influjo de la poesía joven en los campos de batalla'. In it Machado returns to his well-worn thoughts about the generation that produced the *poesía pura* of the 1920s; now, he writes, the Civil War has given this generation a theme that is 'racional y humano, que les obligue a preocuparse, más que de las mismas imágenes, de las relaciones que entre ellas se establecen, para construir ese objeto mental, que es el poema mismo' (IV, 2273). If the war has helped poets in this way, they for their part 'contribuyen a espiritualizar la guerra, a revelar a las masas combatientes, los hondos motivos de la contienda y sus finalidades más altas' (IV, 2274).

I would wish to argue that Machado was able to use the sonnet form to express a wide range of emotions and ideas, personal and civic, and was also able to achieve an overall clarity in his view of the deepest circumstances of the war and of its highest aims. Such achievements outweigh, in my view, the relatively rare strained notes that appear in these sonnets (the address to the 'avión marcial' in sonnet II, the flower metaphors in sonnet IV, and the description of Spain as a 'varona fuerte' in sonnet VIII).[9] The sonnets, of course, cannot be divorced from their historical context. Written from March of 1938 onwards, when Machado began writing his political commentaries for *La Vanguardia*, they must bear the impress of

---

9   The text of the sonnets is from *Hora de España*. Apart from modernizing their accentuation, the following changes have been made:

Sonnet VI:	'ítalo' for 'italo'
	'¡Odio' for 'Odio'
Sonnet VII:	'triste España!' for 'triste España'
	'cuanto' (verses 10, 11, 13) for 'cuánto'
Sonnet VIII:	'Mas' for 'Más'
Sonnet 9:	'Líster' for 'Lister'

the last year of the Civil War. In this chapter, therefore, it will be more than usually necessary to bear in mind some of the issues that this period of the war brought into focus, because Machado's use of the sonnet form leads at times to some condensity of expression that may at first sight seem more remote from the conflict than it really is. The most important of these issues from a European perspective, as fears of another world war pressed on the consciousness of the continent, was the territorial integrity of Spain, and the concern of Britain and France that Spain might remain a prey to foreign influence (or even domination, principally fascist, but communist also) after the Spanish Civil War had ended. A related issue was the lingering suspicion by the European democracies that the Republic's government harboured extreme leftist tendencies. A third concern, which raised huge questions about Western civilization generally, was the aerial bombing in 1938 of great cities such as Barcelona and Valencia. From the perspective of the Republic the promotion of reconciliation (preached by both President Azaña and Prime Minister Negrín) became important, for strategic as well as ethical reasons, as an alternative to the picture of Spanish savagery and blood lust.

The first four sonnets were grouped together by Machado in the manuscript version, extant in the Biblioteca Nacional (Madrid), with the title 'Sonetos escritos una noche de bombardeo, en Rocafort (Valencia) marzo de 1938'.[10] They were therefore written within a matter of hours. (In Valencia Machado regularly wrote late into the night and through to the dawn, according to his brother.)[11] The reason for grouping these four sonnets together is not difficult to ascertain, in the context of the nine sonnets as a whole. While they would broadly conform to the description 'civic poetry', the first four are not overtly political in the way that the last four are, with their reference to foreign invasion, the betrayal of Spain, and the defence of its sovereignty. The oblique references to the political situation that one has to dig for in the first five sonnets

---

10 The B.N. number assigned to this group is MS 22233. They are written on cheap brownish paper: the first letters of some lines are blurred because of the paper's poor quality. This blurring is also due to the fact that these first letters have been changed from lower case to capitals.

11 José Machado, *op. cit.*, 138.

are openly present in the last four. It may be misleading, however, to group the sonnets in this way, as if they formed a sequence. Macrì numbers all nine sonnets sequentially, in Roman (II, 822-26), yet in *Hora de España* only the first eight were numbered in this way. Also, Machado put a date and place at the end of sonnet VIII: 'Rocafort, marzo 1938', referring, it can be assumed, to all eight. The sonnet to Líster is therefore obviously set apart from the other eight in these ways. There remains, none the less, the fact that Machado published all nine sonnets together. The last three of the numbered sonnets (VI, VII and VIII) greatly widen the political scope of the poems by blaming the war on the greed, ambition and treachery that has motivated it both at home and abroad, and showing Spain's dignified sorrow, yet determination at the same time. In other words, where the earlier sonnets had mainly expressed the impact of the war on the individual consciousness, divorced from overt political awareness and calculation, the last three of the eight-sonnet sequence act as a kind of public record of the issues at stake in the Civil War. Seen in this light, the final sonnet, to Líster, expresses the poet's own awakening and a renewal of his commitment, or at least willingness, to play his part as fully as Líster is doing at the Battle of the Ebro.

Of the first four sonnets, three of them (I, II and IV) refer to the war planes circling overhead; the first also mentions the noise and smoke of the air raid. This sonnet reflects the civilian's sense of helplessness as the plane 'sobre el vano techo se retarda', while in the sonnet on the death of the child (IV), the poet describes the city illuminated by the full moon and hence an open target for aerial bombardment. In this poem the warmth of love and life is threatened by the chill of death, which comes as the window rattles from the noise of the plane overhead. K. W. Watkins describes the impact on public opinion, in Britain and elsewhere, of the aerial bombing of Barcelona in the same month of March 1938, when the British Prime Minister Chamberlain was sufficiently concerned to express his 'horror and disgust' at such bombings, which were the heaviest ever experienced until the Second World War.[12] In the first three of these sonnets, however, the poet remains

---

12 *Britain Divided. The Effect of the Spanish Civil War on British Public Opinion* (London: Nelson, 1963), 120-21.

generally serene, because 'a traición' (sonnet II), that is, whether he wishes it or not, the arrival of the month of March suggests an irresistible renewal of life and hope. These three sonnets, poised between sombre reflection and the urge towards the light and life of which he wrote in the last verses of 'A un olmo seco', also bring to mind Machado's words of 1920, which illuminate the poet's attitude to the season of spring, and its attendant flora (and fauna): '¿Podrá cantar [el poeta] a las rosas y los lirios, mientras otros hombres, y aun él mismo luchan por el pan o por el derecho? Sin duda alguna. Las rosas y los lirios no son retórica manida; se producen todas las primaveras' (III, 1616).

Sonnet I

LA PRIMAVERA

Más fuerte que la guerra — espanto y grima —
cuando con torpe vuelo de avutarda
el ominoso trimotor se encima,
y sobre el vano techo se retarda

hoy tu alegre zalema el campo anima,
tu claro verde el chopo en yemas guarda.
Fundida irá la nieve de la cima
al hielo rojo de la tierra parda.

Mientras retumba el monte, el mar humea,
da la sirena el lúgubre alarido,
y en el azul el avión platea,

¡cuán agudo se filtra hasta mi oído,
niña inmortal, infatigable dea,
el agrio son de tu rabel florido!

In this sonnet Spring's friendly greeting of peace ('alegre zalema'), its openness ('fundida irá la nieve de la cima / al hielo rojo de la tierra parda'), its care for life ('tu claro verde el chopo en yemas guarda'), its rough-hewn harmonies ('el agrio son de tu rabel florido') are contrasted with the ugly sounds and movements consequent upon the plane's mission of destruction. The comparison of Spring to an 'infatigable dea' in the penultimate verse calls to mind Machado's use of Demeter — another 'infatigable dea' — in the opening poem of *Nuevas canciones*, 'Olivo del camino'. The noise of the bombs and the siren could be an echo, however different in circumstances, of the screaming of the mother of Demophon ('salió gritando, aullando, como loba / herida en las entrañas') as she tries to save her son from Demeter's purifying flames. These flames are linked by Demeter to the defeat of death and the espousal of eternal youth: 'con la llama que libra de la muerte, / la eterna juventud por compañera'. If we accept the subliminal presence of the Demeter myth in the first Civil-War sonnet and examine the poem in the context of Machado's remarks in 1919, that Demophon represents the 'vástago tardío de la agotada burguesía' (III, 1604), then it is possible to interpret the smoke and flames of the bombing as being the birthpangs of a New Spain, with Spring as its symbolic herald.[13] Machado had indeed expressed this idea of rebirth in 1937, in his poem 'A Méjico', when he wrote of 'el rudo parto de la vieja España y ... la que va a nacer España nueva' (II, 834). And just as Demeter had changed her 'manto azul por burda lana, / como sierva propicia a la tarea / de humilde oficio con que el pan se gana' (II, 604), so in the image of the rebeck's fruitful harmonies and rustic, popular notes there is, perhaps, an implied invitation to see the triumph of the popular cause, in the midst of the apparent destruction.[14]

Even before *Nuevas canciones* Machado had used the image of fire as an expression of the forging of a new Spain. The end of the poem dedicated to Azorín contains the exhortation 'hay que acudir, ya es hora, / con el hacha y el fuego al nuevo día' (II, 594). The axe, while destructive, is overwhelmingly preferable to the attitude of the *campesino* in the opening lines of 'Por tierras de España'. In these lines ('El hombre de estos campos que incendia los pinares / y su despojo aguarda como botín de guerra') there are negative connotations of passivity and looting. It is fascinating to see how Machado's mind moved between the zones of culture and agriculture if some of his words addressed to the Valencia Writers' Conference of 1937 are

---

[13] See Macrì (I, 190-91) for a socio-political interpretation of *Olivo del camino*.

[14] Covarrubias comments on the rebeck: 'usan dél los pastores'. After the Renaissance the rebec was mainly associated with popular rather than with court music. See Sybil Marcuse, *Musical Instruments. A Comprehensive Dictionary* (London: Country Life, 1964), 437, and *The New Grove Dictionary of Musical Instruments*, ed. Stanley Sadie, 3 vols (London: Macmillan, 1984), I, 204.

recalled, words that also lend themselves directly to an interpretation of this sonnet:

> si mañana un vendaval de cinismo, de elementalidad humana, sacude el árbol de la cultura y se lleva algo más que sus hojas secas, no os asustéis. Los árboles demasiado espesos necesitan perder algunas de sus ramas, en beneficio de sus frutas. Y a falta de una poda sabia y consciente, pudiera ser bueno el huracán.
>
> (IV, 2204)

Machado, as we have seen, had already used the image of the hurricane in 'Meditación del día'. There it is purely a destructive force, threatening the peaceful and productive life of the *huertanos* of Valencia. The International Writers' Conference in all likelihood gave Machado an opportunity not just to refine but to give more vigorous expression to his ideas about the renewal of culture. This first sonnet, too, especially in the first five words of its opening phrase, views the war as subordinate to the idea of renewal, a renewal that may be sharp and bitter when seen from a traditional viewpoint but that, like the 'niña inmortal, infatigable dea', is forever full of fruit and power.

Sonnet II

EL POETA RECUERDA LAS TIERRAS DE SORIA

¡Ya su perfil zancudo en el regato,
en el azul el vuelo de ballesta,
o, sobre el ancho nido de ginesta,
en torre, torre y torre, el garabato

de la cigüeña! ... En la memoria mía
tu recuerdo a traición ha florecido;
y hoy comienza tu campo empedernido
el sueño verde de la tierra fría,[15]

---

[15] Macrì (II, 822) places a full stop at the end of verse 8. This reading (if such it is, and not just a typographical error) 'cradles' verse 9 between the past/present memories of the quartets and the present/future hopes and fears of the last five verses. Macrì's reading receives some justification from the manuscript, where the punctuation mark at the end of verse 8 was almost certainly a full stop originally and was then changed to a comma. Also in the manuscript Machado left a space between verses 9 and 10, effectively changing the normal division of the sonnet (8 and 6 lines) to 9 and

> Soria pura, entre montes de violeta.
> Di tú, avión marcial, si el alto Duero
> a donde vas recuerda a su poeta,
>
> al revivir su rojo Romancero;
> ¿o es, otra vez, Caín, sobre el planeta,
> bajo tus alas, moscardón guerrero?

This second poem opens as the poet is imagining the stork appearing on the landscape of Soria: 'en el regato, en el azul ... sobre el ancho nido ... en torre, torre y torre': the sign of the stork is everywhere, and the repetitions serve to underline the bird's ubiquitous presence. In one of his 'Apuntes', published in *Los Lunes de El Imparcial* in 1920 (II, 996), Machado had written: 'Nunca desdeñéis las cópulas / fatales, clásicas, bellas, / del potro con la llanura ... la torre con la cigüeña' (II, 787). He was evidently happy to allow a 'fatal' combination of images to take over when the subject required it. In this sonnet the image of the stork not only attracts the concomitant image of the tower, but also recalls the other associative images of 'Pascua de Resurrección': 'Ya sus hermosos nidos habitan las cigüeñas, / y escriben en las torres sus blancos garabatos'. In 'El poeta recuerda' the images of the stork, especially with the repetition of 'torre', flood the poet's memory, rendering him helpless against such an invasion of his consciousness. The opening word 'Ya', and the exclamatory tone, suggest that these images have already embedded themselves, before the poet has recognized rationally what has happened. It is, of course, a moment of intuitive Bergsonian perception that finds its way into many Machado poems. The poet's memory of the storks in the towers of Soria leads to the thought that one of the enemy planes at present over Valencia may fly back towards that Castilian province. Although the serenity of the poem is troubled by the implication of the question in the last two verses (the image of Cain as a universal and deeply-rooted legacy of violence in human affairs), the two tercets maintain to the end the implied dialogue between the poet and the enemy airman. Not for nothing did this sonnet manage to survive in the truncated section 'Poesías de la guerra' of the Espasa-Calpe/

---

5. The punctuation of *Hora de España* links verse 9 much more closely with the quartets and divides the poem into two invocations, one to Soria (verses 1-9) and one to the enemy plane (verses 10-14).

Austral edition (1975) of the *Poesías completas*. In the poem Machado, who has lived happily in both parts of what is now a divided Spain, recalls without rancour his prophetic bloody tale of the Alto Duero (the 'rojo Romancero' of 'La tierra de Alvargonzález'). Yet this sonnet, however mild in its appearance, is in fact a strong plea by Soria's adopted son (Machado was made an 'hijo adoptivo' of Soria in 1932) to be remembered by its inhabitants, because if he is not, then Cain has come again to cast his shadow on the planet.

The direct reminiscences of *Campos de Castilla* in this poem are in all probability prompted by these memories of Soria, which saturate the sonnet with the vocabulary and diction of the Soria-inspired poems of that collection: words and phrases such as 'ballesta', 'torre', 'el garabato de la cigueña', 'campo empedernido'. The two verses 'el sueño verde de la tierra fría, / Soria pura, entre montes de violeta' are 'borrowed' from stanzas 1, 3 and 6 of 'Campos de Soria'. There are reminscences of at least five *Campos de Castilla* poems in this sonnet. Yet the poem, in spite of its deep-rootedness in the diction and rhetoric of the past, is closely linked to thoughts of the war. In the sonnet Machado's own enforced memory of Soria — 'tu recuerdo a traición ha florecido' — is ambiguously expressed, suggesting primarily the idea of this memory stealing up on him unawares, his own feeling of subliminal guilt, perhaps, of 'day-dreaming' about a place held by the enemy. There is also, however, as in sonnet VI, in which he apparently addresses his brother Manuel in nationalist Burgos, an implied call to a clearer consciousness of the nature of the conflict, aimed at the people of Soria: the idea of the nationalists' betrayal of Spain (which will emerge more strongly in sonnets VI, VII and VIII): 'tu recuerdo a traición ha florecido'. However, in this Soria sonnet the poet principally offers the inhabitants of the region of the Alto Duero a renewal of their solidarity with him, by observing the lessons of spring: 'hoy comienza tu campo empedernido / el sueño verde de la tierra fría'. The beginning and ending of the sonnet contrast the peaceful, life-bringing stork with the 'moscardón guerrero' (in 'Pascua de Resurrección' Machado associates the stork with fertility and birth). While he normally linked the word 'garabato' with the stork (here, 'el garabato de la cigueña') because of its ungainly body and 'perfil zancudo', the use of a writing metaphor, 'garabato', takes on special significance in the context of any 'message' that this poem might have for the inhabitants of the Alto Duero (an antonomasia for the nationalist zone?).[16] The use of landscape as a sign is made clear by Machado through the copulative 'y' in verse 7. Quoting the verses in context will help to make the role of the landscape clearer:

> En la memoria mía
> tu recuerdo a traición ha florecido;
> y hoy comienza tu campo empedernido
> el sueño verde de la tierra fría.

Although the copulative is redundant from a metrical point of view, it is essential to convey the idea of a symbolic landscape, because 'y' continues the train of thought from 'en la memoria mía'. Therefore the 'sueño verde' is a description not so much of the Sorian countryside, as of its presence in the poet's consciousness. Words such as 'empedernido', 'sueño verde' and 'fría' then take on a potential significance for the poet's relationship with the nationalist zone. These signals are sent out with a reticence that is an authentic characteristic of Machado's best poems.

Sonnet III

AMANECER EN VALENCIA
(Desde una torre)

> Estas rachas de marzo, en los desvanes
> — hacia la mar — del tiempo; la paloma
> de pluma tornasol, los tulipanes
> gigantes del jardín, y el sol que asoma,
>
> bola de fuego entre morada bruma,
> a iluminar la tierra valentina ...[17]

---

[16] For a fuller discussion of this aspect of Machado's poetry see Alessandro Martinengo, 'Prehistoria e historia del "garabato de la cigüeña" machadiano', in *Hispanic Studies in Honour of Geoffrey Ribbans*, ed. Ann L. Mackenzie and Dorothy S. Severin (Liverpool: Liverpool U. P., 1992), 205-14.

[17] Macrì gives the last word of this line as 'levantina'. Machado's recent editors (with the exception of the popular Austral edition of the *Poesías completas*) have also employed this reading, which is not authorized by the text of *Hora de España*.

¡Hervor de leche y plata, añil y espuma,
y velas blancas en la mar latina!

Valencia de fecundas primaveras,
de floridas almunias y arrozales,
feliz quiero cantarte, como eras,

domando a un ancho río en tus canales,
al dios marino con tus albuferas,
al centauro de amor con tus rosales.

The same reticence is evident in this poem, with just one verse, 'feliz quiero cantarte como eras', and the title to suggest the poet's presence in the landscape that he is describing. The perspectivist title was toned down in the printed text, which reverses the two phrases of the manuscript's title from '(Desde una torre.) Amanecer en Valencia' to 'Amanecer en Valencia (Desde una torre)' and thereby reduces the poet's distance from his subject.[18] The position of the parenthetical phrase in the revised title gives the phrase the appearance of an afterthought. (The element of intellectual, emotional and aesthetic distance, here expressed spatially, was one that greatly exercised Machado throughout his writings, but especially during the Civil War.) There is also just one word in the poem, 'eras', to suggest that the alliance of hand, brain and abundant natural resources of the region cannot at present yield the happiness of former days. This happiness is expressed in a variety of ways, mostly in terms of the controlled and fruitful use of the exuberant fertility of the surrounding land and water. Machado, in an interview, described the area thus, contrasting it with Castile: 'Castilla es la conquista, la expansión, la fe, lo absoluto; Valencia es el laboreo, la constancia, la conservación de lo por aquélla conquistado' (IV, 2208-09). These images of perseverance and fidelity help to explain somewhat the rather obscure last lines: that of Valencia 'domando ... / al centauro de amor con tus rosales'. A fuller explanation of the 'taming of the centaur of love' is provided by a passage in Machado's essay

---

18 The title of the sonnet in the manuscript is '(*Desde una torre*). *Amanecer en Valencia*', written on the same line. However, the text of *Hora de España* significantly lessens the visual importance of the parenthetical phrase by reducing it to italics that are smaller than the rest of the lower-case text, with the poem's main title in italic capitals, very nearly as we have given it in the body of the text.

'Sobre literatura rusa', where he uses the image of the centaur especially to connote the animalistic aspect of sexual passion: 'Lo que llamamos pornografía, esa baja literatura que halaga no más la parte inferior del centauro humano' (III, 1237). In this light a suggested paraphrase of the final verse of the sonnet would therefore read: 'Valencia ... your rose gardens, whose flowers are destined as offerings of the lover to his beloved, enabling courtesy and generosity to take precedence over sexual passion'.

Is there an implicit political point being made here, as well as in Sonnets I and II? We should not forget that the poem was published in the government's *Servicio Español de Información* as well as in *Hora de España*. The latter had stated in the opening 'Propósito' of its first issue in January 1937 that its contents were aimed more at international than Spanish opinion, and that it hoped to be read by 'los camaradas o simpatizantes esparcidos por el mundo ... hispanófilos, en fin, que recibirán inmensa alegría al ver que España prosigue su vida intelectual o de creación artística en medio del conflicto gigantesco que se debate'. This sonnet is, among other things, an excellent illustration of the 'Propósito' of *Hora de España*. The poem is about the arts of peace: of fishing, of the agriculture and the horticulture of the *huerta valenciana*. Machado had made this point earlier in the year in a greeting to Republican soldiers: 'Ayer obreros de la ciudad y los campos, consagrados a las santas faenas de la paz y de la cultura' (IV, 2229). The images of careful conservation, of conservatism even (the use of the Moorish *albuferas*), of steadiness and self-control in the midst of an exuberant landscape, are far removed from any picture of wanton revolution and anarchy. The ordering of nature in the sonnet may well be an emblem of how Valencia, the newest capital of the Spanish Republic (and its surrounding *huerta*), should be seen, especially by Britain and France, fearful as they appeared to be of communist and anarchist influences. The sonnet, therefore, reinforces the image of Spain, under Negrín's premiership, as a place of order and productive labour. In his *La Vanguardia* article of 23 November 1938 Machado was to express his exasperation at the conservative attitude to republican Spain, at least as far as some aspects of French opinion were concerned, when he wrote: 'Todavía hay en

Francia quien cree de buena fe, que nosotros los llamados rojos, luchamos contra una España auténtica, amante de sus tradiciones' (IV, 2490). Machado may also have been hinting at the socio-economic situation of the *huerta*, as he experienced it following his move from Madrid. Franz Borkenau gives a brief account of the social and political temper of Valencia in the month following the outbreak of the war. He found 'that the peasants here are not in favour of the anarchist drive towards collectivization' and that this was backed by the communists there, who had a 'policy of protecting the individual property of the peasants against anarchist attempts at collectivization'.[19] Although from over a year later, the image in this sonnet of an order that bears even more abundant fruit is the way that the poet sees the landscape and its people, 'desde una torre': that is, as someone who is detached and yet present, a poetic witness for those who will listen to his testimony.

Sonnet IV
LA MUERTE DEL NIÑO HERIDO

Otra vez en la noche ... Es el martillo
de la fiebre en las sienes bien vendadas
del niño. — Madre, ¡el pájaro amarillo!
¡las mariposas negras y moradas!

— Duerme, hijo mío. — Y la manita oprime
la madre, junto al lecho. — ¡Oh, flor de fuego!
¿quién ha de helarte, flor de sangre, dime?
Hay en la pobre alcoba olor de espliego;

fuera, la oronda luna que blanquea
cúpula y torre a la ciudad sombría.
Invisible avión moscardonea.

¿Duermes, oh dulce flor de sangre mía?
El cristal del balcón repiquetea.
— ¡Oh, fría, fría, fría, fría, fría!

'La muerte del niño herido' comes after 'Amanecer en Valencia', which is reflective and rather distanced from the war, while Sonnet IV presents the impact of the war in a directly

---

19 *Op. cit.*, 119 and 118 for the respective quotations.

descriptive fashion. In these sonnets Machado is practising what he was to preach in the next-but-one issue of *Hora de España*, when he discussed the role of the intellectual in times of war. This piece sees two kinds of understanding, the intellectual and the experiential, as necessary to achieve a true perspective on the war: 'en oposición a esta exigencia de distancia para la visión, hay otra de vivencia (admitamos la palabreja) que toda honda visión implica' (IV, 2394), he writes in the third section of his article in the August issue, in the paragraph which begins 'Pero la guerra es un tema de meditación. Los filósofos no pueden eludirlo en nuestros días'. Machado's piece in *La Vanguardia* of 23 July 1938 ('Para el Congreso de la Paz') on the aerial bombing of civilian populations, is a brilliant example of the linking of such experiential and reflective understanding, where he digs deeply into the belligerent culture of Western society in order to try to explain the reason for 'estas mismas aborrecibles bombas que están cayendo sobre nuestros techos [y que son] las que me inspiran estas reflexiones' (IV, 2463). (This piece is also indispensable as a general historical and philosophical illumination of the present poem.)

In 'La muerte del niño herido', as in all nine sonnets, there are various images that are reminiscent of earlier poems. Yet the images, although familiar, are very much a part of Machado's concern to incorporate the consequences of the war into his poems, 'cuya estructura interna y cuya arquitectura total importan sobre todo', as he wrote in 'El influjo de la guerra sobre la poesía ...' (IV, 2273). It is not therefore the reappearance of imagery from earlier days that is significant but rather its place in the new 'estructura interna' of these sonnets. The hammer blows of the fever at the opening of 'La muerte del niño herido' may already suggest the imminent death of the child, since the lines recall those that Machado had written in Poem XII of *Soledades. Galerías. Otros poemas*: 'Los golpes del martillo / dicen la caja negra'. The death in the sonnet, however, has a recognizable cause, the war. Incidentally in Poem XII, verse 11, 'En las sombrías torres' had originally read 'En la ciudad sombría'.[20] The poem's location,

---

20 See *Antonio Machado, Soledades. Galerías. Otros poemas*, ed. Geoffrey Ribbans (Madrid: Cátedra, 1984), 101.

too, is specifically realized, with a hint of how this particular war heaps injustice upon injustice: the child will die in a 'pobre alcoba'. The smell of lavender is not in the poem to add the scent of one of the 'hierbas montaraces / de fuerte olor', as in 'A orillas del Duero'. In the sonnet the products of the herb are almost certainly depicted as being used either as a home-made antiseptic or to protect the wounded child against flies and mosquitoes (or perhaps for both reasons). In other words, in Machado's best lines, including those of his last year of life, the words are saturated with an allusive quality that enriches the language and enhances the reader's experience. The descriptive simplicity of 'Hay en la pobre alcoba olor de espliego' belies the potent reverberations that it can suggest, in the sights and smells of the room that death is about to visit.

The opening lines of Poem CLVII from the 1907 collection ('Fuera, la luna platea / cúpulas, torres, tejados') also anticipate the first two verses of the sonnet's sestet: 'fuera, la oronda luna que blanquea / cúpula y torre a la ciudad sombría'. In the manuscript version of the sonnet, Machado changed the verb in this sentence from 'platea' to 'blanquea', preferring the plainer, colder connotation of the latter verb to describe the moonlit city. The moon here has become bright and threatening: this is not the romantic moonlight of 'Orillas del Duero' or 'Campos de Soria'. The change to 'blanquea' also contributes to a sense of foreboding in the verse, as the sound of a tolling bell, in the phonetic sequence 'on', 'un', 'an'. There is also in the sonnet a reminiscence of Poem LXII, where the poet suddenly awakes and utters the images that have accompanied him in his dream. In the sonnet, however, the dream-images of innocent vulnerability (the bird and the butterfly) are contrasted with the hammer blows of the fever, and the bandages tightly wrapped around the child's head: the freedom and lightness of the dream-images are in this instance no match for the effects of war. One of these images, the butterfly, is not uncommon in Machado's earlier poetry;[21] the butterfly with dark colours (here 'negras y moradas') also has an antecedent in Poem LXXXVI,

---

21 Manuel Ariza, 'Los animales en Antonio Machado', in *Antonio Machado hoy*, IV, 367-80, has counted six appearances of the butterfly in Machado's poems. In this sonnet he sees the dark butterfly as a 'clara metáfora por un avión de guerra' (369).

with connotations of sorrow and the collapse of life.

The cold, bright moon, silhouetting the city, and the invisible, hence anonymous, aircraft also act as a contrast to the closeness of the mother and child, their bodily contact, and dramatically portray Machado's description of war at the end of 1937 as 'el "crimen deshumanizado", la muerte entre ciegas máquinas, para permitirse el lujo de abreviar la vida de los mejores' (IV, 2434). The drumming sound of the window's vibration (of rain in Machado's earlier poems) means that the plane has come closer to the room, and is implicitly compared to a fly that is approaching the now dead body of the child. Even in death the victims of war are not freed from its presence. As the opening line testifies, this is not the first visitation from these anonymous instruments of war; although the line could refer to the return of the fever at night, the suspension points ('Otra vez en la noche ...') also suggest a reference to another enemy plane, and the apprehensive expectation of its return. Another reminiscence of an earlier poem is to be found in the mother's cry, '¿Quién ha de helarte?', which recalls lines from the last of the 'Proverbios y cantares' of *Campos de Castilla*: 'Españolito que vienes / al mundo, te guarde Dios. / Una de las dos Españas / ha de helarte el corazón' (II, 582). The 'dos Españas' in this poem are 'una España que muere / y otra que bosteza'. Is there an intertextual link, an unconscious one perhaps, between these poems of 1917 and 1938? The image in the later poem could be acting as a kind of shorthand for the answer given in the *cantar*: a backward-looking, self-satisfied Spain linked in the sonnet with the plane that is bombing civilian areas of Valencia.

The dramatic directness of this sonnet is an illustration of the experiential understanding of the war, which Machado was to discuss two months later in *Hora de España*, in the article just quoted. On 17 September 1938 the Republic's Ambassador to Britain addressed the League of Nations on the subject of aerial bombings of civilian populations. Having given statistics of the bombs dropped and the casualties caused in Republican Spain, the Ambassador continued:

> Pero hay dos cosas más difíciles de representarse: una, la cobardía y la ausencia total de sentimientos humanos en quienes ordenan o ejecutan los bombardeos aéreos; otra, el heroísmo tranquilo y

sereno, el valor silencioso de todos los días, de todas las horas, de que dan ejemplo al mundo las poblaciones mártires. Lo más espantoso no es el bombardeo mismo, sino la angustia de la incertidumbre, el temor constante de ver aparecer en el horizonte, en cualquier momento del día, tres, seis, nueve puntos negros, y a veces más, siniestros y amenazadores.[22]

It is almost certain that the Ambassador would have read Machado's poem in *Servicio Español de Información*. His words serve to underline the potential political reverberations of Machado's sonnet, in spite of its intimacy and enclosed scale.

In the sonnet Machado runs the gamut of dialogue — or implied dialogue — between mother and child: exclamation, imperative, question and invocation (rhetorical resources that reinforce the contrast between the intimacy within the room and the anonymity without). Yet these resources are not there just to raise the emotional temperature of the poem, through the immediacy and intimacy of the spoken word. The expressionist language of the mother, when speaking to her child ('flor de fuego', 'flor de sangre') conveys the warmth of her love, while her final words (the last verse) tell us that the coldness of death has penetrated into the house. If this last verse can be justified naturalistically, the same cannot be said of the images of fire and blood used earlier; an example, perhaps, of the strain that the demands of public utterance placed on the poet. These images ('fruit of my love, fruit of my body'), in attempting to highlight the intense tragedy for individual lives that war brings, seem artificial by contrast with the naturalistic force of the last verse. Why did Machado end the sonnet in such a repetitive way? The line has no rhetorical parallel in his work. As an expressive instrument, it may represent the repeated sobbing of the mother as she realizes that her child has died. Grammatically, the feminine adjective refers to the 'manita' of verse 5. The line, therefore, is also a civic expression of the 'crimen deshumanizado' of war, which has turned the warmth of love, described in the clasped hands of mother and child in verses 5 and 6, into something cold and lifeless: an adjective or adjunct, forever divorced from its 'manita', no matter how often it is repeated.

---

22 Azcárate, *op. cit.*, 104.

The Manuscript of Sonnet IV, in the Biblioteca Nacional, Madrid.

Sonnet V

De mar a mar entre los dos la guerra,
más honda que la mar. En mi parterre,
miro a la mar que el horizonte cierra.
Tú asomada, Guiomar, a un finisterre,

miras hacia otro mar, la mar de España
que Camoens cantara, tenebrosa.
Acaso a ti mi ausencia te acompaña.
A mí me duele tu recuerdo, diosa.

La guerra dio al amor el tajo fuerte.
Y es la total angustia de la muerte,
con la sombra infecunda de la llama

y la soñada miel de amor tardío,
y la flor imposible de la rama
que ha sentido del hacha el corte frío.

Sonnet I proclaimed the individual poet's belief in a new life for his country, and then in the poems about reconciliation (sonnet II) and peaceful labour (sonnet III) expresses this vision of Spain. Sonnet IV is also a poem about a relationship, but one that is also threatened by the war and even the dramatic finality of death. Sonnet V forms a stark contrast with the relationships depicted in the preceding poems. Although the first two verses state that the war is 'más honda que la mar', the kind of absence portrayed here cuts deeper than the war itself. In one of his *La Vanguardia* articles Machado uses the image of amputation to describe the effects of war: 'la guerra reduce el campo de nuestras razones, nos amputa violentamente todas aquellas en que se fincan nuestros adversarios' (IV, 2240-41). The reduction referred to here is depicted in the poem by the closing in of the Mediterranean horizon, and the ending of a journey ('finisterre'). Guiomar's hesitancy and wariness — her fear of the dark unknown, perhaps — are suggested in the words 'asomada' and 'tenebrosa', reinforced by the contrast with Camões' 'mar de España'. This image from former times is of the Portuguese poet celebrating the conquest of the Atlantic by Spain and Portugal. Frank Pierce has noted that Camões uses 'Espanha' as an equivalent for the Latin 'Hispania'.[23] It is impossible to know whether Machado is using the word in that

---

[23] See his edition of *Os Lusíadas* (Oxford: Clarendon Press, 1973), 8.

way also. Yet even in this very personal poem Machado was concerned to suggest the historical and geographical importance of Spain, as he does more openly in the three subsequent sonnets. Now the picture of Spain and Portugal is of two countries isolated from each other, reflected in the situations of the poet and Guiomar: the poet looks at one sea, and Guiomar looks at another. Both are facing in diametrically opposite directions: an image not just of separation but of alienation, too. Even in verses that suggest some form of dialogue ('Acaso a ti mi ausencia te acompaña, / a mí me duele tu recuerdo, diosa') the oxymoron in the first verse may imply that Guiomar values the poet's absence more than his presence, while the next verse is ambiguous, indicating not a suffering because of absence but, perhaps, because of the poet's painful remembrance of their unsatisfactory relationship. The word 'diosa' recalls, too, the distance evident in the pre-Civil-War poems and letters to Guiomar. The poem depicts not just geographical separation but the realization that a personal relationship, which in any case had never come to fulfilment, has now been given the *coup-de-grâce* by the Civil War.

The tercets of this sonnet are among the most intense and densely-packed lines that Machado has written, in which public utterances about the effects of war are interwoven with the poet's very personal reflections on his relationship with Guiomar. The brutal finality of the war is mirrored in the short first verse of the sestet which also makes the poem a public as well as a personal statement about the horror of war. Unlike most of the other sonnets, which mix the personal and the political, the sense of loss here is not primarily territorial or economic (although these are never overriding considerations in Machado's view of the war) but, as Machado had written in his March 1938 contribution to *Hora de España* ('Alemania o la exageración') of the loss of a peace, 'que haga imposible por muchos años la amorosa convivencia entre los hombres'. In this sonnet, centrally concerned as it is with love or love's absence, he is not interested in blaming any political or national configuration for causing and prosecuting the war. The honey image, always positive in Machado, is here finally productive of neither hope or happiness, but only of frustration. The flame of love casts a sterile shadow because it has been overtaken by the war. Although the last image in the poem could be seen in a positive light, since only one of love's branches has been cut down, leaving the tree intact, there is little sense here that such a pruning is either desirable or necessary. The overall black mood of the poem may, perhaps, be the expression of the poet's feelings at the division of Spain (and of Spain and Portugal) by the war, but it is hard not to sense that an emotion 'más honda que la guerra', or at least as deep as it, is at work here: a personal drawn-out longing (conveyed by the copulatives 'Y ... y ... y' at the beginning of verses 10, 12 and 13) that the poet at the same time knows is based on stillborn futility. This personal and public sense of loss is portrayed in the poem by absence, closure, darkness, violence, amputation, anguish, frustration, impossibility, suffering, sterility and death. The mood of the Guiomar sonnet is sombre indeed. The intensely personal atmosphere that envelops this sonnet may account for its deep pessimism. In a poem that mainly expresses the sadness of a lost personal relationship Machado could perhaps allow himself an anguished cry of sorrow, without any foreseeable hope. The same is true to some extent of the poem on the death of the child: the sonnet is generally kept within the confines of the mother's anguish.

Sonnet VI

Otra vez el ayer. Tras la persiana,
música y sol; en el jardín cercano,
la fruta de oro, al levantar la mano,
el puro azul dormido en la fontana.

Mi Sevilla infantil ¡tan sevillana!
¡cuál muerde el tiempo tu memoria en vano!
¡Tan nuestra! Aviva tu recuerdo, hermano.
No sabemos de quién va a ser mañana.

Alguien vendió la piedra de los lares
al pesado teutón, al hambre mora,
y al ítalo las puertas de los mares.

¡Odio y miedo a la estirpe redentora
que muele el fruto de los olivares,
y ayuna y labra, y siembra y canta y llora!

The sonnet 'Otra vez el ayer' could be seen as a companion piece to 'El poeta recuerda las tierras de Soria', although it is not in the 'noche de marzo' sequence.[24] Both involve memories of places dear to Machado but now in the nationalist zone, and both are addressed to someone on the other side, in this case in all probability to his brother Manuel, in Burgos. This shared memory of something 'nuestra' is sparked off, perhaps, by the 'fruta de oro' of a lemon tree that grew in the courtyard of his childhood and, now in the garden in Valencia, links past and present in the sonnet.[25] Bernard Sesé, commenting on the last two tercets of this sonnet, writes: 'tienen cierta pesadez y torpeza que desentona de la soltura airosa de los seis primeros versos'.[26] Aldo Garosci's criticism of this sonnet is in the same vein: that the poem suffers from 'inspiración dividida' and that 'tampoco tiene suficiente aliento para llegar hasta el final con el mismo tema [of the first six verses]'.[27] Antonio Sánchez Barbudo similarly comments on the same sonnet: 'este tema segundo de la guerra, de los dos bandos y de la actitud de Manuel, no acaba de casar bien con el primero, el recuerdo del jardín de su infancia'.[28] It is not difficult, however, to make an expressive link, at least between the penultimate tercet and what has gone before. The family intimacy depicted in the first 8 verses is contrasted with the anonymity of the 'alguien' of verse 9. The absence of suspension points after the opening phrase of sonnet VI suggests that the phrase does not exclusively lead into what immediately follows, as it does in sonnet IV. This opening of the poem ('Otra vez el ayer') links the birthright of Antonio and his brother to the threat of an invasion that has historical echoes: the archaic-sounding descriptions of the Germans and Italians as 'pesado teutón' and

---

24 The Biblioteca Nacional number for this second group of four sonnets is MS 22233[2]. It comprises the sonnets V to VIII, the latter without a title. They are written on good, thick paper, with only one correction ('siembra' for 'reza') and have the words 'La guerra' as a title at the top of the first page. (Both manuscripts are signed 'Antonio Machado' on their final pages.)

25 José Machado, *op. cit.*, 137, writes of the house in Rocafort: 'Vuelve el Poeta [sic] a sus naranjos y limoneros en esta torre valenciana que le recuerdan su niñez'.

26 *Op. cit.*, 848.

27 *Op. cit.*, 35-36.

28 *Los poemas*, 464.

'ítalo' conjure up historical comparisons with former invasions from Rome and northern Europe.

In his radio address of 22 November 1938, delivered, as the title stated, to 'todos los españoles', Machado was to make the Republic's often-repeated point: that the Spanish war was hardly ever a civil war, but an invasion. In the address, however, he prefaces this remark with a confession that helps to put this sonnet into a context that necessarily transcends family concerns:

> convencido de la ceguera, de los errores, de la injusticia de nuestros adversarios, de cuya índole facciosa no dudé un momento, confieso que nunca pude aborrecerlos; con todos sus yerros, con todos sus pecados, eran españoles; y el lazo fraterno, hondamente fraterno de la patria común, no podía romperse ni con la más enconada guerra civil.
>
> Pero se inició el hecho monstruoso de la invasión extranjera ... Dos pueblos extranjeros habían penetrado en España para disponer de su destino futuro y para borrar por la fuerza su historia pasada. (IV, 2292)

In the sonnet the 'lazo fraterno' is not just of blood, but of the Sevillian *patria chica* and of Andalusia invaded by foreigners. Thus far in this sonnet we can detect a thread of unity, that depicts the safety and peace of the brothers' childhood in Seville (the fountain acts as a cradle for the sleeping water;[29] time cannot threaten these memories of house and garden) and then contrasts these pictures with the anonymous sale of their hearth and home to foreign interests.

The final tercet, with its elliptical opening and the highly compressed phrase 'estirpe redentora', may therefore be paraphrased, as in the following suggested summary: 'To think that a race that is redeeming its birthright by its work, its suffering and culture, should be invaded by hatred and fear!'. Perhaps Machado recalled here the memorable words from Manuel Azaña's speech in Valencia of July 1937: 'Odio y miedo causantes de la desventura de España, los peores consejeros que

---

29 The verse 'el puro azul dormido en la fontana' recalls the 'recuerdo, en el pretil de piedra / de la fuente dormido' of 'El limonero lánguido', where there is a contrast between the security of childhood and the initial hesitations and uncertainties of the present. Machado is able to reuse this basic idea in Sonnet VI and place it in a contemporary political context.

un hombre pueda tomar para su vida personal, y sobre todo en la vida pública. El miedo enloquece y lanza a las mayores extravagancias y a los más feos actos de abyección; el odio enfurece y no lleva más que al derramamiento de sangre.'[30] It is notable how Azaña attributes loss of order and control to the presence of these emotions, and how analogously in the Machado sonnet they appear to destroy, or attempt to destroy, the ordered round of seasonal tasks and events. Machado had used the phrase 'España ... redentora' in his 1913 poem 'Del mañana efímero'. Here the meaning is restricted to the idea of a new salvation, through the antithesis of the verses: 'Esa España que ora y bosteza' and 'Una España implacable y redentora'. In the Civil-War sonnet, however, both the etymological and religious meanings (that is, 'buying back' and 'saving') are possible. The etymological interpretation probably accords better with the linking of the sonnet's personal and political elements, of its private and public tone, centred around a common core of intimate identity. This meaning (the selling and the redemption of one's birthright) in its compressed and oblique way, makes the same point as the impassioned Miguel Hernández in 'Jornaleros':

> ¿Dejaremos llevar cobardemente
> riquezas que han forjado nuestros remos?
> ¿Campos que ha humedecido nuestra frente
> dejaremos? ...
> Jornaleros: España, loma a loma
> es de gañanes, pobres y braceros.

Therefore, it is not correct to assert, as does Lázaro Carreter, that Machado is 'sin progreso, antes bien, recurriendo a la memoria' (133). The idea of redemption in this sonnet contains the new principle of ownership through labour, which was absent from the 1913 poem. Machado was too good a poet merely to reuse words and ideas as if they were, to quote his own words, 'cápsulas lógicas' (III, 1803) untouched by the passing of time. The verbs and conjunctions of the final verse summarize a whole cycle of life which is intimately linked to the region (and is now under threat): the patient preparation of the soil, the sowing, the stoical waiting for harvest, the celebration

---

30 *Al año de guerra*, 25.

and commemoration of joys and sorrows. In addition, the last verse, with its enjambement of copulatives and the final 'a' of the five verb forms, produces the 'ay' sound of the Andalusian *canto jondo* (especially the *saeta*), which Manuel would have recognized and with which he would have felt at home. Machado may be using this shared cultural memory to reach across the division of Spain and to offer his own testimony to a common identity in the face of the uncertainty and anonymity that threatens 'el lazo fraterno, hondamente fraterno de la patria común'.[31]

Sonnet VII

Trazó una odiosa mano, España mía,
— ancha lira, hacia el mar, entre dos mares —
zonas de guerra, crestas militares,
en llano, loma, alcor y serranía.

Manes del odio y de la cobardía
cortan la leña de tus encinares,
pisan la baya de oro en tus lagares,
muelen el grano que tu suelo cría.

Otra vez — ¡otra vez! — ¡oh triste España!,
cuanto se anega en viento y mar se baña
juguete de traición, cuanto se encierra

en los templos de Dios mancha el olvido,
cuanto acrisola el seno de la tierra
se ofrece a la ambición, ¡todo vendido!

Sonnet VIII

(A otro Conde Don Julián)

Mas tú, varona fuerte, madre santa,
sientes tuya la tierra en que se muere,
en ella afincas la desnuda planta,
y a tu Señor suplicas: ¡Miserere!

---

31 Addressing Manuel in the form of a sonnet may also have been an extra gesture of affection by Antonio. Manuel would surely have known Antonio's opinion of him, expressed in *Los complementarios* (III, 1156), as the best Spanish composer of sonnets since Góngora and Calderón.

¿Adónde irá el felón con su falsía?
¿En qué rincón se esconderá, sombrío?
Ten piedad del traidor. Paríle un día,
se engendró en el amor, es hijo mío.

Hijo tuyo es también, Dios de bondades.
Cúrale con amargas soledades.
Haz que su infamia su castigo sea.

Que trepe a un alto pino en la alta cima,
y en él ahorcado, que su crimen vea,
y el horror de su crimen lo redima.

These two sonnets are addressed to Spain, the second using the extended metaphor of Spain as the mother of all her children, including those who have betrayed her, particularly the new Conde Don Julián (presumably General Franco). The link between the two sonnets is provided by the continuation of the invocation to Spain, which is not now the 'triste España' of sonnet VII but is a 'varona fuerte' who is prepared to see her errant son (General Franco?) chastized for his treachery. The first sonnet (essentially the first half of a bipartite poem) ends with the image of Spain being 'todo vendido', while the second half (the second sonnet) strikes a much more vigorous, imperative tone. (The robust tone of the latter is maintained to the end by the five imperatives in the last five verses.) Sonnet VIII redeems the negative sadness of sonnet VII, which cannot effectively be judged as a poem in its own right, because as well as being joined grammatically to the following sonnet by the conjunction 'Mas' it is thematically inseparable from it. Indeed, sonnet VII might not have been approved by the censor had it stood alone: ending with the sigh '¡todo vendido!', the phrase suggests more the musings of an old man than the vigour of the struggle against fascism. In choosing this sonnet for her chapter 'Actitud del poeta ante la guerra', without also including sonnet VIII, Natalia Calamai has surely placed the wrong emphasis on Machado's response to the war in his poetry.[32] Dario Puccini, too, publishes this sonnet on its own and gives it a title ('¡Todo vendido!') that does not appear either in the Biblioteca Nacional manuscript or in *Hora de España*.[33] The

---

[32] *El compromiso de la poesía en la guerra civil española* (Barcelona: Laia, 1979), 119-20.

[33] *Romancero de la resistencia*, ed. Dario Puccini (Mexico D.F.:

practice of separating these two sonnets, while justified on the basis that the two pieces are separate sonnet forms, completely severs the link between them, and therefore misses the contrast between the portrayal of a passive Spain in sonnet VII, in the grip of a military hand, and Spain's firm response in the following sonnet. If we see the sonnets as constituting a unified poem, the 'odiosa mano' at the beginning of VII belongs to the same personage (General Franco) who will die — or deserve to die — by his own hand at the end of sonnet VIII.

The 'crestas militares ... llano, loma, alcor y serranía' of sonnet VII so reminiscent of the Soria poems of *Campos de Castilla* are no longer metaphors for Spain's warrior past, because in the sonnet Machado imagines the general's hand on the map of Spain, turning its geography into war zones and military vantage points (and later selling its resources to further these military ambitions). The initial image also incorporates the idea of Spain as an 'ancha lira' being strummed by an unsympathetic hand. The verse 'ancha lira, hacia el mar, entre dos mares' may not be among Machado's most immediately striking lines but it corresponds in its political resonances with the Republic's effort to make Britain and France realize that because of Spain's strategic importance — 'hacia el mar, entre dos mares' — any help given to the Republic strengthens the position of the other democracies. In the month following the composition of this group of sonnets, the Spanish Ambassador in London, outlining the Republic's view for the diplomatic correspondent of the *News Chronicle*, put forward a scenario that Machado had intimated in this line. In the event of an insurgent victory, he wrote, 'nos encontraríamos ante el hecho de una España dividida en dos zonas de influencia, correspondiendo la zona mediterránea a Italia y la zona atlántica a Alemania'.[34] Manuel Azaña, too, looking back on the war, referred to the importance of Spain's position 'entre dos mares, los Pirineos y el estrecho de Gibraltar'.[35] As with the image of light in sonnet IV, so the image of the lyre that is

---

Ediciones Era, 1967), 153. In spite of my criticism I should add that part of Puccini's Introduction (22-45) is a useful addition to the bibliography of the period.

34 Azcárate, *op. cit.*, 370.
35 *Causas de la guerra de España* (Madrid: Grijalbo, 1986), 36.

normally positive in Machado's work, suggesting beauty and harmony, whether in the immediate surrounds of nature (especially the poplar trees) or whether in the cosmos, is here illustrative of disharmony, because the war has imposed itself on the peaceful concerns of culture and agriculture. The image of Spain in verse 11 as the 'plaything of treachery' ('juguete de traición') brings us back to the initial picture of the general playing war-games on the map of Spain, games that have tragic consequences for the destiny of the country and its resources. Machado had already referred to the military rebels as acting out of 'la rencorosa frivolidad ... que no mide nunca las consecuencias de sus actos' (IV, 2178) in the prose section of 'Meditación del día'. In Sonnet VII he details the enormity of the implications of the selling of Spain: its fish and fowl ('cuanto se anega en viento y mar se baña'), its grain, vines, timber and minerals. The references to 'cobardía' and 'ambición' in this sonnet are perhaps best explained in a piece that Machado wrote in 1937 (for the sixth anniversary of the Republic):

> Y surgió la rebelión de los militares, la traición madura y definitiva que se había gestado durante años enteros. Fue uno de los hechos más cobardes que registra la historia. Los militares rebeldes volvieron contra el pueblo todas las armas que el pueblo había puesto en sus manos para defender la nación, y como no tenían brazos voluntarios para empuñarlas, los compraron al hambre africana, pagaron con oro, que tampoco era suyo, todo un ejército de mercenarios, y como esto no era todavía bastante para triunfar de un pueblo casi inerme, pero heroico y abnegado, abrieron nuestros puertos y nuestros fronteras a los anhelos imperialistas de dos grandes potencias europeas. (IV, 2186)

In sonnet VII the peaceful, productive pursuits of the *pueblo* are plundered by the rebellious military at home and sold off to the military ambitions of Germany and Italy.

Sonnet VIII, although dedicated to 'otro Conde Don Julián', is not primarily a gesture of conciliation (this element is present, however). The last tercet may suggest redemption, but in such terms that the expiation of guilt is only to be achieved by a banishment to 'la alta cima' and by the subsequent suicide of the errant son (the kind of ambiguous reconciliation between the malefactors and their father at the end of 'La tierra de Alvargonzález', when the sons fall into the *Laguna negra*, crying

'¡Padre!'). Some of Machado's remarks in his radio broadcast also appear to make a movement of conciliation towards the insurgents, and may help to put this sonnet into context: 'Dejemos a un lado la parte de culpa que en la invasión de España hayan podido tener los españoles mismos. Si este pecado existe, si alguien lo cometió conscientemente, es de índole tal que escapa al poder de todo tribunal humano' (IV, 2293). In the broadcast Machado appears to suggest an amnesty for the insurgents, not ostensibly for reconciliation's sake but either because (the poet's wording is ambiguous) their motives cannot be judged by a court of law or because their 'sin' is so serious that they are best left to the remorse of their consciences. The choice of the 'alto pino en la alta cima' points in the latter direction, if, apart from the repetition of the adjective to reinforce the isolation of the errant son, Machado's description of the pine tree in 'Las encinas' is recalled: 'El pino es el mar y el cielo / y la montaña: el planeta' (II, 501). (Machado almost always uses the word 'planeta' or 'planetario' to denote isolation.) Yet the note of conciliation is not negligible: 'Ten piedad ... se engendró en el amor, es hijo mío ... Dios de bondades'.

In sonnet VIII, in the mother's willing sacrifice of her son, there is a reminiscence of the integrity of Alonso Pérez de Guzmán, 'el bueno', whom legend portrays as permitting the death of his son, rather than deliver Tarifa to a besieging army. Manuel Machado had already written a sonnet on the theme of a parent's sacrifice of a child, which was also part of a bipartite structure, whereby two sonnets make up the poem to which he gave the title 'Blasón de España'. Manuel's second sonnet recalls the famous incident during the siege of the Alcázar of Toledo, in which General Moscardó is reputed to have allowed his son to die rather than surrender the Alcázar to the Republic. This sonnet is blandly triumphalist and bereft of the expression of any significant thought, shown in such phrases as 'suprema lealtad', 'insuperable hazaña', 'proeza sin nombre', 'suprema gloria' and 'tremenda hazaña', which remain at that simple triumphalist level.[36] Antonio's sonnet VIII appears to start in a

---

36 The text of the second sonnet of 'Blasón de España' in *Horas de Oro* (Valladolid: Biblioteca Nueva, 1938), is as follows:

similar direction also: the rhetoric of the first three verses ('varona fuerte', 'afincas') suggests the fundamental identification of Spaniards with their native land, which no betrayal to outside interests can suborn. The image of Spain as a 'varona fuerte' almost certainly made its way into this poem through the influence of poster art, or graphic art generally, in

---

> General Moscardó: Guzmán el Bueno
> el supremo lealtad el mundo llama.
> Mas hoy tiene la lengua de la Fama
> de Guzmán el Mejor el aire lleno.
>
> Insuperable hazaña — se decía —
> los muros de Tarifa contemplaron.
> Y para nunca más volver pasaron
> aquel hombre y la España de aquel día.
>
> Maravillosamente desmentido
> fue tal decir. A la asombrada Historia
> tu proeza sin nombre desengaña.
>
> Hoy fue más grande que el ayer ha sido.
> No faltó España a la suprema gloria,
> ni otro Guzmán a la tremenda hazaña.

Since I have disagreed with other critics for having separated Antonio's two sonnets, Manuel's other sonnet, under the composite title 'Blasón de España', is included here for reference. It precedes 'General Moscardó ...' in the edition published in 1938, each being given the numbers I and II respectively:

> Las piedras del Alcázar de Toledo —
> piedras preciosas hoy — vieron un día
> al César, cuyo sol no se ponía,
> poner al mundo admiración y miedo.
>
> Sillares para el templo de la Fama,
> palacio militar, a su grandeza
> el arte dio la línea de belleza
> que una vez más desdibujó la llama.
>
> Hoy, ante su magnífica ruina,
> honor universal, sol en la Historia,
> puro blasón del español denuedo,
>
> canta una voz de gesta peregrina:
> '¡Mirad, mirad cómo rezuman gloria
> las piedras del Alcázar de Toledo!'

(I am grateful to Professor Gordon Brotherston, who originally provided me with the text of Manuel's civic sonnets in *Horas de Oro*.)

the Republic of the Civil War. Use of the figure of the heroic woman in these posters or pictures was very popular and owed some of its inspiration to the art of the French Revolution. In the Spanish Pavilion at the Universal Exhibition held in Paris in 1937 the Spanish Republic was represented in relief sculpture by Ricardo Boix as a strong half-naked woman.[37] Carmen Grimau has commented on 'La clara tendencia a la masculinización de la silueta de la mujer' in Republican posters.[38] However, in many of them the physical womanly form is also very noticeable, both in the 'active service' posters as well as more understandably in posters dealing, say, with the evacuation of Madrid or other protective measures. Machado's sonnet VIII brings together softer, emotional images with a picture of Spain's invincible integrity.

A Republican poster by Bardasano, nearer to Machado's poem in its complexity, shows two soldiers with bayonet and machine gun, ready for attack, while above them is a figure of a woman with an olive branch shaped like a laurel of victory.[39] This poster is unusual because women were either depicted as being associated with peace (the dove of peace, the vulnerable, naked female form) or with the determined march to victory, but not with both at the same time. In a fashion similar in some respects to the Bardasano poster, and to the sketch by Ramón Gaya that we mentioned in chapter 4, Antonio's sonnet creates a tension between the ideas of firmness and forgiveness: this latter begins to be expressed in verse 4 of the poem. Its framework is largely religious: verses 4-14 are in the form of a prayer for mercy and redemption. Allied to the poem's general religious sensibility is the depiction that it gives of Spain's care for her treacherous errant son's redemption, rather than her sadness at being a 'juguete de traición', as she was portrayed in sonnet VII. The ethical concern of the prayer is a manifestation of Spain's firmness of purpose (described in the first three verses of sonnet VIII). Machado's gloss on Negrín's words ('al vencedor lo hace el vencido') helps to place sonnet VIII

---

[37] See Rafael Pérez Contel, *Artistas en Valencia*, 2 vols (Valencia: Conselleria de Cultura, Educació i Ciéncia de la Generalitat Valenciana, 1986), II, 555.

[38] *El cartel republicano en la Guerra Civil* (Madrid: Cátedra, 1979), 215.

[39] See Josep Termes, *op. cit.*, 149.

in a light that clearly illustrates the importance of its ethical preoccupation: 'Al vencedor lo hace, en efecto, el éticamente vencido, el que se adelanta a su derrota con el convencimiento de merecerla', Machado had commented.[40] The ethically defeated 'otro Conde Don Julián' in sonnet VIII is not in that position just because of his treachery, but because Machado maintains the prayer for him at a dignified level of ethical concern throughout. The section of the famous ballad 'En Ceuta está don Julián' ('Madre España, ¡ay de ti! / en el mundo tan nombrada') may have inspired the allegory of the Machado sonnet. The ending of another 'Don Julián' ballad may also have suggested the banishment and death in the sonnet:

> ¡Qué mal consejo que diste,
> oh maldito don Julián!
> ¡Maldito fuera aquel día
> en que te fuiste a engendrar!
> más valiera que, en nasciendo,
> te lanzaran en la mar.

The remedy invoked by Machado, however, belies its seemingly straightforward rhetoric, since it involves all the underlying agony of a mother's prayer for her son, whereby Machado underpins the tragedy of the Civil War; and where the balladeer was content to employ crude invective (and Manuel Machado, bland hyperbole) Antonio invoked the ideas of remorse and redemption. In the context of Machado's words about poetry and the war (that poets 'contribuyen a espiritualizar la guerra') we can see how in this bipartite poem Antonio depicts Spain as drawing ethical strength from the sorrow that she experiences at the betrayal by her son. The spiritual element in Sonnet VIII is not necessarily that Spain is a 'madre santa' and addresses a 'Dios de bondades', but that the prayer itself encompasses the ethical dilemma of the inextricable claims of love (here, maternal) and of judgement of wrongdoing.

---

40 Macrì does not include Machado's piece on Negrín, which appeared in *La Vanguardia* of 25 June 1938, in his edition of the *La Vanguardia* articles (IV, 2435-93). Macrì also gives an incorrect speculative date ('07/8-1938') for the portion of the article of 25 June that he reproduces. For the text on Negrín see Antonio Fernández Ferrer, *ed. cit.*, II, 199-200.

Sonnet 9

A LÍSTER

Jefe en los ejércitos del Ebro

> Tu carta — oh noble corazón en vela,
> español indomable, puño fuerte —,
> tu carta, heroico Líster, me consuela
> de esta, que pesa en mí, carne de muerte.
>
> Fragores en tu carta me han llegado
> de lucha santa sobre el campo ibero;
> también mi corazón ha despertado
> entre olores de pólvora y romero.
>
> Donde anuncia marina caracola
> que llega el Ebro, y en la peña fría
> donde brota esa rúbrica española,
>
> de monte a mar, esta palabra mía:
> 'Si mi pluma valiera tu pistola
> de capitán, contento moriría'.

The final sonnet, addressed to Colonel Enrique Líster, contains comments on the Battle of the Ebro, which began at the end of July 1938. Antonio Sánchez Barbudo has recalled that *Hora de España* was running two or three months late, which explains why Machado could refer to this last great battle of the Civil War in the June edition of *Hora de España*.[41] His recurring thoughts of the war years are expressed in this sonnet: the territorial integrity of Spain, the integrity, nobility and heroism of the Republic and its cause, its sacredness even, the indomitable nature of its resistance, and the close alliance of artists and intellectuals with the war effort. Although entitled 'A Líster', and ostensibly constructed around an apparently simple reply to a letter from Líster, the subtitle also suggests that this is a public poem addressed to all Spaniards. It is no casual coincidence that Machado concentrated his poetic powers on the crucial figure of Líster and on this decisive event in the Republic's history: the Battle of the Ebro was the Republic's last supreme military effort to prevent its slow asphyxia.[42] Within the poem's intimate structure of 'tu' and 'mi', Machado is able to

---

41 *Los poemas*, 465.
42 See Jackson, *op. cit.*, 454.

suggest Líster's military and exemplary value for the hard-pressed Republic, and especially its intellectual and artistic *retaguardia*, represented by the poet. Indeed both protagonists in the sonnet act out representative roles as partners in the alliance of 'armas y letras', upon which the Republic had set such great hopes. Linked to this political point is the idea that in the Battle of the Ebro the Republic is fighting for Spain: Líster is the 'español indomable'; the 'lucha santa sobre el campo ibero', as well as its immediate meaning, may also refer to Machado's (and the Republic's) view that the Republic is fighting to preserve Spanish soil against foreign invasion, with 'sobre' meaning the equivalent of 'en torno a'.

In a conceptually complex, though simply expressed image, Machado links the idea of his own artistic testimony with the image of the Ebro, the river of Iberia, as the signature of Spain (the *rúbrica* or typical flourish of the Spanish signature). Machado also uses a variation on the phrase 'doy mi palabra' to witness the signature of the Ebro river as testimony to the integrity of Spain, both nationalist and Republican. Later, in *La Vanguardia*, Machado also used a writing metaphor for the Battle of the Ebro: 'España ... ha adelantado el pecho, para pasar el Ebro, y escribir a su margen la más gloriosa gesta de su historia' (IV, 2482). In this metaphor he links the act of creative writing with heroic witness in battle. Machado traces the path of the river through both parts of a divided Spain, from the 'peña fría' of the province of Santander to the 'marina caracola' of the province of Valencia, and wishes his pledge to be heard at the river's beginning and end, and therefore throughout the whole of Spain. There is also present, in the images of the conch shell announcing the arrival of the Ebro at the Mediterranean coast and the river's flourish written on the parchment of Spain, a strong suggestion of the regal sovereignty, not of any monarch, but of the Spanish State itself (with Líster as one of its heroic and vigilant captains). In the sonnet there is more than one reminiscence of the Spanish Golden Age: the references to heroism and nobility, to the 'lucha santa', to the 'olores de pólvora', the Gongorine hyperbaton of verse 4, and the penultimate verse recalling Garcilaso's famous 'tomando ora la espada, ora la pluma'. Leopoldo de Luis, in his interesting and lengthy analysis of this sonnet, makes the point that Machado's reference to the 'pistola de capitán' highlights it as an arm for personal use, akin to the captain's sword of former times.[43]

These reminiscences of the Renaissance include a rhetorical convention (made necessary by the subventions which patronage offered to art), within which this sonnet situates itself, only to turn it upside down: the dedication of a poem to a person of noble birth. Líster practised the trade of stone-mason before the war; now, because of his work during it he has become part of the new aristocracy of what Machado called 'los mejores'. Therefore in the first verse he is invoked as a 'noble corazón'. Hence while the phrase 'puño fuerte' in the second verse may refer to the socialist salute of the clenched fist or to the physical means by which Líster gained his livelihood, it is also linked to the nobility of spirit which he has earned by his tireless vigil and work as a 'puño fuerte' for the Republic (both phrases, 'noble corazón' and 'puño fuerte', are enclosed within the same set of dashes).[44] Indeed, with these reminiscences of the Renaissance, is it an over-interpretation to suggest that they, and the form of the sonnet itself, contain a subliminal message to the intellectuals of Britain and France (and Italy), reminding them of an aspect of the cultural heritage that the three civilizations share: the cultivation of the Renaissance sonnet? Machado's choice of such a conservative poetic form as the sonnet points to the possibility of a political interpretation.

The references to 'carne de muerte' and 'contento moriría' turn this sonnet into an artistic last will and testament. Machado's valedictory contribution is to attest to the geographical integrity of Spain. The poet increasingly commented in the last months of the war that Spain was not just a recent product of political settlements, such as emerged

---

[43] *Antonio Machado, ejemplo y lección* (Madrid: Sociedad General Española de Librería, 1975), 138.

[44] Machado's poem *Voz de España*, subtitled *A los intelectuales de la Rusia soviética* and dated 'octubre 1937' (II, 834), also uses the idea of a new nobility and sanctity based on manual work rather than on the tradition of authority and power:

¡Oh Rusia, noble Rusia, santa Rusia,
cien voces noble y santa
desde que roto el báculo y el cetro,
empuñas el martillo y la guadaña! (II, 834)

from post-Napoleonic or post-World-War arrangements in Europe, but a country perfectly defined by its history, geography and culture. In this sonnet, and in the others, there are several references to the mountains and the seas of Spain, expressed in sonnet VII in the image of Spain as 'ancha lira, hacia el mar, entre dos mares'. In the sonnet to Líster the invocation of the poet's solemn word intended to ring out all over Spain ('de monte a mar, esta palabra mía') conjoins the double integrity of artistic commitment (the 'word') with an equally ringing belief in Spain's inalienable sovereign rights, based on her geography, history and culture.[45]

With Líster's vigilant example, Machado's own commitment seems to find new life. In the poem he talks of an awakening to a renewed awareness of the struggle for the integrity of Spain: Líster's letter has meant that, 'también', Machado's own poetic sensibilities have been called up to the battlefront. This is, of course, a reminder of Machado's description of culture in an earlier number of *Hora de España* as 'el humano tesoro de conciencia vigilante' (IV, 2317). In the sonnet Líster is described not as a 'capitán en velo' (as he could have been without detriment to the metre) but a 'corazón': a word that, in Machado's verse, has many connotations with creativity. It should also be noted that, on receiving Líster's letter, Machado himself then writes that 'también mi corazón ha despertado': he too has had a renewed cultural awakening by reading what Líster has written. Líster is thus incorporated into the work of culture, in a kind of semiotic way, as a poet/writer who by conjuring up the smells and sounds of war can influence the level of commitment of others. It is unlikely, of course, that

---

[45] See the last paragraphs of Machado's *La Vanguardia* article of 10 November 1938, especially the following: 'España no es una invención de las cancillerías europeas, la resultante de un tratado de paz más o menos inepto. Lleva siglos de vida propia perfectamente definida por su raza, por su lengua, por su geografía, por su historia, por su aportación a la cultura universal' (IV, 2487). Machado, as we saw in his 'Apuntes' in *La Guerra*, was also fond of the image of Spain as an 'ancho promontorio de Europa' to suggest its physical, geographical importance for the Continent (and also its strategic importance as an ally or enemy of Britain and France): see especially his 'Glosario de los 13 Fines de la Guerra' (IV, 2287). As regards the 'ancha lira': is it too fanciful to imagine the land and boundaries of Spain giving the lyre its shape (with Valencia and Barcelona at the top of the lyre) while the great rivers of Spain represent the strings?

Machado needed Líster's example to reinforce his own commitment. It was the threat to Spain's territorial integrity that spurred him on. He made this comment in an interview given a few months after the Líster poem:

> Jamás ... he trabajdo tanto como ahora. De ser un espectador de la política he pasado bruscamente a ser un actor apasionado. Y el motivo que me ha hecho, a mis años, saltar a este plano ha sido el de la invasión de mi patria. ¡España, mi España, a punto de ser convertida en una colonia italiana o alemana ... ! La sola posibilidad de hecho semejante hace vibrar todos mis nervios y conduce mi pluma sobre las cuartillas, despertando energías insospechadas y rebeldías que creía apagadas para siempre.
>
> (IV, 2280)

In the poetic economy of this sonnet, however, where the personal example of Líster is every bit as important as his military strategy, Machado writes that the 'olores de pólvora' in Líster's letter have called the poet to a sense of his duty to witness, to record, and to remember. The phrase 'olores de ... romero' in all probability refers to the rosemary plant as an ancient emblem of fidelity and remembrance. In verses 10 and 11 the recurring Machado image of the water springing from the rock — expressed as 'en la peña fría / donde brota esa rúbrica española' — also suggests the miracle of resurrection in the midst of sterility and death (and which was still abundantly evident some months later, in the interview just quoted). There is, too, in the sequential references to 'olores de pólvora' and '[olores de] romero' an implied analogy of death ('pólvora') and resurrection ('romero'). The action of the wind in 'Caminos' of *Campos de Castilla*, 'levantando en rosados torbellinos / el polvo de la tierra', uses the same idea as the sonnet, where the dust of death is quickened by the poet's awakening to the scent of rosemary. So, in the early poem the dust appears to rise from the dead, through the poet's consciousness of its pink colour, representing human life.

In the *Hora de España* article on the sonnets of José Bergamín Machado described the sonnet as 'esa tardía flor de la escolástica' (IV, 2405), and in choosing the sonnet form for virtually half of his poems published during the Civil War, he is working with a form widely practised in Renaissance Europe. Commenting on Hitler and Mussolini in the September 1937 issue of *Hora de España*, he wrote: 'Ellos no invocan la abrumadora tradición de cultura de sus grandes pueblos respectivos: la declaran superflua' (IV, 2217). Is Machado himself invoking in the very form of these sonnets the 'abrumadora tradición de cultura' of Renaissance Europe and declaring that it is not at all 'superflua'? He had already published three sonnet sequences in *Nuevas canciones* (1924), so it is difficult to decide on the degree of deliberate choice involved where his Civil-War sonnets are concerned. The gap of fourteen years from *Nuevas canciones* could imply a definite, considered return to the sonnet form, especially taking into account that this is the largest of his four sonnet groupings and that these last sonnets are within the context of a total publication of twenty-two poems throughout the Civil War (II, 822-36). If the proportion of nine sonnets out of twenty-two poems published by Machado throughout the Civil War seems high, this is confirmed by another balance of proportions within *Hora de España* itself: here, a total of thirty-four sonnets (or quasi-sonnet forms) were published in the twenty-three numbers, Machado's nine being the largest contribution of a single poet. (J. M. Quiroga Plá and José Bergamín follow closely, with seven each.) Four of Bergamín's sonnets — the sequence 'Europa y el caracol' in *Hora de España*, XXIII, 1938 — are concerned with the blend of appeasement and belligerence in Europe's political climate at that time. Manuel Machado was also to publish in his volume *Horas de Oro* (1938) eight sonnets on civic themes, including the two ('Blasón de España') commented on earlier. One of these eight sonnets was included in the *Corona de sonetos*, published in 1939 in honour of José Antonio.

The small corner occupied by the sonnet form in the house of culture of Civil-War Spain has yet to be investigated in detail. In global terms Serge Salaün has counted four hundred and fourteen sonnets out of a total of eight thousand five hundred poems discovered, in his massive trawl of poems on the Republican side;[46] one hundred and nine of these sonnets were written by a single poet, Pedro Luis de Gálvez.[47] Salaün,

---

46 *La poesía de la guerra de España* (Madrid: Castalia, 1985), 209.
47 See Salaün, *op. cit.*, 337. Apart from distorting the sonnet statistics on the Republican side, Gálvez is also an example of the difficulty of assigning likely relationships between poets, verse forms and politics. Born

observing that the sonnet form remained steadily in favour throughout the war, comments in another study:

> Cette forme de contrainte et de rigueur maximales pour une expressivité également maximale semble avoir joui d'un grand prestige, peut-être parce que la structuration du langage impliquait parallèlement une organization supérieure du monde, sans pour autant négliger les aspects sensibles.[48]

Salaün's statistics (produced ten years after the above quotation) do not quite bear out the position of 'great prestige' that he assigns to the sonnet during the Civil War, but his comment usefully brings to the fore the ideas of order and

---

in 1880, Gálvez led a wild bohemian life in Madrid, becoming one of the most outrageous literary figures of his generation. The judgment of the encyclopaedias, that he was an excellent sonneteer, seems correct, on the evidence of the writings that he was able or willing to publish. His book of poems *Negro y azul* (Madrid: Editorial Rubén Darío, 1930) certainly demonstrates his versatility and his command of the sonnet form. An anarchist during the Civil War, he put his experience as a sonneteer to excellent use in sonnets such as those dedicated to Cipriano Mera and Enrique Líster, from which the quotations that follow are their first quatrains. The sudden, arresting portrayal of each man, the use of broken and end-stopped lines that achieve utter simplicity and immediacy of impact, amply demonstrate Gálvez's mastery of the sonnet:

[To Mera]

> Todo es en este hombre pensamiento.
> Nunca se ha confiado del acaso:
> antes de dar el paso, mide el paso;
> sabe elegir la fecha y el momento.

[To Líster]

> Voluntarioso genio. Es una fiera.
> Arremete al contrario a descubierto.
> Le es igual quedar vivo o quedar muerto.
> El que hay de morir, ese, [sic] que muera.

These extracts are from his *Sonetos de la Guerra (Primera serie)* (Valencia: Socorro Rojo de España, 1938), a publication that is only fifteen pages long, containing just thirteen sonnets. (It is in the Biblioteca Nacional, Madrid.) The vicissitudes of the Civil War may have prevented any other publication in book form. Pedro Luis de Gálvez was executed in Madrid on 20 April 1940.

48 'L'expression poétique pendant la guerre d'Espagne', in *Espagne/Écrivains*, ed. Marc Hanrez, *op. cit.*, 112.

control associated with the sonnet.[49] The implication, as we have seen especially in Machado's 'Amanecer en Valencia', is that if the representatives of the Republic can moderate their thoughts and emotions in this form, then so can the Republic itself in the sphere of politics. Manuel Azaña in his Civil-War speech in Madrid drew together these two strands — of discipline in language and in politics — when citing (doubtless with more hope than certainty) the example for Republican Spain of Madrid's recovery of her equilibrium after the initial shock of the rebellion: 'desde que empezó el asedio [of Madrid] no se ha vuelto a decir una sola palabra excesiva ni hacer un gesto inelegante[:] ese mismo fenómeno maravilloso se ha operado en las filas y en los cuadros de los combatientes'.[50]

On the nationalist side, if we take the *Antología poética del alzamiento. 1936-1939*[51] as a very rough guide, we find that out of a total of seventy-nine poems in the book, eight are hendecasyllabic sonnets, together with two quasi-sonnet forms (one of them a French translation of the other). Four of the traditional sonnets are by Manuel Machado. What is interesting from the point of view of the position enjoyed by the sonnet is that the book begins with one of Manuel's sonnets, and ends with one of the quasi-sonnet forms. In this case, at least, the sonnet has been given a position of prominence in the overall scheme. Dionisio Ridruejo published twenty-three sonnets on aspects of the war. They seem muted and detached, however, including the 'Soneto a Franco' (which may have been a contributory factor to his being omitted from the *Antología poética del alzamiento*). If his sonnet 'En la muerte de Antonio Machado' of that same series is notable for its courage (by the very fact of its publication in 1940) that sonnet's tercets give a good indication of the almost neutral tone of the series as a whole:

---

49 Three unpublished political sonnets by Pedro Salinas, dated 1938, attacking the policies of Neville Chamberlain, have recently come to light. See John Crispin, 'Tres sonetos satíricos inéditos de Pedro Salinas', *Ínsula*, DXL (1991), 9 and 11. Written in the style of Quevedo's satirical sonnets, they would appear to be a highly unusual addition to the exploitation of the sonnet form during the Civil War.

50 *Los españoles en guerra*, 83.

51 (Cadiz: Ediciones Establecimientos Cerón y Librería Cervantes, 1939).

Hoy, cerrado el rencor en la alegría,
al cumplir el volumen de su gloria,
con un ala de fiel melancolía,

trae España tu muerte hacia su historia
y hace hierro de amor tu poesía,
vengando de ti mismo tu memoria.[52]

The sonnet to Líster demonstrates how Machado could endow this classical, conservative poetic form with the potential of a political intrument by suggesting through its form and content that this particular poet is speaking for a pluralist, democratic Republic, the fruit of the alliance of worker, soldier, artist and intellectual. His description in May 1938 of the Republic's government at the time of the outbreak of the Civil War as 'unos cuantos hombres de buena fe, nada extremistas, nada revolucionarios' (IV, 2442) is part of Machado's moderate, pluralist outlook. In Machado's hands these sonnets also become flexible instruments to propose dialogue, conciliation and pardon, yet resistance to the end, if need be. ('No olvidamos que un ejército en orden de combate se parece a un poema' [IV, 2273], he wrote during the Battle of the Ebro.) The dark moments of the child's death and the mother's anguish, of Machado's sadness at the betrayal of Spain to foreign invasion, and at his definitive separation from Guiomar, are counterbalanced by positive resonances: he proclaims the sovereignty of Spain, his affection for the arts of peace, and his enduring faith in nature as a bearer of hope and harmony.

The image projected throughout the poems is that of a people pursuing the peaceful paths of dialogue and the daily tasks of life, who are under mortal threat from the anonymous and unfeeling militarism of the war machine, within and outside Spain. In these Civil-War sonnets, however, the human circumstances of the conflict that produce sadness and anguish are more than compensated for by the poet's reflections on the 'noble corazón en vela' of those who suffer and strive for the renewal of life. This description does not apply only to Líster (although the words just quoted are in the poem dedicated to him). The *huertanos* of Valencia, the olive workers of Andalusia, the mother of the dying child, Spain herself, seen as

---

52 *Poesía en armas* (Barcelona: Ediciones Jerarquía, 1940).

the mother of all her children, are also vigilant, or capable of vigilance, trying to save, or, given the circumstances of the war, to salvage the integrity and identity of Spaniards themselves, threatened by an invisible invasion, hidden under the guise of a civil war. The last phrase of these sonnets, 'contento moriría', although expressed conditionally, is nevertheless an expression of contentment in the face of death. While the use of the conditional courteously concedes the primacy of importance to Líster, Machado has already let it be known in the previous four verses of the sonnet that his own word will ring out across Spain: there is no suggestion of a faint heart or a shortage of breath on Machado's part. These sonnets, therefore, outlive the war: they are in some ways, to quote the first five words of sonnet I, 'más fuerte que la guerra' because the poet's 'corazón en vela' has seen — and heard — beyond the destructive path of the war to the essential integrity of Spain, to her cultural and social sufficiency, and hence to her inevitable renewal.

CHAPTER 6

'Iniquidades envainadas'
Machado's Writings in *La Vanguardia* (1938-1939)

Machado published twenty-eight articles in the Barcelona daily newspaper *La Vanguardia* between 27 March 1938 and 6 January 1939.[1] Nearly all of them appear to have been written specifically for the newspaper, the bulk of them being made up of a series of twenty, under the title *Desde el mirador de la guerra*. (To be exact, the series has nineteen with this title, and one called '*Atalaya*. Desde el mirador de la contienda'.) Of the remaining eight pieces some, such as 'A los voluntarios extranjeros' of 29 October and 'Antonio Machado habla del 7 de noviembre' (this latter not much more than one hundred and fifty words long) were composed for special occasions or anniversaries. The article of 23 November is a transcription of Machado's radio broadcast on *La Voz de España*. In the *La Vanguardia* articles Machado wrote the first three before adopting the *Mirador* title (the first of these begins on 3 May). Therefore, of the remaining twenty-five articles in *La Vanguardia*, twenty were published under the title *Desde el mirador de la guerra* (with the one exception noted).

Only four of the twenty-eight *La Vanguardia* articles approach the same stylistic format as the *Mairena* pieces of 1936 and of *Hora de España*. None, for instance, comes near the miscellaneous form of the first article in *Hora de España*, with its eighteen sections. Two of the *La Vanguardia* articles (the first, of 27 March and also that of 25 September) contain

---

1 The fullest and most correct listing (but not a complete set) of the *La Vanguardia* articles of Machado may be found in Antonio Fernández Ferrer, *ed. cit.*, 235-36. Macrì includes twenty-five of the articles in Vol. IV of *Poesía y prosa*: missing are Machado's contributions for 19 July, 8 November and 6 January 1939. The best edition is by Monique Alonso, *ed. cit.*, which contains all twenty-eight articles.

eight sections each, while the contributions of 1 September and 6 October contain six each. As for the remaining articles, we have already noted that the *La Vanguardia* pieces are generally more discursive in form, with long paragraphs and a more contemporary commentary or political analysis, with special emphasis on British politics, conservative governments in general, and the policy of non-intervention in the Spanish Civil War. Machado was evidently responding to events as they happened, reading about them, perhaps, in the very same newspaper in which his own article was being published. The tone of these articles is sometimes one of exasperation at the folly of the conservative politicians of Britain (and of France, to a lesser extent), but also, as we shall examine in relation to the use of the *mirador* metaphor, that of one who is taking a clear-sighted view of the issues facing Europe at that time. Therefore, the liberal discourse — of dialogue, doubt, questioning, humorous scepticism — which is the hallmark of much of the *Mairena* series, is more often abandoned in the *La Vanguardia* writings, in favour of the certainty that springs from the sufficiency of one's convictions, especially when faced with the evident inadequacies of one's opponents'. Seeking the clearest vision possible is a long standing concern of Machado's.[2] His reference in *Galerías* (Poem LXXXVIII) to the poetic task of articulating 'unas pocas palabras verdaderas' strikes out early in this direction. Machado's work as a whole can also be described in terms of his search for 'creencias últimas' (IV, 2338): basic, irreducible beliefs that have been cleared of all the clutter and accumulated conventions that cloud the vision. It was doubtless these elements of clarity and simplicity that attracted him to nature, as his aphoristic comment in *Juan de Mairena* (1936) illustrates: 'Es en la soledad campesina donde el hombre deja de vivir entre espejos' (IV, 2017). (The aphoristic mode of expression itself is a clearing away of linguistic elements that obstruct clarity of vision.) Machado's instincts for clarity and simplicity, therefore, were admirably suited to the newspaper medium, even though he had to adjust his field of vision from the clarity that he had achieved in his writings set

---

[2] See Rodrigo Álvarez Molina, *Variaciones sobre Antonio Machado* (Madrid: Ínsula, 1973), especially chapter IV: 'Ver y mirar: verbos caracterizadores de la poesía de Antonio Machado' (65-86).

in provincial locations (Soria, Baeza, Mairena's classroom) to the world stage of international politics.

In the *La Vanguardia* articles Machado's tone hardens perceptibly, as he expresses his contempt for what he sees as the trickery and cowardice of the conservative politicians of Britain and France. Machado's angry response to the insurrection was not confined to the pages of *La Vanguardia*: Rodríguez Puértolas and Pérez Herrero, as we have noted, give examples of his 'tono airado' from many other texts, in which, they comment (although we might take issue with their choice of adjective) that Machado 'se vuelve violento como nunca antes'.[3] Yet it is true to say that, as a proportion within the four main elements of Machado's Civil-War writings — his articles in *Hora de España*, his poems, the *La Vanguardia* articles, and his letters and other occasional pieces — the contributions to the Barcelona newspaper display more than any other element the exasperation that he felt at the development of European politics. And as the seemingly insuperable march of events drove the Republic to defeat, the tone of Machado's articles in the autumn and winter of 1938 becomes even more strident and outspoken. To ascribe the following 'ideíca', as he calls it, to Neville Chamberlain after his visits of appeasement to Hitler in Munich in September, betokens a degree of exasperation with official British policy that comes close to despair, and hence is less rational in its assessment of that policy: 'Su ingenio inagotable había tenido una *ideíca* más: ¡Hay que salvar al fascio por encima de todo! ¡Que se hunda Inglaterra, pero que se salve la City!' (IV, 2477).[4] The effect of the prolonged application of Chamberlain's appeasement stance might have led in part to these results, but to depict Chamberlain as part of an international fascist conspiracy is outlandish, unless a cartoon effect of sketchy exaggeration is intended here. Machado also always uses the words 'cancillerías' and 'City' negatively (as synecdoches, in his view, for hypocritical negotiations between governments and for plutocratic financial dealings). Coupled with the idea of clearsightedness in these articles is that of the unmasking of

---

3 *Ed. cit.*, 25.

4 Macrì reads 'ideíta' (unitalicized) for '*ideíca*', which is in *La Vanguardia*, 6 October 1938, 3.

appearances. Machado's attempt to expose what he sees as the 'iniquidades ... envainadas' (IV, 2459), of British politics particularly, is perhaps the most important *leitmotif* of the *La Vanguardia* articles as a whole. Machado's attitude to 'los jefes de las naciones desvergonzadamente imperiales' (IV, 2447), that is, Germany and Italy, is utterly dismissive, while recognizing that they have a formidable military power and a political astuteness, which latter he sees as lamentably lacking in the political leadership of Britain and France.

The beginning of Machado's series in *La Vanguardia* coincided with important events at home and in Britain and France. The Republic's western front had been breached in March and nationalist forces reached the sea at Vinaroz (Valencia) two or three weeks after the first article of 27 March, cutting in two what remained of the beleaguered Republic. Pablo de Azcárate recorded in his diary a meeting with the Republic's Prime Minister Negrín in Paris on 14 March 1938, who informed him bluntly of the situation on the ground as follows: 'Respecto de España situación malísima; desbandada en el frente y derrumbamiento moral en el gobierno y la retaguardia'.[5] Nine days after the date of Machado's first article Churchill wrote: 'Another act of the Spanish tragedy is drawing to its close. The advance of General Franco's three corps attacking on a broad front, and the increasing demoralization of the Republican forces, must, in the absence of some miraculous recovery, be decisive'.[6] In February 1938 Anthony Eden had resigned as British Foreign Secretary and been replaced by Lord Halifax, whose views on appeasement were at one with those of Chamberlain.[7] In France, Leon Blum's Popular Front government gave way in April to the more conservative régime of Edward Daladier. According to Sabina de la Cruz, *La*

---

5 *Op. cit.*, 357.

6 Winston S. Churchill, *Step by Step* (London: Thornton Butterworth, 1939), 227.

7 Eden later wrote in his *Memoirs*: 'At the outbreak of the Spanish civil war, I had no political sympathy with either side ... As the war progressed, however, I became more concerned lest the insurgents should win, because the foreign powers backing them were a menace to peace. From the early months of 1937, if I had had to choose, I would have preferred a Government victory', *Facing the Dictators* (London: Cassell, 1962), 441.

Vanguardia acquired much greater importance, 'Al trasladarse el gobierno a Barcelona a finales de octubre de 1937', when the newspaper 'fue convertida en el portavoz de Negrín'.[8] At the outset of his first article of what was to become the *Desde el mirador de la guerra* series (3 May) Machado explains to his readers in what ways their experience of the Spanish Civil War might help them to see more clearly the important issues in contemporary European politics — and by implication the meaning of their own civil war. Effectively, Machado writes, there are very large principles and strategies at stake in the Spanish conflict, issues that transcend not only Spanish but European politics, because the fascist threat and the response of the conservative government in Britain, and of the French government, reveal moral and political attitudes that have wide-ranging ethical as well as practical reverberations. As Machado remarks at the beginning of the piece: if they did not dig deeply into the reasons for conflict, '¿qué razón habría para que los llamados intelectuales tuvieran una labor específicamente suya que realizar en tiempos de guerra?' (IV, 2441).

These, then, were the very pressing reasons for bringing Machado, by far the best known of all the living artists and writers in Spain, before a much larger Spanish public than *Hora de España* could ever command. The medium of a large-circulation daily newspaper, the more restricted academic background of such an audience, were factors that had pertained in the years from 1934 to 1936 during the first *Mairena* series. Yet these articles in *Diario de Madrid* and *El Sol* are not very different either in form or content from those of *Hora de España*, with the important exception of the way that the Civil War had entered the latter writings and played its part, as we have commented upon in earlier chapters. The *La Vanguardia* articles, however, after a beginning that seemed not much more than a contemporary version of the *Mairena* formula, in the first article of 27 March 1938, immediately afterwards strike out in a different direction, both in style and

---

8 'Una carta inédita de Antonio Machado', in *Antonio Machado, hoy*, I, 404-13. This article also gives an interesting account of some of the very difficult conditions under which Machado had to work, in Barcelona, during the last year of the Civil War.

substance. The fact that Machado persevered with the longer discursive style until the end of the *La Vanguardia* series on 6 January 1939 serves to demonstrate that the new stylistic format was almost certainly a conscious choice on his part.[9]

Allied to this change of style is a change of perspective, or rather a change to a specific perspective: Europe seen from the vantage point of the Civil War. It is unlikely that those readers of *Hora de España* who were committed to the cause of the Republic would have needed Machado to remind them of the political issues arising from the war that were relevant to pre-World-War Europe. Hence the articles in *Hora de España* are more concerned with general philosophical issues of war and peace than with the strategies of European *realpolitik*, such as appeasement and rearmament. The *La Vanguardia* articles, on the other hand, very quickly become tailored to the need to explain to a newspaper readership what the current issues were, in terms of the position and condition of the five Great Powers in Europe, and of the League of Nations in Geneva. The cultural climate throughout the Republic before and during the

---

9   The publication of the letter referred to in the previous note raises an important question as to whether the copy sent by Machado to *La Vanguardia* was accurately reproduced by the newspaper. In the letter (dated 22 November 1938) Machado complained to a high-ranking friend in the Ministry of Defence that 'Los trabajos que escribí para ser radiados y que, probablemente, venían ya plagados de incorrecciones de las máquinas del Ministerio, se han publicado con gran aditamento de erratas, confusiones de líneas, etc.' and he asked 'si pudiéramos evitar el *sabotage*, más o menos consciente, pero indudable de mis artículos' (*art. cit.*, 413). José Machado, who as Antonio's amanuensis would have known his views on correct copy intimately, wrote of his brother's inveterate horror of printing mistakes and tells us that he read his proofs from the bottom up (*op. cit.*, 82). Notwithstanding this aversion, Machado's use of the word *sabotage* has prompted Sabina de la Cruz to interpret it as a reference to 'una "quinta columna" que operara desde dentro de los propios talleres del portavoz oficial ... esa "quinta columna" que se infiltraba en todos los organismos sociales y minaba los esfuerzos de la retaguardia, colaborando eficazmente con el ejército franquista, ya a punto de dar la embestida final a la Barcelona republicana' (*art. cit.*, 406-07). While the theory that Machado's articles were sabotaged by a fifth column seems highly improbable, it would be advisable in the light of the publication of this letter to devote a detailed, line-by-line study to Machado's articles, as they appeared in *La Vanguardia* itself, at least for the months of November, December and January of 1938-39.

Civil War had been leading, with varying success, to a rapprochement between the intelligentsia and those without much formal education (the *Misiones Pedagógicas* of pre-1936, and the various *misiones culturales* that were formed in the wake of the coup). As a reminder of the cultural conditions that prevailed in Valencia during its period as political capital of the Republic, a climate that in all probability made Machado's *La Vanguardia* articles a logical and indeed necessary outcome of these conditions, it is worthwhile quoting at length Ricardo Blasco's description of what it was like:

> Nunca se insistirá bastante en exponer detalles de cómo era la vida cultural entonces. Algo bullente, inmediato, directo; no una actividad de cénaculo o minoría. No había periódico, por modesto que fuese e incluso si se imprimía en el frente, que no tuviera versos o relatos 'literarios' nacidos de la más inmediata realidad. No había acto, partidista o no, en el que no hubiese algún escritor que interviniese. Las 'milicias de la cultura' estaban en todas partes alfabetizando y era algo que 'se veía'. Los 'intelectuales' no eran dioses de un Olimpo. No eran hombres divorciados de sus semejantes.[10]

In such an atmosphere, apart, perhaps, from its activist 'missionary' aspects, Machado the 'humilde profesor de un instituto rural', as he describes himself in 'Poema de un día', would surely have felt at home; but equally he would have sensed the opportunity for clarification and exposure of the issues arising from the Civil War. Moving into the area of political writing, though doubtless an expediency required by the times, was also a natural culmination of Machado's view of culture as a contribution to humanity shared by all who keep a critical yet benevolent vigil over their own affairs and the sayings and doings of others. Such inclusivism — it is potentially too enriching a view of humanity to be called populism — gave Machado an opportunity to discourse on the culture of politics which without the advent of the Civil War he would almost certainly never have had. Since for Machado the

---

[10] Quoted in M. Aznar Soler, *Pensamiento literario y compromiso antifascista*, 214. Juan Gil-Albert also recalls his impressions of Valencia, after the Government's move to Madrid, as of 'una urbe promiscua, en la que codeaban los ministros con los milicianos, la gente de la huerta con los funcionarios madrileños', *op. cit.*, 204.

richest culture is the product of the alert consciousness, his political commentaries in *La Vanguardia* — the scrutiny of some aspects of European politics of the late 1930s — offered him a particularly fruitful source for his cultural endeavours. Although his ideas on culture allowed for a much wider involvement in human affairs than through the conventional realm of art alone, Machado's articles in *La Vanguardia* are his first — and last — sustained entry into the political area. If the fact that Machado left such an incursion so late seems contradictory, given his views on culture, it may well be that he was still reluctant, right up to the last desperate year of the Civil War, to engage in political writing. In this regard we should remember the remarks he made in his 'Discurso a las Juventudes Socialistas Unificadas' recalling his own lack of any serious political formation (IV, 2191). The doom-laden course of the Civil War presented both the dire need and the immediate opportunity to engage in political writing. In the *La Vanguardia* articles, therefore, Machado was able to find a niche for his quietist, contemplative view of culture within the more immediate need for a contemporary analysis of the virtues and vices of the European politics of his day. We should not forget, too, that the 'continuing political moderation of Negrín's Government' made Machado an attractive contributor to the wider forum of the daily newspaper.[11]

The picture of the two senior European democracies that Machado paints is not an attractive one: even the barbaric militarism of the Axis powers is made to seem innocently singleminded compared to his portrayal of the hypocrisy, especially of British conservative policy in Europe at the time. Machado's attempted clarification of the role of contemporary conservative politics *vis-à-vis* the Axis powers and the Spanish Civil War, together with the associated if opposite ideas of probity and integrity in political and national affairs, constitute the single dominant thread that connects all the *La Vanguardia* articles. To achieve such expressive clarity in the midst of the turmoil not merely of Europe, but especially of the conflagration

---

11 Hugh Thomas, *The Spanish Civil War* (Harmondsworth: Penguin Books, 1971), 635. Thomas is referring here to late 1937, but his remark is also true of the Spring of 1938, when Negrín's moderate Thirteen Points were published.

that was ravaging Spain, is one of the measures of the importance of Machado's contribution to the culture of his time. The phrase that Machado uses in his first *Mirador* article could serve as a fitting epigraph to the whole series: 'la hoguera de la guerra nos ilumina'.

Aware, perhaps, that in his new role as a writer on political matters he would be venturing into largely uncharted territory (most of his earlier published political comments were isolated articles or small sections of his pieces in *Hora de España*), the title of Machado's first article appears to be both a disclaimer and a justification for the style of the *Mairena* writings: 'Notas inactuales a la manera de Juan de Mairena'. It is a startling opening to what was to become a newspaper column dominated by commentary on the European crisis. (Machado was later to remark in one of the *Mirador* articles that he was 'el primer convencido de mi insignificancia como escritor político' [IV, 2452].) With its eight short sections, this first article looks back to the 1936 *Juan de Mairena* and to the *Hora de España* series, the latter still ongoing, as Machado opens the series in the breezy, humorous style of Mairena (although Hitler and Chamberlain are also mentioned). José Machado has recalled that, whatever the long-term future of Spain, Antonio saw the Republic's present position during the summer of 1938 as 'completamente perdido'.[12] The predominantly sombre tone that emerges and then predominates in the *La Vanguardia* articles reflects this view, although naturally not in any overt way. In his first article, however, using the editorial plural he states: 'nos declaramos al margen de la historia y de la novela, meros hombres de fantasía'. Yet Machado did not attempt to evade the issues of the day by this declaration. He goes on to explain in the second section what he meant by recommending to his students (in Mairena's voice) that they should not worry about being 'inactuales'. The best of what appears to be innovative, he writes, will turn out not to be new at all in the end, and he uses a paradoxical axiom to illustrate his point: 'Quien avanza hacia atrás, huye hacia adelante'. Lest this should sound like a recipe for traditionalism, Mairena goes on to warn against allowing reactionaries to have a monopoly on the past: in other words, the Mairena dialectic between past and

---

12 *Op. cit.*, 145.

present will continue, even though the emphasis in *La Vanguardia* will be on contemporary features of European society.

Continuing with the *Mairena* format in *La Vanguardia* gave Machado a valuable perspective on the issues of the day, because it enabled him to range more widely over the human condition and helped him to set the Spanish Civil War into a context based on meditations on the nature of Western civilization as well as on current political policies and strategies. While there was no strict need for Machado to invent a character (or continue with him) in order to put forward views on the remote origins of the current European crisis (Machado sometimes advances them in his own voice also), the characterization of Mairena gave a special perspective to Machado's writings. Mairena's fictional vital statistics (1865-1909) meant that he was only ten years older than Machado, but his early death makes his perspective on things essentially from the nineteenth century, with the exception of a few prophecies, which normally do not go beyond the end of the First World War. In *La Vanguardia*, therefore, Machado uses two slices of history, which comprise Mairena's lifetime and his own. In common with other liberal thinkers Machado saw the causes of the current European crisis in the ungenerous settlement of the Treaty of Versailles, but also saw (usually through the eyes of Mairena) the roots of the First World War in the individualism of a nineteenth-century Europe, which was given scientific and intellectual credence by Darwin and Nietszche.

We have very briefly commented earlier on the rhetorical resources used by Machado in the different articles written contemporaneously for *Hora de España* and *La Vanguardia*. The April and 3 May contributions to these respective publications are striking examples of their differences in rhetoric. Both articles deal in whole or in part with the idea of the perspective that war can give on the peace that has been lost. In *Hora de España* the idea is only adumbrated, in the gnomic style that Machado often used for Mairena's *apuntes*: 'Lo más terrible de la guerra es que, desde ella, se ve la paz, la paz que se ha perdido, como algo más terrible todavía' (IV, 2380). The *La Vanguardia* article greatly expands this idea, expressing it more positively and from an overtly socialist point of view. (The publication of Negrín's Thirteen Points, two days earlier, setting out the terms for an armistice and adumbrating a future liberal Constitution for Spain, may have contributed to this more positive tone. Indeed, Machado's new series, 'Desde el mirador de la guerra', begun with this article of 3 May, may have been timed to coincide with their publication.) This piece begins with the assertion that war can be a positive experience, 'un gran avivador de conciencias adormiladas', and that even the vigilant consciousness can find 'nuevos motivos de reflexión' in it (IV, 2440). Machado uses the same paradox in both *Hora de España* and *La Vanguardia* to support his thesis that in the social conditions prevailing in Western Europe there is little to choose between war and peace. In the newspaper the idea is expressed as 'lo que llamamos guerra es, para muchos hombres, un mal menor, una guerra menor, una tregua de esa monstruosa contienda que llamamos *la paz*' (IV, 2241). In *Hora de España* the paradox is similarly expressed, where Mairena imagines the response to war of either the rank and file soldier or those who make up the *retaguardia*: 'dejadme gozar de este mal menor, de esta guerra menor, de esta tregua de la paz que llamamos *la guerra*' (IV, 2380). Machado's italicizing of the last two words in both quotations strongly suggests that, in the form of this emphasis, he was basically making the same point, even though in *La Vanguardia* the peace is condemned as inhuman, while in *Hora de España* it is only 'más terrible' than the war that has replaced it.

The most important difference between the pieces, reflected in their respective lengths, comes in the following humorously ironic sentence in *La Vanguardia*, written in the style of Mairena: 'Os pondré un ejemplo impresionante para ilustrar mi tesis y elevarla al alcance de vuestras cortas luces' (IV, 2441). Machado is at once able to mitigate the severe and solemn tone of the article and yet use the *Mairena* format to comment directly on contemporary affairs. (It begins: 'así hablaría hoy Juan de Mairena a sus alumnos'.) Another important difference is reflected in the title of the *Hora de España* piece: 'Notas y recuerdos de Juan de Mairena'. The cryptic notes and axioms of numbers IX and X of this piece (they are given numbers, in Roman, by Machado) are expanded upon in the *La Vanguardia* article by the long example that Machado gives, to illustrate the paradox that the Civil War in Spain is preferable to the peace prevailing in the rest of Europe. A comparison of sections IX and X with the *La Vanguardia* piece allows us another interesting insight into the creative process in the late Machado writings, if we assume that the *Hora de España* article was written first. Here we see the notes of IX and X, compressed and paradoxical, consigned firstly (in the fiction of the *Mairena* creation) to the privacy of the teacher's notebook, to be later expounded and expanded by Machado, speaking for Mairena, in a Barcelona daily newspaper.

And what of the content of Machado's paradox, illustrated in *La Vanguardia*, that war may sometimes be preferable to peace? Machado's analysis of the peace in Western Europe is frankly socialist, as we said, although it falls short of proposing any solution beyond that of loyalty to the government of the *Frente Popular*, who entertained in peacetime 'la usuraria pretensión de que el pan y la cultura estuvieran un poco al alcance del pueblo' (IV, 2442). The analysis of the peace in Europe is that men, unemployed and lacking basic sustenance during the peace, will be found the necessities and even the luxuries of life in war ('a cambio de sus vidas — claro está —', Mairena adds). This analysis is made, using the metaphor of the vantage point or balcony of the war to see clearly what in peacetime is obscured. Mairena repeats his cherished axiom here — 'toda visión requiere distancia' — suggesting that seeing the paradoxical distance between the conditions of war and those of peace in the plutocracies of Europe (material comforts in the former, misery in the latter) is necessary in order to be able to make a just appraisal of either.

After examining 'la paz circundante' in Europe, Machado turns in Part Two of the 3 May article to the question of the Spanish Civil War. As in the first half, the military and diplomatic peace of Europe is considered a charade: in this instance Britain and France's sacrifice of Spain to the search for a peace at all costs, that is in any event doomed to failure because of the singleminded belligerence of Germany and Italy. Machado touches here on a point that he was to repeat often in his *La Vanguardia* articles, namely that the policy of non-intervention in Spain being pursued by Britain and France was not only unworthy of the issues of justice and freedom at stake but was also bad *Realpolitik*, because it could not give those countries the avoidance of war that they had hoped for through supporting the charade of non-intervention by foreign powers in Spain. Many of the *mirador* articles examine the politics of the British conservative government of Neville Chamberlain *vis-à-vis* the situation in Europe. (French foreign policy is also considered, but Machado recognizes that this is dependent on British politics 'y por ella conducida a remolque' [IV, 2451].) From the point of view of *Realpolitik*, the rhetorical resource used by Machado is a simple one: to stress repeatedly that the British policy of non-intervention (and appeasement generally) will put itself and its empire in jeopardy, because if Britain allows Spain to fall to Germany then Britain will probably lose Gibraltar, 'la más importante llave de su Imperio' (IV, 2452), as a guardian of the route to the Middle and Far East. (Machado comments that France would equally be threatened by Mallorca if it fell under German control.) It is, however, the moral and ethical questions that lie beneath the surface of European social and foreign policies (especially the latter, with particular regard to British conservative politics) that most concern Machado. It is to these issues that we must now turn our attention, in order to attempt to understand the main thrust of Machado's writings for *La Vanguardia*.

In the first place, while aware of the military might of Germany in particular (Mairena's remarks on 'la Alemania prusianizada de nuestros días' as 'la gran maestra de la guerra' in the first *La Vanguardia* article), Machado is dismissive of any complexity in the ideology or political ambitions of the Axis powers. As he commented on the latter's so-called non-intervention in Spain: 'los dos invasores de nuestra patria se quitarán pronto la careta, que ya les sofoca, y aparecerán sus rostros aborrecibles, sin sorpresa de nadie' (IV, 2487). In his brief article of 19 July they are classified as '[Potencias] descaradamente enemigas del género humano'.[13] In other words, the motives and ambitions of the Axis powers are seen as simple and straightforward, if being no less terrifying for such simplicity. Commenting on Germany in his article of 23 November, Machado wrote: 'fiel a sí misma, no gusta de invocar

---

13   *La Vanguardia*, 19 July 1938, 3. (This article is not in Macrì.)

sus razones, mientras pueda inventar alguna sinrazón monstruosa que aterre al mundo' (IV, 2488). Germany's simple, even childish delight in the martial arts, her irreflective militarism is wittily captured by Machado in one of the pieces in *Hora de España* (July 1938) that was contemporaneous with the *La Vanguardia* writings. In the dream related by Mairena in section VI of that same issue he is accused of neglecting his gymnastic classes at a time when Europe is getting ready for war, or, as the voice of his accuser puts it, of neglecting 'el cuidado de fortalecer y agilitar los músculos, de henchir los pulmones a tiempo y compás, de marchar y contramarchar, de erguirse y *encuclillarse*, etc., etc.' (IV, 2389). Incidentally, it is fascinating to see the convergence of thought, and language to some extent, between Azaña and Machado in this regard, when the former in his Madrid speech of November 1937 addressed the Republic's politicians and military in these terms: 'a ninguno de nosotros, ni a estos soldados que están aquí conmigo, nos parece la guerra una fiesta alegre, ni un deporte, ni un entretenimiento de adultos vigorosos'.[14] Since for Machado German militarism exists at a simple, uncomplicated level, and is not in any case amenable to the kind of classroom debate that followed Mairena's account of his dream, Machado does not devote much space to it in the *La Vanguardia* articles. Likewise 'la Italia de Mussolini' is given very little attention, the Italian leader being dismissed in the first *La Vanguardia* article with devastating cartoon-like effect as 'ese faquín endiosado'. One further quotation may suffice to illustrate Machado's view of the simple alternatives that the Axis threat posed for the rest of Europe: 'sin duda el eje Roma-Berlín y el mismo Berlín y la misma Roma, en cuanto focos de ambición imperial, no tienen otra razón de existencia que la aspiración al aniquilamiento de sus rivales' (IV, 2454). The historian David Thomson has suggested that Nazi power achieved its success because politicians simply could not come to terms with the use of such singleminded ferocity and cynicism: 'Statesmen acclimatized to the more rational, humane ways of democracy found — with a few notable exceptions — such a movement

---

[14] *Los españoles en guerra*, 92.

virtually incomprehensible'.[15] From his *mirador de la guerra* Machado was able to see clearly the implications of Nazi expansionism for Europe and the world at large.

Machado's view of Soviet Russia in the *La Vanguardia* articles is expressed as a straightforward belief that the Russian Revolution and its aftermath has been a decisive force, or at least potential, for good in the circumstances of Europe between the wars. The half-dozen or so references to Russia in *La Vanguardia* are all warmly complimentary, praising Moscow (and by antonomasia, Russia) as 'el faro único de la historia que hoy puede iluminar el camino del futuro' (IV, 2447). If there is any caution in Machado's appraisal of post-revolutionary Russia it lies in such references as this to the Soviet experience: that it is the only *present* ('hoy') solution to the social and political problems of Europe in conflict, in particular to prevent the policy of appeasement (and the associated policy of non-intervention) from destroying the democracies in Europe. Machado had already commented in detail on what he saw as the new constructive phase of Soviet policy during the course of 'Sobre la Rusia actual' of September 1937 in *Hora de España*: its renunciation of any claim to an empire beyond its own boundaries and its concentration on improving the standard of living within the Union (a reference to Stalin's victorious policy of 'Socialism in a single country'). With Germany and Italy seeking to create new empires, and Britain and France already in possession of established ones, it is interesting that Machado did not return to his point about Soviet Russia's lack of imperial ambitions in the *La Vanguardia* articles, especially in view of the Spanish Republic's own renunciation of empire in Negrín's Thirteen Points. Did he entertain reservations about the Soviet system? In general he preferred to dwell on what he saw as the essentially Christian qualities of the Russian people. With his 'Carta a David Vigodsky' of April 1937, the September article of the same year, 'Sobre la Rusia actual', and his poem subtitled 'A

---

15 *Europe since Napoleon* (London: Penguin Books, 1970), 758. In his letter of resignation to the King in 1940, Chamberlain wrote: 'I do not feel that I have anything to reproach myself for in my attempts to avoid the present war, which might well have succeeded if they had not come up against the insatiate and inhuman ambitions of a fanatic'; in H. Montgomery Hyde, *Neville Chamberlain* (London: Weidenfeld and Nicolson, 1976), 178.

los intelectuales de la Rusia soviética', dated 'octubre, 1937' (II, 834), Machado's most important reflections on Russia's role in Europe were completed. His strategy in *La Vanguardia* was aimed more at convincing public opinion of the dangers that would follow if Spain became subject to Axis control.

From the evidence of his comments on Stalin in the August 1938 issue of *Hora de España* it is plain that Machado admired Stalin's clarity of thought on the purpose of social revolution. Here, Machado confines himself to discussing a meeting between H. G. Wells and Stalin in 1934, of which he had just read an account; that is, before the Stalinist purges of 1935-1938. Wells, 'a fuer de buen anglo-sajón', comes across as an essentially conservative figure, fearful of any social revolution or upheaval, while Stalin is praised for his 'claridad de ideas'. One can see Machado weighing up the pros and cons of democracy and 'la dictadura del proletariado' in the piece and finding that in the present circumstances liberal democrats cannot hold the ring with the great dictators. A sentence in the 23 November article of *La Vanguardia* on political parties, although mildly expressed and hedged around with the qualification that not all debate is sterile, leads one to conclude that, understandably enough in the Spanish Republic's then parlous state, Machado saw the current political debate of the bourgeois democracies as contributory to the muddying of the waters, which has helped a conservative leadership to hide its own sectional interests and promote these, rather than the public good. Machado wrote in *La Vanguardia*: 'La lucha política, en cuanto tiene de artificial, les ayuda [the governments of Britain and France], porque las verdades más obvias se debilitan en boca de quienes las usan exclusivamente como arma polémica. Sin duda, la verdad no deja de serlo cuando se convierte en proyectil o coincide con intereses de partido, pero pierde para los neutros toda eficacia suasoria' (IV, 2489). Post-revolutionary Russia, on the other hand, is undergoing 'la experiencia maravillosa de una nueva forma de convivencia humana' (IV, 2447).

The dictatorships, therefore, of whatever hue, with their closed systems and patent objectives, were of less interest to Machado than the murky waters of the two great Western European democracies, Britain above all. Machado's singling out of Britain's key role, during 1938 and beyond, is a distinctive feature of the clarity of vision that he sought in the *La Vanguardia* articles, and it will be necessary to deal with this aspect of the articles in detail. But firstly, what of France? Although France is referred to on many occasions, the references are usually tagged on as lesser accompaniments to more searching comments on the British position. Machado's article of 23 November is the only one that devotes any substantial space exclusively to the position of France or French opinion in itself. The subtitle of the article — *La gran tolvanera* — and the reference to a 'cortina de humo' in its first sentence suggests that the main object of Machado's scrutiny is to be what he called in his last article of 6 January 1939 the 'aguas turbias' of British diplomatic politics. In fact both Britain and France are linked equally in the first three paragraphs of the five that constitute the article. There is perhaps some logic in this since the main subject of these paragraphs is the Treaty of Versailles, and how the controversy about its provisions is now distracting public opinion in Britain and France from what Machado argues is the much more pressing question of the huge strategic advantage being gained by the Axis powers through their involvement in the Spanish Civil War.

The article's penultimate paragraph deals almost exclusively with the state of French public opinion on the Spanish Civil War. Using the analogy of the Dreyfus affair Machado expresses his conviction that public opinion favourable to the cause of the Republic is lying hidden waiting to be mobilized by 'la voz inconfundible del *acusador*, voz de timbre francés, que es, como tantas veces lo ha sido, el timbre de lo universal humano' (IV, 2490). Machado's hopes for a rallying of French public opinion, however, are overshadowed in the piece by what he calls 'el mingo de la incomprensión': an article by an unnamed French writer in praise of the *valores eternos* of traditional Spain.[16] Machado quotes in French from the article, content to let the original phrases display for themselves their 'insuperable stolidez', as he terms it. With other French phrases that he uses in these articles and the negative context in which they are quoted, we must conclude that, for Machado, using the French

---

16 Rodríguez Puértolas and Pérez Herrero identify the writer as Paul Claudel (*ed. cit.*, 418).

language during the last year of the Civil War generally evoked less than positive resonances. Machado's use of French phrases in connection with what he sees as the feeble isolationism of France's response to the war in Spain and in the rest of Europe is just a very small but telling rhetorical resource to express his contempt for France's political leadership, which he describes in his last *La Vanguardia* article as being 'en manos de hombres mediocres'.[17] Thus, Machado describes the democracies' policy of appeasement of Hitler as 'una paz ... *'à outrance'* (IV, 2444); the threat of war, and the democracies' response to it, is called 'la guerra como *chantage*' (IV, 2474), and Negrín's radio speech of June 1938 is summarized as meaning 'cuando se lucha por la justicia ¿quién puede estar *au dessus de la mêlée?*'.[18] (Other negative resonances may be found in the description of the League of Nations as *'La Morgue'* [IV, 2474] and in his linking of the phrase *'enfant terrible'* with criticism of the German obsession with war [IV, 2456].) Even in the quotation expressing hope that the lone voice of the French accuser will rouse public opinion, the use of the italicized *acusador* suggests that with a positive resonance such as this Machado preferred the Spanish word, and in this case italicized it in order to link it in some way with Zola's famous accusatorial phrase. In any event it would seem that Machado could not place much reliance on this lone voice: the whole article is overshadowed at the end by what he calls the 'tiranía encubierta' of Chamberlain's government, which was of greater concern to Machado than either that voice or the right-wing romanticism of the writer whose phrases he had quoted with such contempt in his preceding paragraph.

We have seen Machado's expressed views about the general level of mediocrity of France's political leadership. Not so, with regard to Britain, Machado wrote in the same sentence: 'las de Inglaterra [her politics and diplomacy] — en cambio — han venido siendo hasta hace poco el patrimonio de una élite'.[19] Since Machado appears to use the word 'élite' approvingly in

---

17 *La Vanguardia*, 6 January 1939, 3. (This article is not in Macrì; further quotations will be taken from the newspaper itself.)

18 *La Vanguardia*, 25 June 1938, 3. (As we noted in chapter 5, the last section of this article is not in Macrì.)

19 *La Vanguardia*, 6 January 1939, 3.

this context, the phrase 'hasta hace poco' probably refers to the period prior to the premiership of Neville Chamberlain, who had assumed the post in 1937. Machado may also be referring to the appointment of Lord Halifax as British Foreign Secretary in February 1938. Both politicians, mentioned by name in the *La Vanguardia* articles, were determined non-interventionists in Europe generally, effectively abandoning the Spanish Republic to its fate. (Churchill's comment on Britain's foreign policy in 1938 was that 'Chamberlain ... forced Mr Eden's resignation and became, in fact if not in form, his own Foreign Secretary'.[20]) Chamberlain, in particular, is therefore an important target in the *La Vanguardia* writings for Machado's scrutiny, both of his motives and political attitudes. In the article of 25 June 1938 Machado quotes from verses of Milton's *Paradise Regained*, 'born to promote all truth, / All righteous things', as a contrast between the confident sense of mission of the English puritan tradition, implied in Milton's lines, and what Machado sees as the mean-spirited isolationism of the current British conservative leadership. Machado's response to this non-interventionist attitude is many-sided, but chiefly consists of an attempt to clarify issues that have been obscured by the conservative democracies of Britain and France, to bring them out into the light so that they may be seen in their true perspective. The abiding theme of the *La Vanguardia* articles is therefore the gap between appearance and reality in the non-intervention policies of these democracies, especially Britain, and the exposure of the contradictions, both ethical and practical, at the heart of this policy. The historian Dante A. Puzzo by implication endorses Machado's 'Searchlight on Britain' (to turn around the famous title of the Duchess of Atholl's book of that period) in his summary of Britain's role in the Civil War:

> The conclusion is inescapable that the defeat of the Spanish Republic must be attributed as much to British diplomacy from 1936 to 1939 as to German aircraft and Italian infantry. British influence in the determination of French policy toward Spain was decisive, in that of the United States, important.[21]

---

20 *Op. cit.*, 322.
21 *Spain and the Great Powers 1936-1941* (New York: Books for

In general terms, what most exercises Machado's attention concerning the current state of British government politics is that beneath a façade of smooth politeness British policy towards weaker nations can be just as brutal as the more openly aggressive rhetoric of Hitler and Mussolini. Lord Halifax probably epitomized for Machado the anti-progressive conservatism of the British aristocracy, with their attachment to obsolescent ways and unrepresentative political and social values. In an interview given in November of 1934 Machado had commented that 'todo lo que se defiende como un privilegio generalmente son valores muertos' (III, 1811). As a former pupil of the *Institución Libre de Enseñanza* there is no doubt that Machado would have retained something of his old school's affection for British society and institutions, especially its liberalism, which Machado sees as Britain's most important social legacy to the rest of humanity. However, the whimsical example of this legacy that he uses in *Hora de España* (IV, 2344-45), that of boxing (in other words, controlled violence), is a reminder of the critical distance that Machado kept from a society which pursued liberal values at home while maintaining an empire abroad. (Although Machado some months later called the British Empire 'un imperio civilizador' in his commentary on one of Negrín's Thirteen Points, he also interprets with approval Negrín's twelfth Point as meaning that 'España renuncia para siempre a toda ambición imperialista' [IV, 2285].)

To underline the veneer of civility and social respectability that conceals less pleasant realities, Machado in the first *Mirador* article describes the pact of non-intervention in Spain, using the English phrase 'un *gentlemen's agreement*'[22] (a phrase that had been coined some months earlier as a description of an understanding between Mussolini and the British government about the control of the Mediterranean). In the same sentence, however, Machado wonders whether the non-intervention

---

Libraries Press, 1972), 244.

22 The actual phrase used by Machado (or perhaps mistakenly transcribed by his editor) in this article of 3 May 1938 was 'un *gentlemen agreement*'. The phrase was more widely known as the 'Gentleman's Agreement', which was apparently the title given by Mussolini himself to the understanding that had been arrived at with Britain.

arrangement is not just 'un equilibrio entre fieras', where the appearance is suggested by the English word 'gentlemen' and the reality by the Spanish word 'fieras'. The vantage point of the Civil War, Machado implies, enables, (or should enable) Spaniards to see through to the reality of what British conservative policy means: the law of the jungle dressed up as a civilized agreement. Perhaps the most striking image in the *La Vanguardia* series is employed in the fifth *Mirador* article (12 June 1938) when Machado comments on the attitude of the Council of the League of Nations towards the Spanish Republic. Since Machado uses the original Shakespearian phrase 'honourable men' (IV, 2459) to describe the hypocrisy of some of its members, it is possible that he had the British government particularly in mind. Certainly the reference to 'la *no intervención*' in the paragraph that follows the English phrase points the finger at least equally at Britain and France. The image, drawing, perhaps, on the resources of poster art and of the political newspaper cartoon, evokes a stark and sombre picture: that of two or more gentlemen, one of whose gloved hands is helping to strangle the Spanish Republic, while the other points the way to the door of the League of Nations, which will legitimize the assassination. The paragraph merits quotation in full:

> La verdad es que ni Bruto era una buena persona ni pueden ser ejemplos de alta moral los hombres que con una mano, envuelta en el guante de la *no intervención*, ayudan a los estranguladores de la República legítima de España, y con la otra no menos enguantada nos indican la puerta de la Sociedad de las Naciones, en previsión del día en que, con los más inicuos hechos consumados, se consideren abolidos nuestros más legítimos derechos. (IV, 2459-60)

In a short single-sentence paragraph such as this (the penultimate of the 12 June article) Machado could compress in simple form a thick cluster of ideas and sensations. Here, for example, the peculiarly repugnant form of assassination associated with strangulation acts in some degree as an ignoble contrast with the assassination of Julius Caesar, mentioned in the previous paragraph. Now, there is also the idea that a nation is being assassinated, not just an individual, however representative, which magnifies the call for urgent action as well as stressing the enormity of the crime. The contrast between brutality and supposed civility has already been noted: here, the gloved hand softens the impact of the naked aggression on the conscience of the perpetrator, as well as suggesting the supposed gentility of the wearers. There is, too, the contrast often made in these articles between the high ideals of the League of Nations and the iniquity of its actions or omissions.

Hypocrisy is also in part the subject of the next *La Vanguardia* article (25 June 1938) when Mairena discourses on what he calls 'la hipocresía inglesa' (IV, 2464). The switch from the voice of Machado at the end of the 12 June article to that of Mairena at the beginning of this one means that the time framework has once again retreated to 1909 or before. The ideological climate is therefore less immediately contentious and the language is more ironic than the highly-charged description of the gentlemen stranglers in the last section of the previous article. This technique of shuffling the timeframes from Mairena's lifetime to Machado's belongs essentially to the *Hora de España* and *La Vanguardia* writings, although Machado had included some *Mairena póstumo* sections towards the end of *Juan de Mairena* (1936), sections that would have been composed amid the ferment of events in the late spring and early summer of 1936. While the removal of 1909 as a *terminus ad quem* obviously helped the contemporaneity of the writings, the change of temporal perspective also influences the way in which a particular issue, such as that of war and peace, is presented. Here, for example, where Machado had just written on a specific current event — the benign façade of the League of Nations acting as a cloak of legitimacy for the attempt to throttle the Spanish Republic — Mairena in the following section (the first section of the *Mirador* article of 25 June) reverts to a favoured general topic: the aggressive instincts of Western civilization. However, a new emphasis is now added, influenced, perhaps, by the previous section's contrast between civility and brutality: that this aggressiveness is hidden beneath the abstract technical competence, the routinely destructive technocracy of Western civilization. With Swiftian irony, initially masked by a blythe, matter-of-fact style, Mairena prophesies the result for Western society: 'El hombre sobradamente batallón de la civilización occidental va para buena persona, excelente padre de familia, que gana el pan cotidiano contribuyendo en la modesta medida de sus fuerzas al futuro aniquilamiento de la especie humana' (IV, 2463).

Such cool, even chilling irony is a good example of the way that Machado could use the eccentric, sometimes exaggerated expression of Mairena to demand a response from the reader. The sentence previous to the one just quoted also helps us realize the depth of understanding as well as the striking perspective that Machado sought, through continuing to use the wit and wisdom of his apocryphal creation: 'Cierto que esas máquinas [de guerra] serán mucho más destructoras que la quijada asnal que esgrimió Caín: pero no ha de haber más odio en el técnico que las ponga en movimiento que hubo en su constructor'. The sweep in the sentence from myth to modern technology, from the anguish of Cain's theocentric world to the dehumanized technocracy of modern society is in keeping with Mairena's pungent irony. The ideas of *otredad* and *diálogo*, of course, find expression in the creation of Mairena, but in seeking 'distancia para la visión' in the character of the apocryphal professor, Machado was also able to present ideas with a wider range of ironic reference than if he were to address us *voce propria*.

In the following section Mairena turns his thoughts specifically to the English and their ways. His remarks begin in a conciliatory mode, with the recognition that if British society is hypocritical, 'la hipocresía es la sombra de la virtud' (IV, 2464), and he is unsparing in his praise for Shakespeare and Milton. This is a good example of the way that Machado was able to alter the tone of an opinion, seeking refinements of it, from one piece of writing to the next. Here, the image of the gloved hand of the strangler of the Republic, more than likely aimed at British non-interventionist politics, is counteracted by Mairena's attempts to see the other side of the British character. Thus, in this case, 'la hipocresía inglesa es la sombra del puritanismo inglés'. Indeed, it would be tempting to describe all of Machado's writings as a process of rectification and refinement, a search for a judgement that was truer than the last one.

The quotation from Milton's *Paradise Regained* in this

section (Machado quotes two half verses in a single line: 'born to promote all truth, all righteous things') is Mairena's way of expressing his esteem for the seriousness of the British character. Machado's portrayal of Britain as an essentially sober if somewhat self-righteous nation may well be part of his rhetoric: a way of persuading Britain that she is indeed the friend of justice and righteousness. It is unlikely that Machado would have left unread the verses that follow his quotation from *Paradise Regained*. About eight lines later in the poem Jesus tells of how when younger he had aspired to overthrow the Roman yoke, and tyranny everywhere; this, says Jesus, he rejected because he

> Yet held it more humane, more heavn'ly, first
> By winning words to conquer willing hearts
> And make persuasion do the work of fear.

In effect these verses give us a picture of an aspect of Machado's own rhetoric in this piece, 'making persuasion do the work of fear'. Here, he appeals to the British character to be true to its better nature: the love of righteousness and straight dealing. If not, Mairena prophesies, Britain will lose her humanity and become a victim of the rapacious appetite that also lurks within her. The image Mairena uses is a variation on the human/animal contrast that Machado increasingly dwelt on in the Civil-War years, a meditation on images and ideas grouped around Darwinian notions applied to the human condition: whether the human being is, in Machado's words, an *animal batallón* subject to *fatalidades zoológicas*, whether peace is merely an *equilibrio de fieras* or whether, as he put it in *Hora de España* of September 1938, humankind 'puede permitirse el lujo de la animalidad que se llama amor al prójimo'. In this instance Machado appeals to the British sense of propriety when he has Mairena say: 'Si Inglaterra dejase algún día de ser puritana alguien diría: ya se quitó la careta. Yo diría, más bien, que se ha quitado el rostro, para mostrarnos la abominable jeta de pueblo de presa, de lo que algún día llamaremos, con expresión un tanto equívoca, pero irremediable: una potencia totalitaria.' In his gloss on one of Negrín's Thirteen Points Machado explains what he means by a 'pueblo de presa', and it is relevant to his view of Britain's responsibility towards Europe in Mairena's description just quoted. One of the main themes of

Machado's commentary on the Thirteen Points is that Spain's past contribution to world history entitles her present aspirations (as expressed in the Thirteen Points) to be respected and supported by the major powers. 'España', he writes, 'no ha conquistado nunca para sí misma, no ha sido nunca un pueblo de presa, como lo han sido otros muchos' (IV, 2286). To return to the *Mairena* quotation, we may paraphrase its political import as follows: if Britain abandons her sense of strict fair play *vis-à-vis* Europe she will lose her humane, liberal outlook, and join, or re-join, the ranks of the totalitarian powers. (Machado characterizes these latter by their foreign rather than domestic policy: the urge to dominate other nations by force.) Apart from the political implications of Mairena's image — that Britain can either pursue a policy of selfish isolation from Europe or use its high moral principles to contribute to a proper solution of Europe's problems — the image itself is interesting both for its rhetorical power and for the light it sheds on one of the ways that Machado used the *Mairena* format. The close juxtaposition in the image of the human face that hides an animal's snout gives it a surrealistic quality in addition to its Darwinian undertones. Machado is able here to use the nineteenth-/twentieth-century timeframe to bring together two disparate sources of rhetoric, the surreal and the naturalistic, in a highly compressed fashion.

In the following section Machado turns to the poetry of Pope, or as he more circumspectly puts it, to 'una degeneración suya', that is, to that type of writer 'a quien, no sabemos por qué, parece que siempre se le debe algo' (IV, 2464). Machado's attention is still directed towards this lack of magnanimity, not particularly here as a part of the British character, but as a quality that is especially out of place in time of war. His thrust is once more against the kind of self-centred isolationism that refers everything to a sense of petty grievance against others. Machado uses the unpleasant image of animal or insect secretion which not only stains others but drowns its originator in it: 'Este hombre segrega una cierta baba difusa que todo lo mancha, y en la cual es él mismo quien se anega' (IV, 2464-65). As we can readily see from this example, Machado's rhetoric within the same article could move swiftly between the poles of polemic and persuasion. He begins with the utterly deflating irony of Mairena's views on 'el hombre, en su aspecto de *Homo faber*', which is followed by the appeal to the best in British moral principles. There then follows the reference to the type of 'hombre pequeño, esquinado', with its suggestion of a spider's web of petty intrigue and backbiting. The article is rounded off with a rousing gloss on Negrín's June speech and is full of references to the ethical nature of the Republic's cause. The negative and positive resonances of the article as a whole are drawn together into Machado's final aphoristic phrase, which we have commented on earlier: 'cuando se lucha por la justicia, ¿quién puede estar *au dessus de la mêlée*?'.

Although always refusing publicly to accept the possibility of the Republic's military defeat, Machado turned increasingly during the time of the *La Vanguardia* articles to the idea of the importance of honourable conduct in either defeat or victory, as the latter became more remote with the passing of the months of 1938. With regard to Britain and France, Machado had despaired by the end of the series of what he saw as any honourable response by those countries to the Spanish conflict and the European crisis in general. In the last brief paragraph of the series he sees the stand against brute force taken by the Republic as the only hope for the future honour of Western Europe. Thus, Machado's remark in an earlier *La Vanguardia* article (10 November) that 'Chamberlain is an honourable man' (IV, 2486) uses the Shakespearian overtones to question whether the British Prime Minister was capable of making any decision based on ethical principles. In the sentences that follow the Shakespearian paraphrase Machado returns to his theme of the 'iniquidades envainadas' of the two Western European democracies, who keep their masks in place for fear of being found out as sympathizers with fascism. The relevant sentences are worth citing in the light of quotations from *Macbeth* in two of the *La Vanguardia* articles of the previous weeks (6 and 23 October):

> De los cuatro fingidos no intervencionistas, los dos invasores de nuestra patria se quitarán pronto la careta, que ya les sofoca, y aparecerán sus rostros aborrecibles, sin sorpresa de nadie. Las máscaras eran inútiles por demasiado transparentes. Los otros dos procurarán conservarlas, no por miedo a nosotros, sino a sus propias conciencias, quiero decir a sus propios pueblos, a quienes vienen engañando. Son estos mismos pueblos los que han de

arrancárselas. (IV, 2487)

While it would be too fanciful to read into these sentences any influence on Machado of a recent reading of *Macbeth*, the fact that much of Shakespeare's play deals with what one of the victims of duplicity in it (King Duncan) calls 'the mind's construction in the face', enables us to suggest some parallel between Machado's view of the play and of the contemporary European crisis. As we have already seen, even in *La Vanguardia* Machado continued to use analogies from literature to illustrate his articles. Although this was to some extent an inevitable outcome of his background, it also gave Machado a familiar base from which to move into what were for him the uncharted waters of political commentary. In *La Vanguardia* Machado's examples from literature seem to have been deliberately chosen, inasmuch as they seek to express ideas about the British character, either through observations on the writings themselves or on their authors. *Macbeth* is the artistic work that makes its presence felt most in Machado's Civil-War writings, featuring in his poetry, in *Hora de España* and in *La Vanguardia*. (He had also referred to the play on occasions in the 1936 edition of *Juan de Mairena*.) The play's description of the way that Macbeth wades deeper and deeper into blood, together with the stirrings of guilt and hallucination brought on by its shedding, must have impressed Machado as he saw the compromises of appeasement leading to a prolonged nightmare for Europe. More particularly, Machado saw the Shakespearian hero as having been morally defeated from the outset, and hence throughout the whole of the play, in spite of the strategic victories that appear to make his position impregnable. So it is with the insurgents and their allies, Machado wrote to María Luisa Carnelli on 19 November 1938: 'Porque ellos [nuestros adversarios] no pueden dudar de su propia vileza, están moralmente vencidos; y lo estarán en todos los sentidos de la palabra cuando refluya la ola de cinismo que hoy invade la vieja Europa' (IV, 2290). Remembering the reference to *Macbeth* in the final issue of *Hora de España* (which we examined in chapter 4) it would appear that Machado almost to the end clung to some hope of a redemption of democratic Europe, through its willingness sometime in the future to stand up and be counted.

In the article of 6 October, where Machado refers to Chamberlain's *ideíca* before going to Munich, he also quotes in English from *Macbeth*, to comment on what was doubtless a newspaper report that King George VI's mother, Queen Mary, had fainted in an ecstatic House of Commons on hearing Chamberlain's news that he had succeeded in persuading Mussolini to join a four-power conference at Munich. Machado comments: 'Hasta la reina María — *look to the lady* — se desmayó al oírlo'. One wonders how many of Machado's newspaper readers would have understood even the literal meaning of the Shakespearian phrase, let alone have any notion either of its provenance or context. The phrase is used by both Macduff and Banquo when Lady Macbeth faints, or appears to faint, on hearing Macbeth's description of how he has killed King Duncan's servants. Macduff's is the single sentence quoted by Machado, but Banquo adds six verses to the same command. Duncan's sons are also present, and fearing for their lives they agree to leave Scotland. It is easy to see why this scene within a scene from *Macbeth* (Act II, sc. iii) would have made an impression on Machado, particularly if he had been reading or re-reading it in the autumn of 1938. In the scene there is, following all his vacillations, the now outright cynicism of Macbeth, clothed in beautiful protestations of loyalty and love. There is also the ambiguity of Lady Macbeth's fainting fit: does she pretend to faint in order to draw attention away from Macbeth or, more interestingly, does she genuinely faint at the sight of the hypocritical monster that she has helped to create? Finally there is Banquo's speech, not dissimilar in tone to the Milton quotation used by Machado in the *La Vanguardia* article of 25 June: 'In the great hand of God I stand, and thence against the undivulg'd pretence I fight / of treasonous malice.' The contrast between Banquo's integrity and Machado's next description of Chamberlain is startling. They are the sentences that we had occasion to express reservations about earlier in this chapter: 'Su ingenio agotable había tenido una *ideíca* más: ¡Hay que salvar al fascio por encima de todo. Que se hunda Inglaterra, pero que se salve la City!' (IV, 2477). Did Machado envisage the House of Commons' pre-Munich scene in terms of the cynicism, weakness and the opposing virtue of moral integrity that were encapsulated in the little scene from

Shakespeare's play, from which he quoted? The scene from *Macbeth* records hypocrisy, ambiguity and lack of resolve, the qualities that Machado saw revealed in Chamberlain's character, heedless of the lessons of integrity that Shakespeare invests in the probity of a character such as Banquo.

Machado returns to *Macbeth* in the next-but-one *La Vanguardia* article (23 October 1938). The theme of this article, as of others in the series, is of the need for vigilance, both within the gates, and beyond the frontiers of Spain. In the article Machado contrasts the hypocrisy and bad faith of the proponents of non-intervention in Spain, with the ethical consistency of the Republic. Although Chamberlain is not mentioned by name in this piece, there are several references to a single unnamed person, which given the context of this and other articles can only refer to the British Prime Minister. Such a pseudo-anonymity is effective within the overall rhetoric of the piece, since one of the pictures conveyed in it is that of fear, pretence and calculation, in opposition to the consistent and open proclamation of 'valores éticos universales' (IV, 2482-83) by the representatives of the Spanish Republic both at Geneva and at the Battle of the Ebro. The last section of the article returns to the idea of the need for vigilance, especially with regard to an unnamed person, presumably the same one (that is, Chamberlain) mentioned earlier in the piece.

Almost the whole of the article's last paragraph uses analogies from *Macbeth* as a comparison between Macbeth and the anonymous person, that we assume to be Chamberlain. All parallels between Macbeth and Chamberlain result in the latter being portrayed in a much worse light than the gory protagonist of Shakespeare's play: 'en la brumosa Albión, hay alguien que no duerme, porque, como Macbeth, ha asesinado el sueño y no precisamente en su castillo de Escocia, sino en el corazón de la City' (IV, 2483).[23] Indeed, what Machado has done here in his portrayal of Chamberlain is to combine, in a compressed reference, the evil deeds of Macbeth, who in the play imagines himself as the one who 'does murder sleep', with the bad

---

[23] The text in *La Vanguardia* reads 'ha asesinado el sueño'. Monique Alonso (*op. cit.*, 401) follows this reading, but Rodríguez Puértolas and Pérez Herrero (*op. cit.*, 280) and Macrì have 'un sueño', a very suggestive reading, but one that is not authorized by the original edition.

conscience of Lady Macbeth (who cannot sleep). As the quotation shows, the blame is laid, however anonymously, at the door of the British Prime Minister. Machado uses the English word 'City' in a context that was wider than its merely financial ramifications; he drew a distinction between what he saw as the appearance of democracy and the reality of plutocracy in conservative Britain. In drawing a contrast between Macbeth's Scottish castle and the 'corazón de la City' he also wanted, perhaps, to draw a distinction between Macbeth's warrior-like courage and the counting-house mentality of Chamberlain. A few sentences before, Machado had praised the Republic's crossing of the Ebro as Spain's 'más gloriosa gesta de su historia'. As with the reference to 'los valores éticos universales' in the paragraph before the *Macbeth* paraphrase, the implication is that Chamberlain knows nothing of these imperatives. Incidentally, T. S. Eliot expressed similar sentiments in 1939, reflecting on the events of 1938, although he did not wish it to be taken as 'a criticism of the [British] government', when he wrote:

> Was our society, which had always been so assured of its superiority and rectitude, so confident of its unexamined premises, assembled round anything more permanent than a congeries of banks, insurance companies and industries, and had it any beliefs more essential than a belief in compound interest and the maintenance of dividends?[24]

'Por lo demás', Machado continues, 'sus brujas lo engañarán con la verdad, hasta el fin. Tampoco él ha de creer en el milagro del bosque semoviente, ni en el invulnerable ardimiento del hijo de la loba ... romana'. [The suspension points are Machado's]. This last phrase is probably linked to Macbeth's naive belief in his own invulnerability, following the witches' prophecy, but is here transferred to Mussolini. The preceding image, however, must have confounded most of Machado's *La Vanguardia* readers not familiar with *Macbeth*. The whole paragraph, indeed, with its sustained literary references would have been more suitable for *Hora de España*, except that Machado nearly always avoided 'raw' political analysis in that journal. There is

---

24 Quoted by Raymond Williams, *Culture and Society 1780-1950* (Harmondsworth: Penguin, 1966), 225.

no doubt, however, that the rhetorical wires of communication have become crossed here: how many of Machado's readers of this article in *La Vanguardia* could have picked up the significance of the reference to the trees that move in *Macbeth*? In the play these trees are soldiers carrying boughs as camouflage, and in Machado's piece they refer to the armed forces of Germany and Italy fighting covertly in Spain. In contrast with the foolish Macbeth, Machado implies, Chamberlain can easily see through the farcical camouflage of non-intervention in Spain, just as easily as he must surely be able to see through Mussolini's bluff and bluster. Chamberlain is not the type, Machado suggests, to believe, like Macbeth, in the seemingly miraculous prophecies of the witches, but in the end he will be morally defeated by his recognition of the falseness of his position: 'sus brujas lo engañarán con la verdad, hasta el fin ... que no lleva trazas de ser demasiado gallardo'. The piece finishes with another exhortation to keep a careful watch on this latter-day Macbeth, keeping out of his way, and making sure that any cry of alarm is loud enough to be heard across the Atlantic.

In this brief paragraph Machado uses rhetorical effects that are, in however faint a degree, reminiscent of a ballad technique and of his own 'La tierra de Alvargonzález' (which he had re-published during this same year, 1938). As in that ballad or *romancero* there are here similar supernatural and allegorical effects: witches, a miraculous wood, a fiery wolf. The 'pendiente' is not a natural slope, but 'la pendiente del crimen y del miedo'; the assassination is of a country's ideals; the cry of alarm is to be heard thousands of miles away. (The dark tone of the piece also has some similarities with much of the black, nightmarish atmosphere of many of the Republic's posters of the period.) All mention of politicians or politics is veiled either in anonymity or oblique references, such as 'alguien ... ha asesinado el sueño'. This has the effect of creating a sense of hidden menace, of an unknown hand at work in evil ways. The references to *Macbeth* tend to distance the piece from current political events, reminding readers that they are reading literary analogies. Indeed, Machado himself draws attention to the paragraph as a literary construct when he remarks at the end of the *Macbeth* analogy: 'No agotemos el símil'. Whether the piece, with its strong literary overtones, would have effectively communicated its contempt for the deceit of modern-day politics is debatable. It stands, however, as an example of the way that Machado blended ideas from Shakespeare with the primal, even primeval, sensibility of the ballad atmosphere in order to expose what he saw as the calculating hypocrisy of the conservative politicians of his day. Machado's examples from *Macbeth* demonstrate the way that his experience of the play's protagonist formed a sounding board for his meditations on the meaning of the the war. The example from *La Vanguardia* that we have just seen suggests a naive but dangerous Macbeth, a victim of the partial truths told him by the witches. The contrast is with the portrayal of a devious British politician, more a knave than a fool, but one who will finally succumb to defeat; in other words, failing as well as deserving to fail.

Hypocrisy, mean-spiritedness, lack of ethical principles: these are the charges in the *La Vanguardia* articles that Machado persistently levels against the politics of the leaders of the conservative democracies, qualities which he sees mostly personified in the figure of the British Prime Minister, Chamberlain. In the first article Machado refers to one of Chamberlain's remarks about not getting his fingers burnt in the Spanish Civil War, and suggests that there is something unmanly in that remark. There is, indeed, a series of references throughout these articles when Machado discusses the conservative democracies, that suggest a lack of manliness or even humanity on the part of their leaders: words such as *homúnculos*, *pigmeos*, *monstruoso*, *abominable* are used more than once in this connection. There are also, as we mentioned earlier, associated images from the animal world, especially the word *fieras*, to denote a hidden savagery beneath the political or diplomatic mask. Machado sums up the lack of enlightened ethics in the conservative democracies as follows: 'allí donde a la razón y a la moral se jubila, sólo la bestialidad conserva su empleo' (IV, 2451). This lapidary conclusion could serve as an epigraph for the way that Chamberlain, and conservative politics generally, are described in these articles. In his first article referred to earlier, Machado goes on to distinguish between the Prime Minister and the British people, described as 'un gran pueblo de varones' (IV, 2438). This point is also made on several occasions throughout the series: that the present political leadership in Britain has divorced itself from the people on the issue of intervention in Europe.[25] A consequence of such a false position, in Machado's view, is that the British conservative government (and the French) remain indecisive and give away advantages to the fascist powers because such governments are not supported by the people on European matters.[26]

The piece that Machado wrote for publication in *La Vanguardia* on 23 July, and also for delivery to a meeting in Paris to protest against the aerial bombing of the civilian areas of the Republic's major cities, is another very good example of the way that he sought to expose the civilized veneer of Western society, which hides the aggressive instincts underneath.

---

[25] Anthony Eden's personal private secretary, Oliver Harvey, had the following view of the Chamberlain government (excepting Eden himself): 'the Cabinet are far too right, both of the House of Commons and of the country'; quoted in Jill Edwards, *op. cit.*, 165. Denis Smyth, *Diplomacy and Strategy of Survival. British Policy and Franco's Spain, 1940-41* (Cambridge: Cambridge U. P., 1986), makes the same point in relation to the British Government: that they were 'almost all sympathetic to the Spanish Nationalist cause' (10). See also the note to his chapter 'Britain and the birth of Franco's Spain, 1936-39', 253. K. W. Watkins (*op. cit.*, 109) goes so far as to suggest that the Axis powers 'worked on the assumption that the continued existence of the Chamberlain administration would enable them to obtain what they desired'. William Laird Kleine-Ahlbrandt, *The Policy of Simmering. A Study of British Policy during the Spanish Civil War* (The Hague: Martinus Nijhoff, 1962), comments, in a wider context: 'In reality the British people were more pro-Republican than pro-Nationalist. Although savagery was by no means uncommon to both sides, under Franco it seemed to be more organized and deliberate. For this reason the image of Spanish democracy being eaten by the wolves of Fascism seemed to be generally accepted' (22).

[26] There is an interesting coincidence of views on these issues between Machado and Pandit Nehru, the latter writing of the situation as he saw it on 14 November 1938: 'The British Government has throughout played a reactionary role in Asia, Africa and Europe, and has given every encouragement to fascism and nazism. It has done so, curiously enough, even at the cost of endangering the security of the British Empire, so great was its fear of real democracy and its class sympathy with the leaders of fascism'; quoted in K. W. Watkins, *op. cit.*, 136. (Nehru visited Spain in 1938 to show his support for the Republic.)

Machado achieves this by a series of oppositions between what he calls 'nuestra retórica' and 'nuestras realidades efectivas' (IV, 2462). In the article he speaks of the need to 'mirar la verdad cara a cara' in order to lay bare the lies that conceal the monstrous truth about the Western civilization of his time, where preparations for war are dressed up as 'fecundas actividades de la paz', and where technocratic progress is in reality a regression to the level of jungle warfare, but without the curbs placed on it by technical limitations. In such a society the mutual nature of the family unit is not only insufficient to effect a change of direction but may actually contribute to its regression by a too-narrow definition of what may constitute 'un buen padre, un buen hijo, un buen esposo y hasta un excelente vecino' (IV, 2461), when a man may be regarded as such and yet go off to his work of dropping bombs on children, the sick, women and the aged.

At the end of the article Machado describes how he is writing the piece as the bombs drop on the roofs of Barcelona. The criticism of the inadequacy of family values in times like these seems to spell the end of the Krausist ideal of humanity for Machado. Krause (or in the Spanish context his adapter Julián Sanz del Río) had placed the family at the beginning, middle and end of the road to the perfection of humanity. ('Con la familia principia la historia, de ella se alimenta, mediante ella se continúa hoy, y con ella acabará en el ocaso de su vida terrena ... en su seno son preparados estos miembros para toda ulterior obra y función histórica', Sanz had written in 1860.[27]) The conditions pertaining in Spain in 1938 explain Machado's perception of the ever widening gap between what he sees as 'monstrous' and 'abominable' in human conduct (words that are used more than once in the article) and the kind of programme for peace that he had expounded nine months before in *Hora de España*.

Machado's articles of 14 and 22 May reflect on the similarities and differences between the causes of the 1914-18 War and the political situation of Europe in 1938. A key word in the first long paragraph of the 14 May article is contained in Machado's condemnation of the conservative democracies (or

---

[27] Krause/J. Sanz del Río, *Ideal de la humanidad para la vida* (Barcelona: Ediciones Orbis, 1985), 74.

rather their leaders: the 'esos hombres' of the following quotation): 'Lo verdaderamente monstruoso es que esos hombres sigan simulando echar sus viejas cuentas como si entre el año 14 y el año 38 de nuestro siglo no hubiese pasado nada sobre el mísero planeta que habitamos' (IV, 2445). The first half of this quotation will sound familiar to most students of Machado's poetry because he had used a similar expression just after the 1914-18 War in his highly political *Prólogo* to the 1919 edition of *Soledades. Galerías. Otros poemas*: 'Los defensores de una economía social definitivamente rota seguirán echando sus viejas cuentas, y soñarán con toda suerte de restauraciones' (III, 1603). Although separated by nearly twenty years, the basic idea in the two quotations is the same: that there can be no going back over old solutions to social ills because, as Machado goes on to say in the 1919 *Prólogo*: 'la vida ... se renueva o perece'. The significant difference, however, between the 1919 and the 1938 quotations is the word 'simulando', whereby Machado not only condemns the making of out-of-date calculations about society, but suggests that the present-day conservative politicians, while acting in the same way as of old, now hypocritically do not believe in what they profess. In the article of 14 May Machado imagines the conservative politicians of 1938 making the same patriotic speeches as in 1914 and using the same fatuous rhetoric as then. Machado's charge, however, against the current conservative leadership of democratic Western Europe is much more serious because, he implies, they have knowingly stood still at a time when their peoples have moved on to a more democratic and liberal stage of development. Such iniquity, knowingly hidden, represents both a social and moral bankruptcy, and hence is the chief target for Machado's censure throughout the *La Vanguardia* articles.

The remainder of the article of 14 May is taken up with nine numbered points in which Machado underlines the way that time has moved on since 1914-18, bringing with it liberal movements in Britain and France and a new creative and constructive phase to 'la gran Revolución rusa' (IV, 2447). These two observations are made in points 6 and 8, respectively, of the nine points, whose general import is that the leaders of the conservative democracies are out of touch with the progressive sentiments of their peoples. At the end of the article

Machado humorously refers to Negrín's famous *Trece Puntos*, which had been published just two weeks before Machado's article. Wall posters were made of the Thirteen Points and they therefore received extensive circulation. Machado did not need any lessons in the art of succinct communication but he may have been influenced sufficiently to use a similar headline technique. However, the sentence that he employs to introduce his points becomes highly significant, because each of the points begins with 'Que': a relative clause dependent on the introductory clause, which reads: 'Porque sus pueblos [Britain and France] saben y ellos mismos [the conservative leaders] no ignoran lo siguiente' (IV, 2446). Therefore, most of the nine accusations not only carry with them the charge that is made in the numbered point but also, simply by being prefaced in this way, the additional one of hypocrisy, because in it the conservative leadership is accused of continuing to practise what it knows to be wrong. Numbers 2, 6 and 8 also contain very brief commentaries by Machado, and hence are not governed entirely by the relative pronoun 'Que' at the beginning. Generally, however, linking the introductory clause in a direct grammatical way with the nine points does have a startling ethical effect on the light in which the conduct of the conservative leaders is seen. Without the introductory sentence they are merely fools; with it they are knaves as well.

Given the import of Machado's other remarks in *La Vanguardia* that we have examined, it is likely that he did indeed wish to portray them this way; the thrust of the nine points is part and parcel of the 'iniquidades envainadas' of the conservatism of the period that Machado continually attempts to expose throughout the series. But what about the phrase 'sus pueblos' in the governing clause? One of the effects of the link between the peoples and their governments is to suggest some degree of either complicity or at least complacency on the part of the former, when the emphasis was meant to be on the 'conciencia vigilante' of the ordinary people, who would not be fooled by a conservatism 'que deshonra a sus pueblos', as Machado goes on to say later in the piece. In using a headline technique Machado gave his argument greater visual force and hence made it more easily assimilated, but it seems evident that he was not fully in control of his material in this article, an unusual blemish which is most likely attributable to the pressures of the war.

In the following article (22 May) Machado takes his comparison between 1914 and 1938 a step further. It is another example of the 'sedimentary' process in Machado's thought, whereby an earlier idea is subjected to further reflection and refinement — a crucial part of the process of the development of culture, added to by a vigilant consciousness, or to quote yet again Machado's own description of the product and its process: 'aumentar en el mundo el humano tesoro de conciencia vigilante'. In this article Machado recalls his own personal attitude towards the First World War (he was approaching forty at its outbreak). Although hedged around with qualifications, Machado concedes the ethical superiority to the Allied cause in that war, based on their respect for treaties and the rights of peoples. The real contrast, however, is not between the *then* and *now* of British and French politics, although this acts as an important backdrop to Machado's assessment of the contemporary situation, but between the 'actuación hipócrita y perversa' (IV, 2449) of the proponents of Non-Intervention (Britain and France) at the League of Nations, and the cultured representations of the Spanish Republic, especially the contributions of the Republic's Foreign Minister, Álvarez del Vayo: 'como flecha trémula de conciencias adormiladas' (IV, 2449). Machado does not mention the word 'culture' in the article, but his description of culture quoted earlier in this paragraph underlies his portrayal of the speeches of Britain, France and the Spanish Republic. The British and French speeches are described as stale, predictable pieces of oratory that refuse any engagement with Álvarez del Vayo's speech. If culture for Machado is 'el *humano* tesoro' (our emphasis), then neither the British nor the French representative can make any contribution to it: both men are therefore described as 'homúnculos' (IV, 2449) in the piece.

The result of Machado's two-pronged attack in the article as a whole is that contemporary conservative politics stands condemned not only in its derogation from historical conservatism, the latter exemplified in the Allied attitude towards the 1914-18 War, but more damningly in its present hidden collaboration with fascism (through non-intervention in

Spain) acting thereby as 'torpes disimuladores de una iniquidad sin ejemplo en la Historia' (IV, 2451). Such a claim leads Machado to describe its perpetrators as the outcasts of culture. We have commented before on the power of Machado's lapidary rhetoric. At the end of this piece Machado sums up what he saw as the pathetic charade of the League of Nations in a phrase that envelops within its brief compass deep meditations on humanist culture, on politics, war and peace: 'allí donde a la razón y a la moral se jubila, sólo la bestialidad conserva su empleo' (IV, 2451). Not only have reason and morality been pensioned off: the force of the metaphor also leads us to conclude that Machado saw the League of Nations as having been made redundant for the pursuit of good works and is now employed only to promote iniquity.

The *mirador de la guerra*, while it gave Machado a valuable vantage point from which to survey and analyse the events on the wider European stage, produces, of course, a viewpoint whereby, as we have seen, a character in the drama of Spain and Europe such as Neville Chamberlain is seen in a particularly harsh light. (Chamberlain, seen in the light of Machado's portrayal, is arguably the most important figure in the Spanish Civil War.) An interesting example of the way that the *mirador de la guerra* conditioned Machado's view of British politics may be found in his *La Vanguardia* article of 2 June 1938. In this piece Machado uses the views of the British Nobel Peace laureate Norman Angell, which had been summarized in *La Vanguardia* five days earlier. Angell is best known as the author of the book *The Great Illusion* (1907) which he then revised and updated in the light of developing circumstances through the 1920s and 1930s. A popular, Penguin edition of the book, re-titled *The Great Illusion Now*, was published towards the end of 1938. Angell's analysis there of the contemporary European crisis is different in several important respects, while there are also significant convergences of view, from the analysis on to which Machado fastens for his own meditations on the conservative democracies in the article of 2 June.

At the outset of the article Machado states that British conservative politics, and 'en cierto modo' those of France, are 'una política de clase, en pugna con la totalidad de los intereses nacionales ... pero que, no obstante, se presenta ante el mundo y ante sus pueblos respectivos como política nacional' (IV, 2541-42); a point repeatedly made, as we have noted, throughout the *La Vanguardia* articles. Another point repeated in the series is that the leaders of the conservative democracies are aware of the lack of democratic support for their greater sympathy towards the Axis powers than towards Russia (and by extension Republican Spain). Indeed Machado, in the 2 June article, goes further and accuses these leaders of 'honda fascistofilia' (IV, 2453). Their position, therefore, as Machado sees it, is one of hypocrisy, trickery and guilt. As he writes in the same article, this latter condition results in 'su línea de conducta política ... indecisa y temblorosa'.

Machado mentions Angell five times in this article, mainly as an authority on international affairs, but also as having produced an analysis of the European crisis that was broadly in harmony with Machado's own views. ('Es esto lo que vengo diciendo desde hace varios meses', he writes at the beginning of the article.) One of the principal points of convergence between the two writers is the need for cooperation between the powers — which must include Russia — to secure just, collective solutions (and peaceful ones, if possible) to international disputes. The plea for cooperation with Russia is the crucial point of agreement between the writers, because Machado is understandably scathing about the appeasement-dominated League of Nations, whose actual and effective motto, as distinct from its original 'primitiva concepción de [Woodrow] Wilson', Machado transcribes as follows: 'Defendemos la paz como finalidad suprema, la paz a todo trance y ello por el camino más corto, que es, naturalmente[,] el del exterminio de los débiles, es decir, defendemos la paz para mantener el imperio de la iniquidad' (IV, 2459). Another important point of agreement between the writers is that the so-called conservative *Realpolitik* has been ineffective in halting the hegemony of fascism. However, the differences of view between the writers are just as significant. A couple of paragraphs from Angell's *The Great Illusion Now* neatly illustrate the points of agreement and disagreement:

> we [in Britain] are deeply divided as to whether a German or a Bolshevist Europe is the greater danger. These deep and sincere divisions of opinion have produced an oscillation of policy that has

in fact made the country for the time being defenceless, as the events of September, 1938, tragically reveal.

Resistance to totalitarian aggression has not been possible because great sections of our people refused to pay the price of effective resistance, that price necessarily including such things as close cooperation with Russia, (it is patently impossible to create a balance of forces in Europe which can meet the totalitarian challenge without Russia); and economic and financial aid to the governments of China and Spain engaged in resisting totalitarian invaders who were attempting to destroy them.[28]

Taking them in the order in which they arise from the above quotation, the points of agreement between Angell and Machado are:

1) Antipathy to Russia is a powerful factor in any ambivalent feelings towards fascism.

2) Inasmuch as it is a Conservative government which is in power, it has left Britain defenceless against the fascist threat, or as Machado expresses it in his own article: '[la] política conservadora ... nada puede conservar' (IV, 2454).

3) Refusal to cooperate with Russia has resulted in the imbalance of forces in Europe.

4) Likewise, the refusal to help the Spanish government has given the advantage to totalitarianism.

The differences between Angell and Machado are almost as striking:

1) Nowhere in *The Great Illusion Now* (and these paragraphs are no exception) does Angell accuse the Conservative government of being 'fascistophile'.

2) Angell does not see the divisions of opinion in Britain as being between the Conservative leadership and the great bulk of the British people, but rather as a division, probably, between conservative and liberal opinion (see his reference to 'great sections of our people').

---

28 *The Great Illusion Now* (London: Penguin Books, 1938), 25-26.

3) Such divisions as exist are described here and in other places by Angell as being 'deep and sincere', whereas Machado stresses the hypocrisy of the Conservative leadership and its fear of having its true motives — plutocracy and crypto-fascism — brought out into the open. (In the paragraph that follows the two quoted above, for example, Angell also refers to British opposition to Russia as being mistaken, but describes it as 'sincere and high minded'.)

Machado appears to have depended completely on Fabián Vidal's *La Vanguardia* article for his use of Norman Angell's views. Vidal (and Machado follows him in this) states (unlike Angell) that it is those British and French capitalists most unsympathetic to the Republic who claim to represent national policy towards Spain, or as Vidal expressed it: 'se arrogan la representación total de sus pariguales'.[29] There is finally, however, one piece of evidence in Machado's writings which sheds some light on the way that Machado was prepared to revise or refine a view in the light, perhaps, of further thought on the matter. The text is the *Prólogo* (IV, 2303-07) that Machado wrote to Manuel Azaña's collection of speeches, *Los españoles en guerra*. In it Machado's appraisal of those political leaders — conservatives 'de tipo *realista*' he calls them — is in accord with Angell's views, on two important counts. It is, of course, a very late text: one of only a very few that are considered to be properly allocated to the year 1939. It is the only time in his political writings — and the *Prólogo* is a political text — in which Machado concedes that the views taken by the conservative leaders of Britain and France might be sincerely held. 'Yo no quiero dudar aquí de su sinceridad' (IV, 2304), he writes of them in the *Prólogo*. While the use of the adverb in this sentence suggests that Machado is reserving any final position on their sincerity or otherwise, the statement is a significant rectification of the approach taken by Machado in the *La Vanguardia* articles.

Another important concession in the same paragraph of the *Prólogo* also marks a point of agreement with Angell's analysis,

---

[29] Vidal's article is titled 'El asombro del *Times*. La España eterna que describió Macaulay', in *La Vanguardia*, 28 May 1938, 3.

but which Machado had omitted, or opposed, throughout the *La Vanguardia* articles. 'Yo no creo', he writes, 'que estos hombres hayan caído de otro planeta, y que no representen corrientes de opinión más o menos impetuosas de sus pueblos. Estoy convencido de todo lo contrario' (IV, 2304). Such a statement, too, is in stark contrast with others in his *La Vanguardia* writings: that the conservative leadership of Britain and France is not representative but regressive, and out of touch with the 'tendencia realmente liberal y democrática y ... el sentido de la corriente más impetuosa y profunda de sus pueblos' (IV, 2447). This quotation comes from Machado's article in *La Vanguardia* of 14 May 1938, a date that represents a gap of seven or eight months between that article and his Prologue to Azaña's work. A comparison of both texts is surely one of the most telling instances of Machado's acute awareness that the vantage point or *mirador* should be recognized as such: a viewpoint from which both the one who perceives and that which is perceived are susceptible to change, revision and refinement.

This briefest of comparisons between two liberally-minded intellectuals, writing at the same time about broadly similar problems, serves to highlight the importance of the *mirador* or vantage point of the writer. Machado's metaphor of the *mirador* suggests height, and thus a clearer view that enables him to see through words and actions to a better appraisal of their motivation and meaning. Angell's title, *The Great Illusion*, is not altogether dissimilar to Machado's: the element of seeing through illusions and mistakes is common to both writers. However, the English writer's analysis of the motivation of his government is much more benign than Machado's. Spain, of course, is usually bracketed in Angell's analysis with the other failures of the democracies to counter the totalitarian aggression of the 1930s. One further quotation from Angell may suffice to illustrate the different 'balconies' from which both writers viewed the European (and indeed world) crisis in 1938:

> For very frankly, very fully, supporters of the Government's policy [of non-involvement in foreign conflicts] have repeatedly declared that if resistance to Japan in 1931, Italy in 1935, Italy and Germany in Spain, could have been completely successful without war, that resistance should not have been made, since, in their view, the victory of Japan was preferable to that of a Communist China, the presence of Italy in Abysinnia preferable to

a success for Geneva, the victory of Franco with German and Italian aid preferable to the victory of the Spanish Government with its Socialist tendencies.[30]

For Machado the balcony of the Spanish Civil War was also its cockpit, and he was necessarily drawn into the conflict in a way that Angell was not, for whom Spain remained as just one more example among others of the failure of conservative democratic politics in the 1930s. Manuel Azaña, writing in 1939, saw this dispersal of Britain's interests as an important political factor in her attitude to the Spanish Civil War: 'Naturalmente', he wrote, 'el conflicto de España era para los británicos una parte, y no la principal, del problema europeo que aspiraban a desenlazar, si era posible, dentro de la paz'.[31] The urbane and detached tone of Angell's prose, indeed, makes it closer to Machado's own analogy of the balcony as productive of an elevated and hence clearsighted viewpoint, than is Machado's prose itself at times, which in *La Vanguardia* demonstrates less patience with human folly than anywhere else in his writings.

One of the ways in which Machado was able to vary the viewpoint, or at least experiment with an altered perspective, was through the use of the *Mairena* format. He uses Mairena twice in the Angell article. On the first occasion Machado quotes some of Mairena's words, consigned to an apocryphal notebook at the beginning of the *Mairena* series in 1934:

> La verdad es la verdad, dígala Agamemnón o su porquero.
> Agamemnón: Conforme.
> Su porquero: no me convence.

As Tuñón de Lara has pointed out, it is possible to interpret this scepticism about Platonic truth on the part of the *porquero* as a bitter recognition by the latter that acceptance of the authority of truth may well depend upon the social status of that authority, for as Tuñón comments: 'Agamemnón gozaba de todas las circunstancias favorables para presentar *su* verdad, como *la* verdad de todos'.[32] In the Angell article Machado truncates the original note, leaving the proposition only: 'Pero dejemos a un lado todo criterio basado en la autoridad, no sin

---

30 *Op. cit.*, 43.
31 *Causas de la guerra de España*, 44.
32 *Op. cit.*, 244.

antes recordar la frase de Mairena: "La verdad es la verdad, dígala Agamemnón o su porquero" ' (IV, 2542). The original is therefore altered from its scepticism about the status of a truth issued by an authority, to an acceptance that truth is truth, no matter who says it, provided such a person is a genuine authority on the subject, whether it be epic battles or the raising of pigs, or in the case of Norman Angell, the politics of Europe. Of course, as the first part of the quotation indicates, Machado here leaves behind any appeal to authority for authority's sake and goes on to argue the case against the conservative democracies on its merits. As we have seen, much of the first *Mairena* series is a questioning of authority, both classical and modern, and in the Angell article Machado also ploughs his own furrow, using Angell's analysis, but putting his own views almost as it were against the promptings of Mairena, who on this occasion appears to favour the truth of authority. Machado, in fact, is both refining or revising his earlier sceptical view of authority as expressed in the quotation from the first *Mairena* article of 1934, and at the same time using the sceptical view to pursue his own analysis. Angell's strictures *vis-à-vis* the conservative democracies are thereby incorporated into Machado's much more scathing criticisms of these democracies.

In the following paragraph Machado brings in Mairena in a way that appears ironic and whimsical, when he again uses his apocryphal figure to shift the perspective, this time towards that of Germany's view of the paradoxical spectacle of appeasement and massive rearmament keeping step with each other in Britain. Mairena explains the German attitude in terms of Prussian military chivalry: a willingness to wait until Britain is sufficiently armed for the fray, in order to have a decent contest. Such exaggerated chivalry, Machado argues, cannot be a part of the national psyche of Britain and France. Machado then proceeds to explore deeper reasons, helped by Angell's analysis: what Machado describes as the 'honda fascistofilia' of the conservative governments. Perhaps the most significant aspect of Machado's use of Mairena here is that Mairena's analysis, like Angell's, does not go far enough for Machado. It is one of the rare occasions in the four-year-long *Mairena* series when Mairena's somewhat whimsical analysis is counterposed by Machado's much more serious examination. Machado's independence of criterion is seen in this piece to telling effect, where he uses Angell's views and goes beyond them to a much more searching analysis of the contradictions, as he sees them, at the heart of political conservatism. 'Soy yo el primer convencido de mi insignificancia como escritor político', he writes at the beginning of the article. Yet his analysis provides an indictment of the conservative democracies that in its urgent clarity effectively sweeps aside Angell's gentler examination of Europe and finally also looks elsewhere for hope for the future: to 'las grandes democracias ricas de porvenir, en el Viejo y Nuevo Continente' (IV, 2454), rather than to what Machado calls the 'reacción desmedida' of the political leadership of Britain (and France).

The English writer's appeal is above all a pragmatic one, to the enlightened self-interest of his readers. In this he is at one with Machado's stance in the article of 2 June, because Machado, basing his argument on Angell's analysis, keeps his own examination within the bounds of an exposure of the inadequacies of conservative *Realpolitik*. But Machado consistently goes beyond considerations of pragmatism, even of this enlightened kind. The 'hidden iniquities' that he attempts to expose in these articles are ethical as well as practical. It is this extra element in his writings that compensates for his inexperience, and inevitable limitations, as a political writer. His forecast in the final article of the series for the future of the conservative democracies' policy of appeasement encapsulates both the practical and the ethical in eight simple words: 'Ni dignidad ni precio; ni honra ni provecho'.[33] In this same paragraph, the penultimate of the series, Machado turns to the words of another English writer (and politician) Winston Churchill, to express the essence of his own final position with regard to any imperative: 'Porque entre el deshonor y la guerra — recordemos las palabras de Churchill — [las llamadas democracias] habrían elegido el deshonor y tendrían la guerra, una guerra sin honor — añadimos nosotros — y que de ningún modo merecería la victoria'. It was this assurance of occupying the high moral ground in the Spanish Civil War that gave Machado the confidence that he could clearly see through what

---

33 *La Vanguardia*, 6 January 1939, 3.

he called the 'claudicación' of the conservative democracies in 1938. Such an assurance also led him to the belief — less firmly expressed, however, than in our last quotation — that the Republic, against all the technical, strategic and political appearances, would emerge as the 'human' victors in the Civil War. In his interview with Ilya Ehrenberg at the end of 1938, Machado expressed his opinion of the war's conclusion as follows: 'Esto es el final, cualquier día caerá Barcelona. Para los estrategas, para los políticos, para los historiadores, todo está claro: hemos perdido la guerra. Pero humanamente, no estoy seguro ... Quizá la hemos ganado' (IV, 2300).

In his attempt to seek a clear vision of the plight of Western Europe in 1938 Machado brought to the surface deep crosscurrents of affinities and antipathies, and laid bare the motives and prejudices of British Conservative opinion, in particular those of the Prime Minister Neville Chamberlain. Especially in the last three months of his writings in *La Vanguardia* Machado's prose has the kind of reiterative simplicity that sought to make his points come to his readers with the maximum clarity that the urgency of the times required. Any failures in immediacy of communication in the *La Vanguardia* articles are due, not to the use of a highly compressed form of language, such as we sometimes see in *Hora de España* — aphorisms saturated with a lifetime's meditation — but rather to a tendency at times to see events through the prism of literature. In a happier outcome to the circumstances of the Civil War Machado might have looked forward to seeing his political articles published in some more permanent form, so that what was lost to the immediate persuasive impact of the daily newspaper could be left for future study. It was perhaps Machado's conscious will for Spain to deserve a 'razón de continuidad en la historia' that made him persist with literary analogies in *La Vanguardia*, whereby the continuity of the work of culture acted as a mirror for the continuing legality of the Republic itself: he, too, was not to be deflected from his own deeply sensed literary vocation by a rebellion of the military or by the fascist menace. Within the discursive mode and political subject matter of the *La Vanguardia* articles Machado could write with great economy and precision. The first sentence of his last article of 6 January 1939 makes its points in this way:

'La política de Chamberlain se caracteriza por su incansable pertinacia para navegar en aguas turbias, por la ocultación constante de sus motivos y por la gran ceguera para el porvenir de Europa y, en primer término, para el porvenir de Inglaterra'. Here, Machado highlights Chamberlain's lack of any vision for the future of Europe, his secretive and autocratic tendencies especially where the conduct of foreign policy is concerned, tendencies that have led him out of his depth in dealing with the fascist dictators, thereby putting the future of Europe and of Britain herself in grave danger. Simplicity and a forthright clarity are indeed two of the dominant characteristics of Machado's prose pieces in *La Vanguardia*, the very manner of his prose acting as a counterpoint to what Machado saw as the dishonourable and ultimately futile manoeuvrings of British Conservative politics at the time.

The use of the word 'humanamente' in the Ehrenberg interview brings us back again to Machado's description of culture as 'el humano tesoro de conciencia vigilante'. Such a broad definition made it natural and indeed inevitable that Machado should be given a chance to play a prominent part in the debate about the significance of the Spanish Civil War. Given Machado's view that worthwhile culture can only be created by the critical consciousness at work on everything that comes within its vision, it was also inevitable that, unlike his brother Manuel, he would speak for the cause of democratic, participatory politics rather than authoritarian modes of government. But even in the case of a well established democracy such as Britain, the consensual basis of ruling Conservative opinion is given close and severe scrutiny by Machado. The fact that Machado was prepared to venture publicly into the political arena at all amply demonstrates that, in his case at least, one of the Republic's cherished objectives was to be achieved: the gap between the intellectual and the general public had effectively been bridged. Notwithstanding the political outcome of the Spanish Civil War, Machado's articles in *La Vanguardia* are a net gain for culture, viewed in the light of his emphasis on culture as dependent on the exercise of the 'vigilant consciousness' in every sphere.

CONCLUSION

E. Allison Peers was evidently not the kind of scholar who was daunted by the challenge of contemporary, up-to-the-minute literature. Yet even he, in his Taylorian Lecture on Antonio Machado in 1939, preferred not to venture beyond 1930, effectively writing off Machado's final years, or at least his writings, as a barren area of study, when he observed that 'About 1930 the road which the poet had been following for some thirty years came to an abrupt end and those who would follow it farther must wander along bypaths over the uncultivated hillside'. And he concluded: 'It is more profitable to leave the Machado who will surely be soon forgotten for the Machado whose name is already written large in the history of Spanish literature in the twentieth century'.[1] This attitude is still reflected in the small proportion of studies devoted to Machado's writings during the Republic and the Spanish Civil War. Octavio Paz attempted to redress the balance in favour of Machado's late writings when he wrote that 'sus poemas sólo pueden ser comprendidos cabalmente a la luz de sus últimas meditaciones'.[2] It is tempting to agree with this opinion when within these late works we can encounter such reflections as the one that follows, in which a lifetime's thought has been distilled, and in which clarity and profundity are inseparable partners in the attempt to begin to strike through to the heart of the enigmas of human existence. Machado opened his July 1937 contribution to *Hora de España* with the following observations:

> Sería conveniente — habla Juan de Mairena a sus alumnos — que el hombre más o menos occidental de nuestros días, ese hombre al margen de todas las iglesias — o incluido sin fe en alguna de ellas — que ha vuelto la espalda a determinados dogmas, intentase una profunda investigación de sus creencias últimas. Porque todos — sin excluir a los herejes, coleccionistas de excomuniones, etc. —

---

[1] *Antonio Machado* (Oxford: Clarendon Press, 1940), 27-28.
[2] 'Antonio Machado', in *Antonio Machado*, ed. Gullón and Phillips, 61.

creemos en algo y es este algo, a fin de cuentas, lo que pudiera explicar el sentido total de nuestra conducta. (IV, 2338)

These sentences could have been clipped for the purposes of quotation, but leaving them with all their clauses and asides gives us one of the most authentic spiritual portraits of Machado that we could get from all of his writings. One can immediately see that the heterodox legacy of the *Institución Libre de Enseñanza* still lives on in 1937, as well as the deeply serious commitment to a re-discovery of human values that are inclusive rather than exclusive. The sense of intellectual isolation caused by the insufficiency or intransigence of traditional religious belief is also captured, together with the concomitant need to re-think one's ideas from first principles. The sentences, indeed, graphically sum up the way in which Machado's thought moved between the poles of solitude and solidarity throughout his life. Dionisio Ridruejo shrewdly used this latter point, but without any validity in my view, in his famous Preface to the first post-Civil-War edition of Machado's *Poesías Completas* of 1941: that Machado's intellectual isolation made him an easy target for the 'reds' to bamboozle with progressive ideas and win him over for their propaganda machine, because Machado was 'un abismado, un ausente, un desencantado, un errante, un solitario, un absorto, un alma de Dios'.[3]

Machado began to take up sustained serious writing again at the end of 1934, a time of deep crisis for Spain, with the polarization of opinion to the right and left of the political spectrum, particularly in the wake of the revolution of Asturias in October of that year, and the declaration of a State of War by the Republic's government, with its attendant consequences. Gabriel Jackson has seen the tragedy of the Republic in its impossible ambition, during its two main phases of existence, to have the equivalent of the French Revolution in the pre-war Republic and of the Russian Revolution during the Civil War itself.[4] Such an unleashing of liberal middle-class and radical proletarian energy within the space of a few years was bound to cause social and political upheavals of gigantic proportions. Of the Spanish October revolution of 1934 Carlos Seco Serrano has

---

3   *Ed. cit.*, XI.
4   *Op. cit.*, 479.

written: 'La gravedad de la revolución de octubre no reside exclusivamente en su violencia — preludio ya de la guerra civil — sino en el rompimiento efectivo del socialismo y de las izquierdas catalanas con las normas de convivencia democrática hasta entonces vigentes en la República'.[5] *Juan de Mairena* (1936), which began publication in November 1934, seen in the light of the escalating tensions within the country and its political system, is an attempt to bring to the fore the proper grounds for agreement or disagreement between contending opinions. It therefore rises to the occasion rather than remaining removed from the conflict. Machado's claims to be considered as a writer of the first importance during these two periods of the Republic stem from his readiness to seek out the wealth that both classical and popular culture had to offer, in particular relating such culture to the critical response that it induced in the personal consciousness. If Hamlet's view was that 'conscience [that is, consciousness] doth make cowards of us all', Machado's was that consciousness is an enriching experience, a cultural treasury open to all who are endowed — 'quién más, quién menos' (IV, 2340) — with the desire to reflect deeply and seriously on the human condition. *Juan de Mairena* (1936), however, transcends the liberal ethos of the pre-war Republic's showpiece for the meeting of the intellectuals and the people, the *Misiones Pedagógicas*. While such an element is a powerful motor within the book, as we saw in Chapter 1, the way that *Juan de Mairena* (1936) charts the map of culture places the so-called 'desheredados de la cultura' (IV, 1975) within their own cultural treasure-house of popular wisdom, and pointedly implies that any transfer of culture from 'high' to 'popular' is ultimately sterile, unless it becomes a two-way process.

The Civil War gave an extraordinary impetus to the enthusiastic efforts at *rapprochement* between the liberal intelligentsia and the conventionally uneducated or undereducated class, a *rapprochement* that was represented in the pre-war years by the *Misiones Pedagógicas*. After the outbreak of the war, Antonio Sánchez Barbudo, writing in the first issue of *Hora de España* of January 1937, recalled his stay as a *misionero* in Yeste just before the war, during the death of

---

5   *Historia de España*, 7 vols (Barcelona: Océano, 1982), VI, 123.

twenty civilians at the hands of the *guardia civil*, and wrote of the villagers: 'Parecía imposible que aquellos hombres, ávidos de todo, hambrientos y miserables, fuesen cada día a escuchar con atención grave y profunda nuestras charlas culturales'. If they continued to listen after the outbreak of the war, it was to a much more radical platform of anti-illiteracy programmes and political consciousness-raising. Machado's *La Guerra*, slimmed down to Giacometti-like proportions, responds both to the need for a reasoned calm and to the stimulus of individual example, that of Lorca and Barral, for example. Above all there is, in *La Guerra*, the ideal that transcends the individual: the immortality of the best culture that is strengthened through its links of solidarity with the *pueblo*, that 'muchedumbre de hombres que temen, desean y esperan aproximadamente las mismas cosas', as Machado expressed it in *La Guerra*.

Machado's ideas on the democratization of culture meant that he was well placed to make his own critical contribution to the collectivist ethos that emerged in the Republic in the wake of the Civil War. Later, in the sonnets, written in the spring of 1938 (except for the one to Líster), Republican Spain is projected as a place where the civilized life of dialogue and pluralism is under threat, very much in the spirit of Negrín's Thirteen Points of 1 May of that year, which sought to appeal to the democracies on a similar basis. As the consequences of the war became more apparent, in terms of its likely extension and logistical ramifications, and of the consequent loss of human life, the questions of militarism and pacifism were ones that Machado addressed at greater length. While both these extremes are rejected, the activist militarism of the dictators is essentially consigned to nineteenth-century Darwinian and Nietzschean ideas, and hence quickly dismissed as inappropriate for progressive twentieth-century democracies. Indeed, Machado saw the whole theory of a balance of forces within Europe as an out-of-date legacy of the nineteenth century (IV, 2454). With regard to pacifism Machado doubtless was a man of peace, but his views on the subject were shaped by the Spanish Civil War and the fascist threat to the parliamentary democracies of Europe. For Machado, the basic ethical position of true democracies in any present or future conflict is secure in the long term because they have not or will not have provoked conflict. Since Machado saw Chamberlain's European policy as a prevarication, a muddying of a clear ethical imperative, he invokes the motto 'o guerrear por la justicia o cruzarnos de brazos ante la iniquidad', to enscapulate both a justification of the Republic's position and a rejection of the theory of pacificism in the 1930s.

The *La Vanguardia* articles represent the most direct *rapprochement* between Machado and the general public in all his writings. At the beginning of 1934 Machado was asked in an interview: '¿Qué deberes tiene el arte en los momentos actuales?', and he replied: 'Acaso el deber del arte en los momentos actuales, como en todo momento, sea el de ser actual'.[6] All his meditations on the extension and accessibility of culture, as well as on the flowering and expansion of human consciousness, the 'muchas horas de mi vida gastadas — alguien dirá: perdidas — en meditar sobre los enigmas del hombre y del mundo' (III, 1595), as he wrote in his Prologue to *Campos de Castilla*; these hours and years thus spent were to be tested in the pressing need to explain, not enigmas now, but the problems of the senior European democracies, and to identify solutions based on *Realpolitik* as well as on ethical imperatives. Machado's achievement in *La Vanguardia* may best be summed up by his own simile in his article of 22 May in the newspaper when he wrote in praise of a speech made by the Republic's Foreign Minister, Álvarez del Vayo, to the League of Nations: 'ahí queda, hincado en el blanco, sin agotar su impulso, el discurso de nuestro compatriota, como flecha trémula y vibrante para inquietud y escándalo de conciencias adormiladas' (IV, 2449). This is Machado's technique in *La Vanguardia:* his own arrows 'desde el mirador de la guerra' were also aimed to make direct hits at the targets of non-intervention, appeasement and undemocratic manoeuvres. In *La Vanguardia* Machado seized the opportunity to forge new cultural links with society in a way that he could never have dreamed of at the outbreak of the Civil War. One can see from these articles that he certainly

---

6   Rosario del Olmo, 'Al comenzar el año 1934. Deberes del Arte en el momento actual', originally published in *La Libertad*, 12 January 1934; collected in *Los novelistas sociales españoles (1928-1936). Antología*, ed. José Esteban and Gonzalo Santonja (Madrid: Ayuso, 1977), 65-67. (The interview is not in Macrì.)

encountered difficulties in sorting out the appropriate level at which to pitch his argument, given his innate attachment to literature and literary analogies. Yet it could be argued that in using literature he was able to avoid too great an immersion in the political issues of the day, for which, in any event, he had insufficient training or experience. And while some of his pragmatic criticisms of the democracies concerning trade routes and communication with overseas branches of empires have passed into history, the ethical questions of openness and democratic accountability, and of fighting in defence of a just cause, remain as issues — in Machado's own words 'sin agotar su impulso' — that will never allow these articles to fall into irrelevance and obscurity.

Machado's last four or five years were lived in a period of the utmost uncertainty: the Spanish Republic's swing to the right after 1933, the revolution of Asturias and Cataluña's virtual declaration of itself as an independent state, in 1934, the 1936 coup d'état, the unimaginable duration and devastating course of the Civil War itself,[7] the cataclysmic prospects for Europe and even the world as a whole. There is, therefore, a sense of the provisional about Machado's work of this period, of work in progress, without a finished synthesis. The stresses and strains of conflict, the immediate, harsh imperatives of war, combined to test Machado's will to express his deepest convictions. That he did so with such vigour, clearsightedness and the highest ethical standards is a measure of his success as a writer. *Hora de España* must have been a blessed boon, offering him a regular outlet for the expression of his ideas, which he continued to expound in the style of *Mairena*, and by analogy claiming the right for the Republic to continue its existence as the incorporation of the Spanish State. If on rare occasions in the journal he lapsed into an over-compressed form of writing, the *Mairena* style was one to which he had become accustomed, thus enabling him to deepen his meditations on issues affecting

---

[7] In Manuel Azaña's first Civil-War speech, delivered on 21 January 1937, he observed: 'seis meses de guerra ... plazo que ... ahora nos parece breve y encontramos en nuestra alma el vigor suficiente para duplicarlo, y triplicarlo si es menester, con tal de sacar adelante la causa de la República', *Hacia la victoria*, 8. The actual duration, of course, more than quintupled those first six months.

the human spirit, typically seeking illumination rather than heat from the conflagration that was engulfing Spain. And as in *Juan de Mairena* (1936), Machado in *Hora de España* used the *Mairena* formula with the truthful humility of one who was only too aware that discoursing on such issues required all the wit, perspective and humanity that he could muster, in order to deal with them with integrity, although the tone in the latter series necessarily on occasions inclines towards a more direct and sober rhetoric. In the end Machado returned to the medium in which he began his *Mairena* series — the daily newspaper — the final proof of his enthusiastic will to rise to the occasion that the Civil War had demanded of every Spaniard. In answering the call Machado did no more than his duty. In so doing, however, he has left us with writings that will continuously yield fruit to patient study and to the meditative sensibility of all who are curious about the brief life of Spain's Second Republic and about Machado's work during its existence, in peace and war. Remaining at his post until he was materially worn out, he bequeathed the best of himself through these writings of his last years.

BIBLIOGRAPHY

The reader should consult Oreste Macrì's Bibliography in Volume I of his edition of Machado's *Poesía y prosa* (see chapter I, note 18) which contains over one thousand entries spanning the whole of Machado's life and work. This present Bibliography is mainly confined to works on Machado that deal with the period 1934-1939, and to other studies consulted, that are relevant to that period.

Abellá, Rafael, *La vida cotidiana durante la guerra civil. La España Republicana* (Barcelona: Planeta, 1975).
Abellán, José Luis, 'Antonio Machado: la teoría de lo apócrifo y su radicalización ideológica', *Diwán*, XI (1981), 57-74.
Albornoz, Aurora de, ' "Un miliciano más" ... — entre otras cosas', *La Calle*, LVI (1979), 41-43.
Alonso, Monique, in collaboration with Antonio Tello, *Antonio Machado. Poeta en el exilio* (Barcelona: Anthropos, 1985).
Anderson Imbert, Enrique, 'El pícaro Juan de Mairena', *Antonio Machado*, ed. Ricardo Gullón and Allen W. Phillips (Madrid: Taurus, 1973), 365-69.
Aubert, Paul, 'La Cultura y los intelectuales en la obra y vida de Antonio Machado', *Boletín de la Asociación Europea de Profesores de Español*, X (1977), 17-34.
_____ , 'En torno a las ideas pedagógicas de Antonio Machado', *Cuadernos para el Diálogo*, XLIX (1975), 105-13.
¡Ayuda!, I-XII (1936).
Ayuda, XIII-CXIII (1936-1938).
Azaña, Manuel, *Los españoles en guerra*. Prólogo de Antonio Machado (Barcelona: Editorial Crítica, 1977).
Azcárate, Pablo de, *Mi embajada en Londres durante la guerra civil española* (Esplugues de Llobregat [Barcelona]: Editorial Ariel, 1976).
Aznar Soler, M., *II Congreso Internacional de Escritores Antifascistas (1937)*. Vol I: *Pensamiento literario y compromiso antifascista de la inteligencia española republicana* (Barcelona: Laia, 1978).
Aznar Soler, M. and Luis María Schneider, *II Congreso Internacional de Escritores Antifascistas (1937). Ponencias, documentos y testimonios* (Barcelona: Laia, 1979).

Barbachano, Carlos and Agustín Sánchez Vidal, 'Tres pilares del diálogo en la prosa de Antonio Machado: Sócrates, Cristo y Cervantes', *Cuadernos Hispanoamericanos*, CCCIV-CCCVII (1975-1976), 614-24.

Barjau, E., 'Juan de Mairena: teoría del diálogo', *Instituto de Bachillerato 'Cervantes'. Miscelánea en su cincuentenario, 1931-1981* (Madrid: Ministerio de Educación y Ciencia, 1982), 247-64.

Bécarud, J. and E. López Campillo, *Los intelectuales durante la II República* (Madrid: Siglo Veintiuno Editores, 1978).

Beceiro, Carlos, 'Una frase del "Juan de Mairena" ', *Ínsula*, XIV (1960), 13 and 15.

Borkenau, Franz, *The Spanish Cockpit. An Eye-Witness Account of the Political and Social Conflicts of the Spanish Civil War* (London: Faber and Faber, 1937).

Calamai, Natalia. *El compromiso de la poesía en la guerra civil española* (Barcelona: Laia, 1979).

Cano, J. L., *Antonio Machado* (Barcelona: Bruguera, 1982).

____ , 'Guerra y amor en un soneto de Machado', *Ínsula*, DVI-DVII (1989), 15.

Caudet, Francisco, 'Juan de Mairena durante la guerra', *Antonio Machado hoy. Actas del Congreso Internacional Conmemorativo del Cincuentenario de la Muerte de Antonio Machado* (Seville: Alfar, 1990), 4 vols, I, 267-85.

____ , 'Las Misiones Pedagógicas: 1931-1935', *Cuadernos Hispanoamericanos*, DCLIII (1988), 93-108.

Cerezo Galán, P., *Palabra en el tiempo. Poesía y filosofía en Antonio Machado* (Madrid: Gredos, 1975).

Cobb, Christopher H., *La cultura y el pueblo. España, 1930-1939* (Barcelona: Laia, 1980).

Cobos, P. A. de., *El pensamiento de Antonio Machado en Juan de Mairena* (Madrid: Ínsula, 1971).

Crispin, John, 'Tres sonetos satíricos inéditos de Pedro Salinas', *Ínsula*, DXL (1991), 9 and 11.

Cruz, Sabina de la, 'Una carta inédita de Antonio Machado', *Antonio Machado hoy. Actas del Congreso Internacional Conmemorativo del Cincuentenario de la Muerte de Antonio Machado* (Seville: Alfar, 1990), I, 405-13.

Díaz de Castro, Francisco J., *El último Antonio Machado (Juan de Mairena y el ideal pedagógico machadiano)* (Palma de Mallorca: Universitat de Palma de Mallorca, 1984).

Díaz Plaja, Fernando, *La Guerra Civil y los poetas españoles* (Madrid: Editorial San Martín, 1981).
Dieste, Rafael, *Testimonios y homenajes*, ed. Manuel Aznar Soler (Barcelona: Laia, 1983).

Edwards, Jill, *The British Government and the Spanish Civil War 1936-1939* (London: Macmillan, 1979).
Escolar Sobrino, Hipólito, *La cultura durante la guerra civil* (Madrid: Alhambra, 1987).
España. Nuestro siglo. Texto, imágenes y sonido. Guerra Civil 1936-1939, ed. Guillem Burrel i Floria (Barcelona: Plaza y Janés, 1986).

Fernández Ferrer, Antonio, 'En busca del archilector imaginario', *Antonio Machado hoy. Actas del Congreso Internacional Conmemorativo del Cincuentenario de la Muerte de Antonio Machado* (Seville: Alfar, 1990), IV, 9-17.
Fernández Soria, Juan Manuel, 'La asistencia cultural de la República en guerra', *València, capital cultural de la República (1936-1937). Antologia de textos i documents*, ed. M. Aznar Soler *et al.* (Valencia: Generalitat Valenciana, 1986), 43-98.
____ , *Educación y cultura en la Guerra Civil (España 1936-39)* (Valencia: Nau Llibres, 1984).
Ferreres, Rafael, 'Antonio Machado en Valencia', *Cuadernos Hispanoamericanos*, CCCIV-CCCVII (1975-1976), 374-85.

García de la Concha, Víctor, 'La nueva retórica de Antonio Machado', *Antonio Machado hoy. Actas del Congreso Internacional Conmemorativo del Cincuentenario de la Muerte de Antonio Machado* (Seville: Alfar, 1990), I, 13-32.
García Padrino, Jaime, 'Antonio Machado y la atención al niño en la guerra civil', *Antonio Machado hoy. Actas del Congreso Internacional Conmemorativo del Cincuentenario de la Muerte de Antonio Machado* (Seville: Alfar, 1990), I, 441-48.
Garosci, Aldo, *Los intelectuales y la Guerra de España* (Madrid: Ediciones Júcar, 1981).
Gil-Albert, Juan, *Memorabilia* (Barcelona: Jusquets Editor, 1975).
Gil Novales, Alberto, *Antonio Machado* (Barcelona: Editorial Fontanella, 1966).
Glendinning, Nigel, 'Art and the Spanish Civil War', *¡No pasarán!': Art, Literature and the Spanish Civil War*, ed. Stephen M. Hart (London: Tamesis, 1988), 20-45.
Gómez Molleda, D., *Guerra de ideas y lucha social en Machado* (Madrid: Narcea, 1977).

González, Rafael A., 'Las ideas políticas de Antonio Machado', *La Torre*, XLV-XLVI (1964), 151-70.
Grimau, Carmen, *El cartel republicano en la Guerra Civil* (Madrid: Cátedra, 1979).
Guadalajara Solera, Simón, *El compromiso en Antonio Machado (a la ética por la estética)* (Madrid: Emiliano Escolar, 1984).
La guerra de España en sus documentos, ed. Fernando Díaz-Plaja (Madrid: Sarpe, 1986).
Guerrero Ruiz, Pedro, 'Don Antonio Machado, escritura de un compromiso', *Antonio Machado hoy. Actas del Congreso Internacional Conmemorativo del Cincuentenario de la Muerte de Antonio Machado* (Seville: Alfar, 1990), IV, 33-41.
Gullón, Ricardo, *Espacios poéticos de Antonio Machado* (Madrid: Fundación Juan March/Cátedra, 1987).

Hamilton, Thomas J., *Appeasement's Child. The Franco Régime in Spain* (London: Victor Gollancz, 1943).
Hart, Stephen M., 'War within a War: Poetry and the Spanish Civil War', *¡No pasarán!': Art, Literature and the Spanish Civil War*, ed. Stephen M. Hart (London: Tamesis, 1988), 106-22.
Hernández, Jesús, *A los intelectuales de España* (Barcelona: Ediciones del Partido Comunista de España, 1937).
Hora de España, I-XXII (1936-1937), introd. E. M. [sic] (Glashütten im Taunus: Verlag Detlev Auvermann KG, 1972), 5 vols [facsimile ed.].
Hora de España, XXIII (1937), introd. María Zambrano (Glashütten im Taunus: Verlag Detlev Auvermann KG, 1974) [facsimile ed.].
Hora de España (Antología), ed. Francisco Caudet (Madrid: Ediciones Turner, 1975).

Jackson, Gabriel, *The Spanish Republic and the Civil War 1931-1939* (Princeton: Princeton U. P., 1965).

Kleine-Ahlbrandt, William Laird, *The Policy of Simmering. A Study of British Policy during the Spanish Civil War* (The Hague: Martinus Nijhoff, 1962).

Lázaro Carreter, Fernando, 'El último Machado', *Curso en homenaje a Antonio Machado*, ed. Eugenio de Bustos (Salamanca: Univ. de Salamanca, 1975), 119-34.
Lechner, J., *El compromiso en la poesía española del siglo XX* (Leiden: Univ. Pers Leiden, 1968), 2 vols.
Lida, Raimundo, 'Elogio de Mairena', *Antonio Machado*, ed. Ricardo Gullón and Allen W. Phillips (Madrid: Taurus, 1973), 365-69.

Luis, Leopoldo de, *Antonio Machado, ejemplo y lección* (Madrid: Sociedad General Española de Librería, 1975).

Machado, Antonio, *Antología de su prosa*, ed. Aurora de Albornoz (Madrid: Editorial Cuadernos para el Diálogo, EDICUSA, 1971), 4 vols.
———, *La guerra. Escritos: 1936-1939*, ed. Julio Rodríguez Puértolas and Gerardo Pérez Herrero (Madrid: Emiliano Escolar, 1983).
———, *Juan de Mairena*, ed. Antonio Fernández Ferrer (Madrid: Cátedra, 1986), 2 vols.
———, *Poesías completas* ed. Dionisio Ridruejo (Madrid: Espasa-Calpe, 1941).
———, *Poesía y prosa*, ed. Oreste Macrì in collaboration with Gaetano Chiappini (Madrid: Espasa-Calpe/Fundación Antonio Machado, 1988), 4 vols.
Machado, José, *Últimas soledades del poeta Antonio Machado* (Soria: Imprenta Provincial, 1973).
Machado, Manuel, *Horas de Oro* (Valladolid: Biblioteca Nueva, 1938).
Los Machado y su tiempo (Madrid: Fundación Española Antonio Machado, 1987).
Madrid. Cuadernos de la Casa de la Cultura, introd. Robert Marrast (Glashütten im Taunus: Verlag Auvermann KG, 1974) [facsimile ed.].
Marrast, R., 'Antonio Machado, collaborateur de *La Vanguardia*', *Les Langues Néo-Latines*, CLXXXIII-CLXXXIV (1968), 88-93.
Moliner, Matilde, 'Mis encuentros con Machado', *Instituto de Bachillerato 'Cervantes'. Miscelánea en su cincuentenario. 1931-1981* (Madrid: Ministerio de Educación y Ciencia, 1982), 297-305.

Nadal, José María, 'Narratología y persuasión en el "Discurso a las Juventudes Socialistas Unificadas" ', *Antonio Machado hoy. Actas del Congreso Internacional Conmemorativo del Cincuentenario de la Muerte de Antonio Machado* (Seville: Alfar, 1990), IV, 357-68.
Nueva Cultura, introd. Josep Renau (Vaduz, Liechtenstein: Topos Verlag AG, n.d.) [facsimile ed.].

D'Ors, Eugenio, 'Carta de Octavio de Romeu al Profesor Juan de Mairena', *Cuadernos Hispanoamericanos*, XI-XII (1949), 289-300.
Otero Urtaza, Eugenio, *Las Misiones Pedagógicas: una experiencia de educación popular* (La Coruña: Ediciós do Castro, 1982).

Patronato de Misiones Pedagógicas (Madrid, 1934).
____, *Memoria de la Misión Pedagógica-social en Sanabria (Zamora). Resumen de trabajos realizados en el año 1934* (Madrid, 1935).
Paucker, Eleanor Krane, 'Cinco años de misiones', *Revista de Occidente* (April 1981), 233-68.
Paz, Octavio, 'Antonio Machado', *Antonio Machado*, ed. Ricardo Gullón and Allen W. Phillips (Madrid: Taurus, 1973).
Peers, E. Allison, *Antonio Machado* (Oxford: Clarendon Press, 1940).
Peirats, J., *Los intelectuales en la revolución* (Barcelona: Ediciones 'Tierra y Libertad', 1938).
Pérez Contel, Rafael, *Artistas en Valencia* (Valencia: Conselleria de Cultura, Educació i Ciéncia de la Generalitat Valenciana, 1986), 2 vols.
Pérez Galán, Mariano, *La enseñanza en la II República española* (Madrid: Editorial Cuadernos para el Diálogo, 1975).
Pont, Jaume, 'Sobre *La guerra* de Antonio Machado', *Antonio Machado hoy. Actas del Congreso Internacional Conmemorativo del Cincuentenario de la Muerte de Antonio Machado* (Seville: Alfar, 1990), I, 477-86.
Puccini, Dario, *Romancero de la resistencia española [1936-1965]* (Mexico D. F.: Ediciones Era, 1967).
Puzzo, Dante A., *Spain and the Great Powers 1936-1941* (New York: Books for Libraries Press, 1972 [first published 1962]).

Ridruejo, Dionisio, *Poesía en armas* (Barcelona: Ediciones Jerarquía, 1940).
Rodríguez Puértolas, Julio, 'Antonio Machado, Luis Cernuda y los poetas en la España leal', *Ínsula*, DVI-DVII (1989), 68-69.
Rojo, Vicente, *Así fue la defensa de Madrid. [Aportación a la historia de la guerra de España / 1936-39]* (Mexico: Ediciones Era, 1967).
Roumette, Monique, 'Hora de España', *Espagne/Écrivains. Guerre civile*, ed. Marc Hanrez (Paris: Les Dossiers H., 1975), 201-13.
Rovira, José Carlos, 'Acerca del modelo moral del Mairena de *Hora de España*', *Camp de l'Arpa*, XXIII-XXIV (1975), 20-21.

Salaün, Serge, 'L'expression poétique pendant la guerre d'Espagne', *Espagne/Écrivains. Guerre civile*, ed. Marc Hanrez (Paris: Les Dossiers H., 1975), 105-13.
____, *La poesía de la guerra de España* (Madrid: Castalia, 1985).
Sánchez Barbudo, Antonio, 'Antonio Machado en los años de la Guerra Civil', *Estudios sobre Antonio Machado*, ed. José Ángeles (Barcelona: Ariel, 1977), 259-96.
____, *Ensayos y recuerdos* (Barcelona: Laia, 1980).

———, *Los poemas de Antonio Machado* (Madrid: Editorial Lumen, 1967).
Sesé, Bernard, *Antonio Machado (1875-1939). El hombre. El poeta. El pensador* (Madrid: Gredos, 1980).
Si mi pluma valiera tu pistola. Los escritores españoles en la guerra civil, ed. Fernando Díaz-Plaja (Esplugues de Llobregat [Barcelona]: Plaza y Janés, 1979).
Somolinos D'Ardois, Germán, 'Las misiones pedagógicas de España (1931-36)', *Cuadernos Americanos*, XII (1953), 206-24.
Soria, Georges, *Guerra y revolución en España (1936-1939)* (Barcelona: Ediciones Océano, 1978), 5 vols.
Sotelo Vázquez, Marisa, 'Las colaboraciones de Antonio Machado en *Hora de España*', *Antonio Machado y su doble* (Barcelona: Univ. de Barcelona, 1989).

Termes, Josep, *Carteles de la República y de la Guerra Civil* (Barcelona: Centre D'Estudis D'Història Contemporània/Editorial La Gaya Ciencia, 1978).
Tierra Firme. Revista de la Sección Hispanoamericana del Centro de Estudios Históricos, 'Testimonios. Un año de labor cultural de la República Española (julio 1936-julio 1937)', III-IV (1936), 579-614 (various authors).
Tuñón de Lara, Manuel, 'Antonio Machado y la Institución Libre de Enseñanza', *Cuadernos para el Diálogo*, XLIX (1975), 98-104.
———, *Antonio Machado, poeta del pueblo* (Barcelona: Nova Terra: 1967).
———, 'La position de Machado', *Espagne/Écrivains. Guerre civile*, ed. Marc Hanrez (Paris: Les Dossiers H., 1975), 137-44.

Valencia a Machado (Valencia: Generalitat Valenciana, 1984).
Valencia, capital cultural de la República (1936-1937), ed. M. Aznar Soler *et al.* (Valencia: Generalitat Valenciana, 1986).
Valverde, José María, *Antonio Machado* (Madrid: Siglo Veintiuno, 1975).
Vidaković Petrov, Krinka, 'La poesía de Antonio Machado y la guerra civil', *Antonio Machado hoy. Actas del Congreso Internacional Conmemorativo del Cincuentenario de la Muerte de Antonio Machado* (Seville: Alfar, 1990), I, 567-72.

Wardropper, Bruce W., 'The Modern Spanish Elegy: Antonio Machado's Lament for Federico García Lorca', *Symposium*, XVI (1965), 162-70.
Watkins, K. W., *Britain Divided. The Effect of the Spanish Civil War on British Public Opinion* (London: Nelson, 1963).

Whiston, James, 'The "Cubing" of Language in Antonio Machado's *Juan de Mairena* (1936)', *Essays on Hispanic Themes in Honour of E. C. Riley*, ed. Jennifer Lowe and Philip Swanson (Edinburgh: Dept of Hispanic Studies, Univ. of Edinburgh, 1989), 148-69.

─── , ' "Más fuerte que la guerra": The Civil-War Sonnets of Antonio Machado', *Modern Language Review*, LXXXVIII (1993), 644-65.

─── , 'Las "misiones paradójicas" de Antonio Machado', *Antonio Machado hoy. Actas del Congreso Internacional Conmemorativo del Cincuentenario de la Muerte de Antonio Machado* (Seville: Alfar, 1990), I, 345-56.

Zambrano, María, *Los intelectuales en el drama de España. Ensayos y notas (1936-1939)* (Madrid: Editorial Hispamérica, 1977).

Zaragoza Such, Francisco, *Lectura ética de Antonio Machado* (Murcia: Editora Regional de Murcia, 1982).

Zardoya, Concha, 'Los autorretratos de Antonio Machado', *Estudios sobre Antonio Machado*, ed. José Ángeles (Barcelona: Ariel, 1977), 309-53.

INDEX

Abellá, R., 56n
Abellán, J. L., 9
Achilles, 34
Agamemnon, 37, 235-36
Alba, Duke of, 51
Alberti, R., 65n, 79, 109
Albornoz, A. de, 9, 83n
Alonso, M., 9, 49, 193n, 221n
Álvarez del Vayo, J., 229, 245
Álvarez Molina, R., 194n
Andrés, T., 56n
Ángeles, J., 72n, 149n
Angell, N., 230-37
Anselm, St, 26, 30
Antología poética del alzamiento. 1936-1939, 189
Aristotle, 26, 32
Ariza, M., 164n
Armas y Letras, 55n, 56n, 135
Atholl, Duchess of, 211
Aubert, P., 40, 98n
Averroes, 33
Ayuda, 49, 51, 57-58, 73
Azaña, M., 18, 59, 63, 65n, 152, 172-73, 176, 189, 206, 233-35, 246n
Azcárate, P. de, 58, 165-66, 176, 196
Azcoaga, E., 14n
Aznar Soler, M., 17, 100n, 143n, 199n

Barbachano, C., 146
Bardasano, J., 180
Barral, E., 52, 57, 69, 83, 244
Bataillon, M., 142
Bécarud, J., 18
Beceiro, C., 25-26
Benavente, J., 73
Bergamín, J., 62, 186-87
Bergson, H., 61-62, 157
Blasco, R., 199
Blum, L., 196

Boix, R., 180
Borkenau, F., 58n, 162
Brancaforte, B., 17n
Brigadas volantes, 56
Britain, 54, 118-19, 132-33, 152, 161, 176, 184, 185n, 194-97, 200, 204-05, 207-25, 227-39
Brotherston, G., 179n
Bustos, E. de, 150n

Calamai, N., 175
Calderón, 79, 174n
Camões, 168
Cano, J. L, 13n, 104n
Carnelli, M. L., 219
Carta colectiva, 113-14, 116, 122, 124
Casona, A., 14
Caudet, F., 15, 17, 85n, 108n
Cerezo Galán, P., 101, 110
Cervantes, 33-34, 39, 42, 79, 101, 132, 146
Chamberlain, N., 130, 153, 189n, 195-96, 201, 205, 207, 210-11, 218-25, 230, 238-39, 245
Chiappini, G., 10, 16n
Christ, 45, 94-95, 114, 216
Christianity, 79, 91, 94-99, 114, 119, 207
Churchill, W., 196, 211, 237
Claudel, P., 209n
Cobb, C., 149
Cobos, P. A. de, 19n
Cossío, M. B., 13-15, 38, 41, 43, 47
Covarrubias, 155n
Cruz, S. de la, 196, 198n
Cultura Popular, 41, 56

Daladier, E., 196
Darwin, 26, 30, 111, 114, 118, 202, 216-17, 244
Demeter, 154-55

Democritus, 26-27, 29, 31-32
Descartes, 118
Diario de Madrid, 17-19, 85, 98, 107, 115, 120, 197
Díaz de Castro, F. J., 40
Díaz-Plaja, F., 113n, 124n
Diego, G., 67, 149
Dieste, R., 14, 39, 85n
Domenchina, J., 150
Don Quixote, 33, 37, 42, 128-32, 146
Dostoievsky, 79
Durán, M., 55n

Eden, A., 196, 211, 225n
Edwards, J., 225n
Ehrenberg, I., 238-39
Eliot, T. S., 222
Epicurus, 26, 28
Escolar Sobrino, H., 55n, 79n
Esteban, J., 245n

Fascism, 50, 54, 62, 84, 87, 152, 175, 195, 218, 220, 225n, 229, 231-33, 236, 244
Fernández Ferrer, A., 10, 19, 52n, 67n, 98n, 111, 115n, 116, 134n, 138, 181n, 193n
Fernández Soria, J. M., 38n, 47, 56n, 102-03
Ferreres, R., 52n
France, 54, 73, 119, 133, 138, 152, 161-62, 176, 184, 185n, 194-96, 200, 204-05, 207-11, 213, 218, 225, 227-31, 233-34, 236-37
Franco, F., 51, 54, 90, 130, 144, 175-76, 189, 196, 225n, 235

Galileo, 26, 29, 31, 103
Gálvez, P. de, 187-88
García de la Concha, V., 26
García Lorca, 49-50, 52, 57, 64-71, 75, 77, 79, 83, 109, 244
Garcilaso, 55, 183
Garosci, A., 69-70, 171
Gaya, R., 14, 121, 180

Germany, 59, 72, 109-12, 118, 130, 132-33, 144, 146, 169, 171, 177, 186, 196, 200, 204-08, 210-11, 223, 231, 234-36
Gil-Albert, J., 60n, 199n
Gil Novales, A., 90, 104-05
Giner de los Ríos, F., 66
Góngora, 174n, 183
González, R., 117n
Goya, 64-65, 68
Gramsci, A., 45
Grimau, C., 180
Guiomar, 113, 168-70, 190
Gullón, R., 22n, 119, 148, 241n

Halifax, Lord, 196, 211-12
Hamilton, T. J., 90
Hanrez, M., 85n, 188n
Hart, S. M., 65n
Harvey, O., 225n
Heidegger, 53, 61-62, 83, 125-26
Hernández, J., 52-53, 55-56, 135
Hernández, M., 65n, 135-36, 173
Hitler, 125, 127, 130, 186, 195, 201, 210, 212
Homer, 29
Hora de España, 20, 36, 47, 49, 57, 60n, 76, 79-80, 84n, 85-191, 193, 195, 197-98, 201-04, 206-07, 212, 214, 216, 219, 222, 226, 238, 241, 243, 246-47
Hume, D., 33
Hyde, H. M., 205n

Iglesias, P., 87
Institución Libre de Enseñanza, 38, 40, 212, 242
Italy, 54, 72, 144, 146, 171, 177, 184, 186, 196, 200, 204-08, 211, 223, 231, 234-35

Jackson, G., 58n, 96, 182n, 242
Julián, Conde Don, 145, 174-75, 177, 181

Kant, 26, 30-31, 33-34, 118
Kleine-Ahlbrandt, W., 225n
Krausism, 117, 226

Lázaro Carreter, F., 150, 173
League of Nations, 119, 165, 198, 210, 213-14, 221, 229-31, 234, 245
Lechner, J., 149
Leibnitz, 26, 31-32
León, M. T., 79
Lerroux, A., 18, 24, 82
Lida, R., 22, 111
Líster, E., 137, 153, 182-86, 188n, 190-91, 244
López Campillo, E., 18
Lowe, J., 11
Luis, L. de, 183

Macbeth, 129-32, 218-24
Machado, A., writings:
  Abel Martín, 34-36, 42-43, 74, 94-96, 117, 123
  'A Emiliano Barral', 69, 74, 77-78, 83
  'Alemania o la exageración', 128, 132-33, 169
  'Algunas ideas de Juan de Mairena sobre la guerra y la paz', 113, 116-24, 127-28, 148
  'A Méjico', 155
  'Apuntes', 57, 60-62, 83, 185n
  Campos de Castilla, 9, 46, 81, 158, 176, 186, 245
  'Canciones del Alto Duero', 60n
  'Carta a David Vigodsky. Leningrado', 57, 61, 66, 74-75, 79-80, 83, 89-91, 107, 109, 114, 207
  'El crimen fue en Granada', 57, 64-71, 77, 83
  'Desde el mirador de la guerra', 193-97, 200-239, 245
  'Discurso a las Juventudes Socialistas Unificadas', 57, 63, 79-82, 200
  'Discurso pronunciado en Valencia en la sesión de clausura del Congreso Internacional de Escritores', 88, 91, 100-04, 115n

'El dos de mayo de 1808', 65
La Guerra, 49-84, 88, 185n, 241n
Guiomar, 113, 168-70, 190
Juan de Mairena, in *Poesías completas*, 74; in *Juan de Mairena* (1936), 10, 16-49, 56-57, 85-88, 93-99, 102-04, 107, 110-12, 115-16, 120-21, 123-24, 131, 193-94, 197, 201, 214, 235-36, 243, 247; during the Civil War, 10-11, 26, 61, 85-148, 194, 197, 201-05, 214-19, 235-36, 241, 246-47
'¡Madrid! ¡Madrid! ¡Qué bien tu nombre suena!', 65-66
'Meditación del día', 57, 71-77, 83, 88-89, 98, 131, 137, 156, 177
'Los milicianos de 1936', 57-60, 88, 91, 100-01, 126, 136-37, 142-44
'Notas de actualidad', 60, 126
'Notas del tiempo. Voces de calidad', 125-28
Nuevas canciones, 46, 57, 62, 77, 187
'Nueve sonetos y una cuarteta', 107, 113, 137, 147-90
Poesías completas, 158, 159n
Poesías completas, ed. D. Ridruejo, 79n, 242
'Proverbios y cantares', 46, 165
'(Sobre la Alemania guerrera)', 109-12, 132
'(Sobre la guerra)', 123-25, 128
'Sobre literatura rusa', 161
'Sobre la maleza', 128-30
'Sobre el pacifismo', 112-13, 116-17, 120
'Sobre la Rusia actual', 107, 110, 113-14, 116, 207
Soledades. Galerías. Otros poemas, 9, 21, 46, 69, 81, 163, 194, 227
'La tierra de Alvargonzález', 74, 158, 177-78, 223

'Voz de España. A los intelectuales de la Rusia soviética', 184n, 207-08
Machado, J., 13, 14n, 16n, 49, 52-55, 59-60, 100n, 152n, 171n, 198n, 201
Machado, M., 10, 49, 67-68, 171-74, 178-79, 181, 187, 189, 239
Machiavelli, 26, 29, 31
Mackenzie, A. L., 159n
Macrì, O., 10, 22n, 23n, 48-49, 57n, 63n, 98n, 115n, 128, 131n, 134n, 153, 155n, 156-57n, 159n, 181n, 193n, 195n, 205n, 210n, 221n, 245n
Madrid. Cuadernos de la Casa de la Cultura, 57, 86
Manaut Viglietti, J., 42n
Mann, T., 125, 127
Manrique, J., 28-29, 58, 77
Marcuse, S., 155n
Martinengo, A., 159n
Marxism, 53, 76, 80-82, 92
Mera, C., 188n
Miaja, J., 52-53
Milicias de la Cultura, 38, 55n, 55-56, 103n, 135
Milton, 211, 215-16, 220
Misiones Pedagógicas, 13-17, 20-22, 36-39, 41, 43, 46-47, 55, 103n, 199, 243-44
Moliner, M., 16
Mono Azul, El, 49, 58
Moscardó, J., 178-79
Mulvihill, E., 17n
Mussolini, 130, 186, 206, 212, 220, 222-23

Nadal, J. M., 82n
Navarro Tomás, T., 55
Negrín, J., 152, 161, 180-81, 196-97, 200, 203, 207, 210, 212, 216, 218, 228
Nehru, Pandit, 225n
Nietzsche, 26, 111-12, 114, 118, 202, 244
Nueva Cultura, 39n, 52n, 62n

Olmo, R. del, 245n
D'Ors, E., 117n
Ortega y Gasset, J., 31, 40
Otero Urtaza, E., 14n, 15, 39

Paucker, E., 14n, 17n
Paul, St, 26
Paz, O., 241
Peers, E. A., 241
Peirats, J., 102n
Pérez Contel, R., 180
Pérez Herrero, G., 9, 49, 57n, 77n, 104n, 118, 130, 134n, 195, 209n, 221n
Phillips, A., 22n, 241n
Pierce, F., 168
Pius XI, 114
Plato, 27, 38, 118
Pla y Beltrán, P., 71
Poema de Mío Cid, 50, 59-60, 142-45
Poetas en la España leal, 70
Pont, J., 51, 83n
Pope, A., 217-18
Prieto, M., 52
Protagoras, 26-28
Puccini, D., 175-76
Puzzo, D., 211

Queipo de Llano, G., 90
Quevedo, 189n
Quinto Regimento, 49
Quiroga Plá, J., 187

Renau, J., 38
Ribbans, G., 20, 159n, 163n
Ridruejo, D., 79n, 189-90, 242
Riley, E. C., 11
Rodríguez Puértolas, J., 9, 49, 57n, 77n, 104n, 118, 130, 134n, 195, 209, 221n
Rojo, V., 63-64
Rolland, R., 138
Romancero de la guerra civil, 58n-59n, 99
Romano García, V., 140n
Roumette, M., 85n

INDEX   261

Russia, 54, 78-79, 107-08, 110, 113-14, 184, 207-08, 227, 231-33, 242

Sadie, S., 155n
Salas Viu, G., 56
Salaün, S., 187-88
Salinas, P., 14, 189n
Sánchez, R., 17n
Sánchez Barbudo, A., 17n, 60n, 72-73, 76, 129-30, 137, 147, 150, 171, 182, 243-44
Sánchez Vidal, A., 146
Santonja, G., 245n
Santullano, L., 13-14, 16, 18
Sanz del Río, J., 226
Seco Serrano, C., 242
Segarra Bañales, I., 114n
Segundo Congreso Internacional de Escritores Antifascistas, 84, 88, 91-92, 100, 155-56
Seneca, 26, 33
Serrano Plaja, A., 14, 100n
Servicio Español de Información, 125, 150, 161, 166
Sesé, B., 65n, 67n, 88, 150, 171
Severin, D., 159n
Shakespeare, 42, 101, 130-32, 213, 215, 218-24
Smyth, D., 225n
Socorro Rojo Internacional, 73-74, 77
Socrates, 26-27, 45
Sol, El, 18, 102, 107, 115, 197
Somolinos D'Ardois, G., 43
Soria, G., 38n, 54, 56n
Sotelo Vázquez, M., 85n
Spinoza, 26, 32
Stalin, 207-08

Swanson, P., 11
Swift, 94, 214

Tello, A., 9
Termes, J., 80, 180n
Thomas, H., 200n
Thomson, D., 206-07
Tolstoy, 101, 132
Tuñón de Lara, M., 17, 19, 39, 235

Unamuno, M. de, 20, 53, 61, 79, 107n, 109

Valle Inclán, 23n, 39
Valverde, J. M., 115n, 149
Vanguardia, La, 10, 58n, 72, 88, 93, 107, 116, 119, 131-34, 136-37, 139, 148, 151, 161-62, 168, 181n, 185n, 193-239, 245-46
Velázquez, 20, 34-35, 48
Vidal, F., 233
Viñas, R., 80n
Virgil, 29

Wardropper, B., 67n
Watkins, K., 153, 225n
Wells, H. G., 208
Whiston, J., 11
Williams, R., 222n
Wilson, W., 231
Wordsworth, 72

Xirau, J., 14n, 21, 140-41

Zambrano, B., 131
Zambrano, M., 14, 86
Zaragoza Such, F., 101, 117n
Zardoya, C., 149
Zola, E., 210